MEANING AND MYTH
IN THE STUDY OF LIVES

MEANING AND MYTH IN THE STUDY OF LIVES

A SARTREAN PERSPECTIVE
STUART L. CHARMÉ

UNIVERSITY OF PENNSYLVANIA PRESS

PHILADELPHIA · 1984

Library of Congress Cataloging in Publication Data

Charmé, Stuart L.
    Meaning and myth in the study of lives.
    Bibliography: p.
    Includes index.
    1. Sartre, Jean Paul, 1905–1980. 2. Meaning
(Philosophy) 3. Self. 4. Existential psychology.
5. Psychoanalysis
I. Title.
B2430.S34C524 1984   194   83-12330
ISBN 0-8122-7908-5

Printed in the United States of America

Designed by Adrianne Onderdonk Dudden

CONTENTS

ABBREVIATIONS FOR FREQUENTLY CITED WORKS
    OF JEAN-PAUL SARTRE   *vii*
INTRODUCTION   1

1 THE NATURE OF CONSCIOUSNESS AND THE STORY
    OF THE SELF   5
    The Reflective Construction of the Self   5
    The Role of Stories in Self-Understanding   9
    Language and the Self   15
    The Image of One's Life   17

2 STRUCTURES OF HUMAN MEANING AND THEIR
    INTERPRETATION   23
    "Choosing" the Meaning of One's Life   24
    Conscious versus Unconscious Meaning   25
    Sartre and Freud on the Nature of Memory   30
    The Fundamental Project and the Totality of the Self   34
    The Original Choice as Mythic Event   39
    Changing One's Fundamental Project   44
    The Fundamental Project as a Literary Work   46

3 DIALECTIC AND TOTALIZATION: NEW THEORETICAL
   DEVELOPMENTS   *54*
   Sartre's Reevaluation of Psychoanalysis and the Unconscious   55
   "Lived Experience" versus "The Unconscious"   58
   The Dialectical Development of the Self   60
   The Nature of "Totalization"   62
   Working on the Spiral of Life   65
   Sartre and Ego Psychology   67
   Biological and Biographical Instincts   70

4 EXISTENTIAL PSYCHOANALYSIS AND "TRUE
   NOVELS"   *73*
   Transference and the Clinical Situation   73
   Living with Style   76
   The Nature of Truth in Existential Psychoanalysis   78
   Novelistic Elements in Freud's Case Studies   82
   A Myth to Believe In   84

5 TWO EARLY "TRUE NOVELS"   *87*
   Baudelaire's Fall From Grace   87
   The Sacred World of Genet   92

6 EXISTENTIAL PSYCHOANALYSIS AS IDEOLOGY
   AND MYTH   *101*
   The Structure of Sartre's Autobiography   101
   The "Singular Universal"   107
   Erik Erikson and Religious Biography   109
   Sartre as Religious Autobiographer   113
   Life Without Father: The Protean Style   117
   The Retrospective Illusion   120
   Sartre as Religious Biographer   123

7 "WHAT CAN WE KNOW ABOUT A MAN?"   *126*
   "For Example, Gustave Flaubert"   126
   The Myth of Flaubert's Childhood   132
   Flaubert's Hysterical Conversion: The Crisis at Pont l'Evêque   143

8 IDENTITY, NARRATIVE, AND MYTH   *149*
   The Fullness of Time   151
   Cosmogony and the Self   152

   NOTES   *159*
   SELECTED BIBLIOGRAPHY   *177*
   INDEX   *187*

ABBREVIATIONS FOR FREQUENTLY CITED WORKS
OF JEAN-PAUL SARTRE

B	Baudelaire
BEM	Between Existentialism and Marxism
BN	Being and Nothingness
CDR	Critique of Dialectical Reason
E	The Emotions
I	Imagination
IF	L'Idiot de la Famille
LPE	Literary and Philosophical Essays
LS	Life/Situations
N	Nausea
PI	The Psychology of Imagination
SG	Saint Genet
SM	Search for a Method
TE	The Transcendence of the Ego
W	The Words
WL	What Is Literature?

INTRODUCTION

This book deals with the question, How can one determine and describe the meaning of a person's life? It touches on both the autobiographical and the biographical dimension of this question. In particular, it focuses on the work of Jean-Paul Sartre to examine a number of theoretical issues involved in the study of individual human lives. Much of Sartre's work was dedicated to the development and practice of what he calls "existential psychoanalysis." As his career progressed, Sartre gradually turned away from plays and novels, which initially brought him fame, toward the goal of presenting a method for interpreting the meaning of a particular human life.

A good deal of Sartre's theory of existential psychoanalysis can only be appreciated in relation to the twentieth century's most important interpreter of human lives, Sigmund Freud. A prominent French psychoanalyst has described Sartre's lifelong intellectual encounter with psychoanalysis as "an ambiguous mixture of *equally* deep attraction and repulsion" (*BEM*, 220). At times, Sartre seems to stand on Freud's shoulders. At other times, he is content with nothing less than standing

Freud on his head. Existential psychoanalysis, therefore, represents both an appropriation of, and a reaction against, traditional Freudian psychoanalysis. Throughout this study I will try to illustrate both of these elements in Sartre's theories.

To a great extent, Sartre's ambivalence about psychoanalysis reflects the fundamental ambiguity in Freud himself over whether the central metaphor for human personality should emphasize "mechanisms" or "meanings."[1] When Freud acts as spokesman for the deterministic power of blind desires and the mechanistic operation of unconscious forces, he offends Sartre's convictions about the absolute freedom and responsibility possessed by every person. However, when Freud directs the main concern of psychoanalysis to the systems of meaning found by interpreting images, symbols, and myths, Sartre finds much that he admires and that is compatible with his own hermeneutical system.

Sartre believes that every human being is a source of meaning. He continually analyzes the active dimension of consciousness that creatively participates in the establishment of structure and meaning in the world. Human consciousness cannot help but color the world it apprehends. It is never merely a passive reflection of a world whose meanings are already fixed. Sartre's existentialist work popularized the maxim that every person is "condemned to be free." Implied in this notion of inescapable freedom is the fact that as human beings we are also condemned to endless interpretation of ourselves, other people, and the world created by our encounters with each other. Like Freud, Sartre has tried to help make explicit the meanings embedded in the actions, feelings, desires, and goals that comprise human life.

The succeeding chapters will analyze the gradual emergence of Sartre's hermeneutical system, his theory of the interpretation of human reality. We begin with Sartre's earliest discussions of the nature of consciousness and the self. Sartre emphasizes that the meaning of the self only emerges through a complex mixture of reflection, narration, and imagination. The nature of the self is not that of an object with fixed attributes determined by the past which can simply be discovered or analyzed into component parts. Rather, the essential form of the self is that of a retrospective story that creates order out of the chaos of experience. Sartre develops the concept of the "fundamental project" that undergirds the meaning of every person's life. This project—often misunderstood as a lonely and radically free decision—is actually the cumulative structure of meaning that unfolds slowly in the course of life and links together a person's past, present, and future into a coherent whole. In its highly dialectical understanding of human development, Sartre's position resembles in significant ways recent ideas within psychoanalytic ego psychology, particularly those of Erik Erikson.

Aspects of Sartre's fiction and literary theory offer further insights into how he understands the process of presenting and interpreting the experience of a person's life. In some ways, interpreting a person's life may fruitfully be compared with the process of creating and interpreting texts. Thus, the full implications of Sartre's theory of existential psychoanalysis only become clear in relation to his theory of the literary text and the nature of language. It will be evident that psychoanalytic interpretation has an important literary dimension for two reasons. First, it produces a text, a narrative account of a specific life. Second, its human subject has certain characteristics in common with a literary text and must be analyzed accordingly.

In time, Sartre modifies some of his earlier ideas while continuing to build on others. The theoretical positions developed in such later works as *The Critique of Dialectical Reason, The Words, The Family Idiot*, and other essays and interviews, present a significant development in Sartre's attitude toward psychoanalysis, especially in relation to the unconscious and the external determining influences that shape an individual's original project. While retaining many elements from his earlier approach to the interpretation of human lives, Sartre does come a long way in appropriating psychoanalytic concepts and in clarifying some of the limits of human freedom.

Sartre's theory of existential psychoanalysis has produced several major case histories. These include the early studies of Baudelaire and Genet, Sartre's own autobiographical analysis, and finally the massive study of Flaubert that preoccupied him during the final portion of his life. Sartre has called these studies "true novels," thereby raising the interesting epistemological question of their truth value while at the same time suggesting the importance of certain literary and narrative elements within them. Both these elements are involved in what can be called the *mythic* dimension of Sartre's reconstructions. The purpose of reconstructing certain climactic events in the lives of his subjects is not historical in any ordinary sense. Rather, Sartre uses such events as symbolic condensations of overall attitudes toward reality. His analyses elaborate a mythic structure in each subject in terms of which every specific moment of that person's life acquires a transcendent meaning. In this sense, Sartre's work begins to resemble the kind of narratives commonly found in religious traditions. Existential psychoanalysis becomes a vehicle for the sense of sacrality that modern life has displaced from its original context.

Historian of religion Mircea Eliade characterizes modern man by his refusal of any transcendent models for his life that point beyond human history or experience.[2] Unlike the member of the traditional religious society of the past who finds meaning in his or her life only when it is valorized by sacred paradigms, modern man *"makes himself, and he* only makes himself completely in proportion as he desacralizes himself and the world. The sacred is the prime obstacle to his freedom. . . . He will not be truly free until he has killed the last god."[3] The sense of the sacred, however, has never really disappeared from modern life; it has simply been relocated. Sartre has identified the fundamental human goal as "the desire to be God." This effort to be the ultimate architect of one's own self results in a *sacralizing of the self*. The classic role of religion to provide the overarching stories that unify the fragments of our experience is increasingly usurped by the modern obsession with the self. Philippe Lejeune describes "the myth of the self" ("le mythe du MOI") as one of the great myths of modern Western civilization whose hypnotizing effect appears in our fascination with autobiography and biography.[4] To understand the self as a "myth" is not to discredit it but to recognize it as an entity that transcends any given moment of experience and whose story valorizes human life in the same way that the stories of the gods did in earlier cultures. There is a quasi-theological quality in the "cosmic" drama that unfolds in the life of the self. Culturally, the existential psychoanalysis of the self arises only after the traditional religious issue of cosmogony has been demythologized. The process of establishing the meaning or myth of a person's life has now become one of humankind's major creative acts, since through it every person repeats the cosmogonic task of constructing a unique place in the world.

The study of the mythic dimension of existential psychoanalysis leads to a further aspect of Sartre's work. Sartre's objectives in existential psychoanalysis include using the study of individual lives as a means of investigating larger historical and cultural issues. He is interested in how every person internalizes the cultural values of his or her epoch and in turn acts on them to create new cultural values. Individual human development is thus related to the development of history. Furthermore, the lives of certain persons may acquire an archetypal or paradigmatic status for a whole society. Traditionally, it has been the role of religious biographies to present such lives. Existential psychoanalysis takes on a deeper religious and ideological quality when it uses particular lives as a way to endorse or condemn various normative models of human existence. In addition to his other studies, Sartre presented his own life in precisely this light.

[1] *THE NATURE OF CONSCIOUSNESS AND THE STORY OF THE SELF*

THE REFLECTIVE CONSTRUCTION OF THE SELF

In classical Freudian psychoanalysis, as well as much of traditional Western philosophy, the self or psyche has normally been treated as an object at the center of experience. Freud frequently presents the psyche as a quasi-mechanical apparatus that generates and contains various desires, memories, images, and feelings. Large portions of the psyche and its contents, which Freud treats analogously to physical objects, remain hidden or unconscious at any given moment.

To a great extent, Freud's view of the mind rests on an archeological metaphor that presents a person's thought and memory as a site to be excavated in order to reconstruct his or her past from the surviving fragments.[1] The archeological model of the mind implies that repressed events and the accompanying affect are thinglike entities which are preserved intact in the mind. When uncovered, they give an accurate picture of a person's past mental life. A repressed memory is thus like an ordinary object that has been buried. From this point of view, the task of interpretation for Freud is to disclose the true contents of an individual's psyche. Interpretation permits the recovery of hidden desires, thoughts, memories, and feelings as if they were quasi-physical traces waiting to be found in dark corners of the psyche, reactivated, and brought to consciousness. The interpreter is essentially an explorer in search of buried treasure. Freud continues to maintain at the end of his career that "All the essentials are preserved, even things that seem completely forgotten are present somehow and somewhere, and have merely been buried and made inaccessible to the subject. Indeed, it may . . . be doubted whether any psychical structure can really be the victim of total destruction. It depends only upon analytic technique whether we shall succeed in bringing what is concealed completely to light."[2]

Psychoanalytic interpretation presumably culminates in the reexperiencing or at least reconstruction of the past exactly as it happened, just as "correctly" interpreting a literary text, according to some theorists, allows one to reexperience the author's original feelings and intentions. Since the goal of the process is to find the objects or thoughts which are preserved in a psychic container, it is logical that only one interpretation can be correct, that which corresponds with the buried past. Although alternate ways of construing both the psyche and the process of interpretation are possible, this spatial conception of the psyche influences much of Freud's work.

In the same year (1937) that Freud published the essay from which the passage above is taken, Sartre published *The Transcendence of the Ego*. Freud's essay was one of the final ones of his career, whereas Sartre's was only the beginning of a lifelong effort to understand the self. Sartre's early analysis of the nature of consciousness, self-reflection, and the ego fights the container view of the psyche found in Freud (and much Western philosophy) and its implications for interpreting the self.

Sartre rejects the notion that the self or psyche is a permanent structure *in* consciousness which produces feelings, thoughts, and desires or contains them in a disguised form.[3] Sartre argues that the experience of the self is something which may exist *for* consciousness, but the self is neither materially present behind each moment of consciousness nor the source of all thoughts and desires (*TE*, 31). While his aim is primarily to repudiate Husserl's notion of a "transcendental ego" that unifies a person's experience, his position will also have significant implications for understanding the process of interpretation in psychoanalysis. Sartre's theory of the self requires that interpretation be something other than trying to uncover psychic structures, as though they were objects found after having been misplaced, ignored, or hidden. If the self is not a kind of psychic container within which these psychic realities could be stored, then a different hermeneutical system is necessary.

Sartre's position is based on expanding the phenomenological principle of intentionality, which he takes as the essential characteristic of all consciousness. Intentionality means that consciousness is always directed outward toward objects in the world, or as it is commonly put, "all consciousness is consciousness of something." One never simply sees, knows, or feels. One sees *something*, knows *something*, or feels *something*. Consciousness is thus a *relation* to objects beyond itself, rather than a *thing* or *place* that contains objects. Sartre criticizes the prevalent "digestive philosophy" that metamorphoses each thing in the world into a "content" of consciousness. According to that view, "the spidery mind trapped things in its web, covered them with white spit, and slowly swallowed them, reducing them to its own substance."[4]

Sartre deprives the self of its usual privileged status as the force outside or behind consciousness that directs and unifies one's experience of the world in accordance with its desires. The self loses this privileged status since it, too, is a special kind of object *for* consciousness. Sartre reaches this conclusion because he believes that consciousness is originally "pre-personal" (*TE*, 36).[5] In a person's immediate, direct consciousness of objects or situations in the world there is no need to refer to an implicit self or "I." For example, while one is involved in an activity such as reading, there is no self experienced in consciousness, but only consciousness of the book, of the heroes in the novel, and so on.

Sartre insists that the absence of a phenomenological experience of the self in immediate consciousness cannot merely be attributed to momentary lapses of attention to the self. Like James and others, Sartre sees the original structure of consciousness as a continual flux. There is no need to posit an additional self to unify this flux. Each successive moment of consciousness simply represents a synthesis of past moments of consciousness and present consciousness resulting in an ideal object we call the self (*TE*, 39).

The self is thus not a concrete structure immanent within consciousness. Sartre calls it a "transcendent object," which arises only when one reflects (*TE*, 52-53). The self "transcends" any individual moment of consciousness. It "constitutes the ideal and indirect . . . unity of the infinite series of our reflected consciousnesses" (*TE*, 60). In other words, the self represents a reflective unity of mental facts, actions, and feelings, although it is not a special entity distinct from these elements. When I accept an act or feeling as "mine" I place it within this unified and organized whole. In reflection, I take my own past experience of the world as an object for a further act of consciousness. Reflection is thus a synthesis of two moments of consciousness, one of which is conscious of the other. Reflection is a "project of recovery"[6] in which one moment of consciousness is always trying to assimilate or incorporate past moments of consciousness within itself.

Sartre suggests the analogy of a melody to describe the nature of the self. The individual notes of a melody are not attributes, predicates, or emanations of a fixed object that is the "melody"; rather a melody consists of the unity produced by the relations between the individual notes (*TE*, 73). A melody appears "through" each note, but it is not any one of them nor something in addition to all of them. In the same way, the self or personality "appears through" individual feelings, desires, and acts, but it is not any one of them, nor is it a separate source or support of any of them.[7] This musical analogy emphasizes the temporal nature of the self. The self unfolds in time like a melody. It includes a series of moments that are united in reflection, just as a melody links a sequence of notes together.

Implicit in the view that the self, like a melody, is a transcendent object which appears "through" individual acts is the central Sartrean concept of the "project." The self and the melody are both "projects" in the sense that neither is a fixed or static object. This "transcendent object" only exists when the temporal sequence of individual acts is synthesized into a whole. But the sense of the whole can always be altered by events or notes which have not yet been played out.

Sartre thus concludes that through reflection one *produces* a temporary self. He makes it clear that reflection does not uncover a fixed psychic structure which existed before the act of reflection. Rather reflection constitutes a new object, the psyche, or self. It is a "synthetic totality" of psychological facts just as the "world" is the synthetic totality of all things (*TE*, 75). Neither the self nor the world is something in addition to the elements that comprise it.

Sartre recognizes that once reflection has constituted a self, it is common to attribute creative power to that self. As a result, the self seems to produce certain acts, yet it is simultaneously modified by those acts. As Sartre puts it, "the ego which produces undergoes the reverberation of what it produces. The ego is 'compromised' by what it produces. . . . Each new state produced by the ego colors and tinges the ego slightly the moment the ego produces it" (*TE*, 82). The self thus exists as a "totalizing synthesis" (*TE*, 86) whereby each new psychological state is incorporated in the existing totality to constitute the next moment in the life of the self.

Since the self is an ideal or transcendent unity of individual acts of consciousness, its final "nature" is always uncertain. For Sartre, it is not the self which determines the character of one's acts, but rather one's acts which determine the character of the self. To say that my self-awareness is always tentative and questionable does not mean that there is "a *true me* which I am unaware of" (*TE*, 76) but which I could find if I looked hard enough. In reflective interpretation, one is not uncovering a hidden preexistent self. Reflection simply constructs a synthesis out of an ambiguous series of past acts and feelings, which may even include "memories" that are distorted or completely imagined.

THE ROLE OF STORIES IN SELF-UNDERSTANDING

In *Nausea*, a novel written several years after *The Transcendence of the Ego*, Sartre dramatically illustrates his view that the meaning of a person's past and the nature of his or her self is not something hidden which needs only to be uncovered, but rather is creatively produced in the process of reflection. *Nausea* confronts the question of what can be written about a person's life, and what structure can be given to it. Just as self-reflection modifies immediate consciousness by synthesizing it into a totality which I call my "self," so narrating my life, argues Sartre, involves a fundamental modification of actual lived experience. This crucial dimension of narrative in the shaping of self-consciousness is echoed by Gabriel Marcel: "My life presents itself to reflection as something whose essential nature is that it can be related as a story . . . and this is so very true that one may be permitted to wonder whether the words 'my life' retain any precise meaning at all, if we abstract from the meaning we attach to them any reference whatsoever to the act of narration."[8]

Nausea focuses on the difficulties inherent in the narrative recording of a person's life. The structure of the novel illustrates these difficulties on two levels. *Nausea* is the fictional diary of a historian who is also trying to write a biography of an eighteenth-century French nobleman. On one level, we see the difficulties the protagonist faces in telling the story of his own life and in understanding his own experience. Within his own story, moreover, we find the additional problems he encounters in trying to write the story of another person's life.

Sartre suggests that reflective consciousness provides an overall meaning to events in a person's life by placing them within a narrative. The meaning of events is constituted according to the way the events are incorporated within a totality (a story) by subsequent acts of consciousness. Although an autobiographer or biographer would like to record the nuances and details of a portion of a particular life exactly as it was experienced, Sartre indicates that this is a goal which could never be achieved. The very process of telling stories about oneself or another inevitably introduces structure and form by selecting, condensing, or possibly distorting elements of the past. As Marcel puts it, "in fact this rebuilding of the past is really a new building, a fresh construction on an old site, modelled more or less on the former edifice there, but not identical with it. What I mean is that it would be an illusion to claim that my life, as I turn it into a story, corresponds at all completely with my life as I have actually lived it."⁹

Roquentin immediately realizes the "danger" of keeping a diary or attempting to represent oneself. One seldom simply records the events of his or her life. He warns: "You exaggerate everything. You continually force the truth because you're always looking for something" (N, 7). By looking for the meaning or direction of one's life, a person chooses which events will be emphasized and how they will be linked together. In so doing, he or she inevitably "exaggerates" or "forces" the truth. How to describe one's past is neither self-evident nor unequivocal. The very selection and organization of recollections has a tendency to add a fictional or literary quality to events.

While one is living, events flow, but one does not usually make the necessary distinctions to tell about them. At first, most people are like Roquentin, who confesses: "I am not in the habit of telling myself what happens to me, so I cannot quite recapture the succession of events, I cannot distinguish what is important" (N, 18). Only in reflection does one learn to place events in narrative succession, determine which aspects of them are important or relevant, and simplify or clarify them accordingly. This is both difficult and risky, since one must always be cautious that reflection does not "put in strangeness where there is none" (N, 7). In the same way, André Gide complains, "What hampers me most is having to represent states that are really one confused blend of simultaneous happenings as though they were successive. . . . Memoirs are never more than half sincere, however great the desire for truth; everything is always more complicated than one makes out."¹⁰

When he reflects as a historian on the life of another person, Roquentin again struggles with the absence of any compelling pattern in the material he is studying. After a long study of the Marquis de Rollebon, Roquentin questions whether he really understands the Marquis's life. Although he has plenty of letters, fragments of memoirs, secret reports, and so forth, he discovers, "I have almost too many of them. What is lacking in all this testimony is firmness and consistency. They do not contradict each other, neither do they agree with each other" (N, 22). In Sartre's view, we are always presented with "too much" data. To tell the story of a person's life requires a creative, imaginative process whereby we reduce or arrange this data to something firm and consistent.

Roquentin gradually realizes that it is this artistic arrangement of the data that really interests him. Through him, Sartre insists that the meaning of a person's life is indeterminate, and depends on the way one organizes it. In this sense, to reconstruct the meaning of a person's life is an aesthetic task, not unlike writing a novel. If *The Transcendence of the Ego* shows that the self is not an immanent structure within consciousness but a product of reflection, *Nausea* shows that the episodes in a person's life assume a particular pattern or structure only when one begins to make a narrative of them: "for the most banal event to become an adventure, you must (and this is enough) begin to recount it. This is what fools people: a man is always a teller of tales, he lives surrounded by his stories and the stories of others, he sees everything that happens to him through them; and he tries to live his life as if he were telling a story. But you have to choose: live or tell" (N, 56).

The occasional failure of Roquentin to distinguish between living and telling results in the deceptive sense of "suspense" and "adventure" that he experiences from time to time. This is the experience that "something is going to happen" and that he is "advancing with a sense of fatality" (N, 76). On such occasions, the present moment acquires a transcendent dimension or meaning that comes from the undefined destination to which events are leading. Roquentin then feels "as happy as the hero of a novel" (N, 76). He simply awaits the endpoint of the "adventure" which will make each step he is now taking essential.

Yet Roquentin finally realizes that his sense of "adventure" presupposes the introduction of a narrative unit, that is, a sequence with a beginning and an end. The "beginning" of his adventure is defined and makes sense only in light of the subsequent "end"; consequently, he can genuinely understand the meaning of his adventure only in retrospect. Roquentin says: "Something is beginning in order to end: adventure does not let itself be drawn out; it only makes sense when dead. . . . Each instant appears only as part of a sequence" (N, 54). He further realizes that "this feeling of adventure definitely does not come from events: . . . It's rather the way in which the moments are linked together" (N, 79). Since we experience time irreversibly flowing from one instant to the next we tend to think that the events in our lives are already linked in a meaningful way. However, it is in narrating the events that links are provided.

In short, imaginative retelling is what dramatizes life into extraordinary events and "adventures."

Nothing happens while you live. The scenery changes, people come in and go out, that's all. There are no beginnings. Days are tacked on to days without rhyme or reason, an indeterminable, monotonous addition. From time to time you make a semi-total: you say: I've been travelling for three years, I've been in Bouville for three years. Neither is there any end: you never leave a woman, a friend, a city in one go. . . .

That's living. But everything changes when you tell about life; it's a change no one notices: the proof is that people talk about true stories [histoires]. As if there could possibly be true stories; things happen one way and we tell about them in the opposite sense.[11] *You seem to start at the beginning: "It was a fine autumn evening in 1922. I was a notary's clerk in Marommes." And in reality you have started at the end. It was there, invisible and present, it is the one which gives to words the pomp and value of a beginning. . . . But the end is there, transforming everything. For us, the man is already the hero of the story. . . . And the story goes on in reverse: instants have stopped piling themselves in a lighthearted way one on top of the other, they are snapped up by the end of the story which draws them and each one of them in turn, draws out the preceding instant* (N, 57–58).

According to Sartre, as we actually live through projects and actions minute by minute, they are uncertain and risky. Their final meaning is inescapably opaque, since we must always wait for future results and the perspective of the larger whole in order to judge present endeavors. When *telling* a story, however, we can examine an event and its meaning in every temporal direction. We are not constrained by the irreversibility of lived time. We can clarify the past by what came later, evaluate enterprises by their results, or judge the sincerity of intentions by the consequences.[12] We inevitably interpret events and experiences by taking into account results that were not foreseeable at the time the events occurred. We produce a sense of retrospective destiny in the events of a person's life by "giving particular weight to events whose effects left their mark on him at a later time but which he lived through casually. That's the mirage: the future more real than the present" (W, 45).

Each event within our story receives meaning by providing a step leading to the conclusion. We look back from the present and see causes for it inscribed in every moment of the past. When a life becomes a story, no detail remains superfluous. Every detail seems to be an annunciation of something to come. But the appearance of necessity in the unfolding of a life is based on an illusion. "We forget that the future was not yet there" (N, 58). Since we cannot use the future to illuminate an event when it first occurs, a story that presupposes the future end to give meaning to the events along the way is dishonest in a certain sense. As Louis Mink puts it, "Stories are not lived but told. Life has no beginnings, middles, ends; there are meetings, but the start of the affair belongs to the story we tell ourselves later, and there are partings, but final partings only in the story. There are hopes, plans, battles, and ideas, but only in retrospective stories are hopes unfulfilled, plans miscarried, battles decisive, and ideas terminal."[13] The only reliable "predictions" we make are about what has already happened. We see necessary links between past and present. Yet even Freud reminds us that our ability to construct retrospective interpretations falls far short of offering a genuine predictive synthesis. He says:

So long as we trace the development from its final stage backwards, the connection appears continuous, and we feel we have gained an insight which is completely satisfactory or even exhaustive. But if we proceed the reverse way, if we start from the premises inferred from the analysis and try to follow these up to the final result, then we no longer get the impression of an inevitable sequence of events which could not be otherwise determined. We notice at once that there might have been another result, and that we might have been just as well able to understand and explain the latter. The synthesis is thus not so satisfactory as the analysis; in other words, from a knowledge of the premises we could not have foretold the nature of the result.[14]

Sartre is fond of the ambiguity in the French word "histoire," which means both history and story. In one sense all history is merely a series of stories, no one of which is "true" in the sense of reproducing lived experience. For Sartre, there is an intrinsic contradiction in the idea of a "true story." All stories are false in one sense, since they are modifications of actual lived experience; the structure they provide is never "true" to experience since it violates the irreversibility of time, thus tampering with the reality of life. A story assumes knowledge of the conclusion to dictate relevant facts along the way. Thus, stories cannot really constitute either my own life or that of another person.

Since a story is to some extent an imaginative construction, it lacks logical necessity. It is always possible to doubt a plausible and coherent story, and to offer an alternative. Any number of stories can emerge from the same life. Roquentin says, "I am beginning to believe that nothing can ever be proved. These are honest hypotheses which take the facts into account: but I sense so definitely that they come from me, and that they are simply a way of unifying my own knowledge. Not a glimmer comes from Rollebon's side. Slow, lazy, sulky, the facts adapt themselves to the rigour of the order I wish to give them; but it remains outside of them. *I have the feeling of doing a work of pure imagination* [italics mine]. And I am certain that the characters in a novel would have a more genuine appearance" (N, 23). By a curious reversal, Roquentin discovers that it is not so much novels which imitate life, but "true" life-narratives which imitate the novel. The meaning of a person's life arises out of an imaginative interaction between reflective narration and the brute facts of his or her life. This process is futile and self-deceptive if it is treated merely as a way of discovering a hidden order or pattern. I never achieve permanent knowledge of myself, since I know myself only in terms of a merely possible story. Simone de Beauvoir has said that "On ne peut jamais se connaître, mais seulement se raconter."[15] The desire to live my life as though I were telling a story is the desire to escape the amorphous chaos of my present experience by locating an intrinsic structure in it. It is the wish for "the moments of my life to follow and order themselves like those of a *life remembered*" (italics mine) (N, 58). In retrospect, life's events follow each other with the inevitability of a familiar melody. By *telling* the story of my life, I begin to achieve a purification of what is foggy and ambiguous. Sartre believes stories and words have a "subtle" and "magical power" (*LPE*, 81–82). He compares the story to a lightning rod; it attracts nameless, fleeting actions and experiences like lightning flashes and joins them together.

Sartre's interest in the way stories transform the immediate experience of events is reflected in his basic attitudes toward the novel. Since he will later characterize existential psychoanalyses as "true novels," it is important to understand his basic attitudes concerning novelistic technique.

The main characteristic Sartre finds in traditional novels is that immediate experience, the "direct onrush of the event" (*WL*, 132–33), is lost. Most often, narratives are reflective and relate events retrospectively. Ordinarily, the story presented by a novel has already been carefully "plotted"; it has been "set in order, pruned, and clarified" (*WL*, 132) by the reflections of the narrator. The reader does not so much reexperience real events as remember them with an omniscient narrator who knows past and future simultaneously. Sartre disparages such novelistic techniques that describe events as though they already existed in a network of fixed logical relationships. A novel that was true to experience would "restore to the event its brutal freshness, its ambiguity, its unforeseeability, . . . to time its actual course, to the world its rich and threatening opacity, and to man his long patience" (*WL*, 220). The novel would not try to intellectualize or offer explanations that posit an underlying order to the disorder of events.[16]

Sartre links the temporal structure of the traditional novel with the structure of memory. Neither of them reproduces events with the temporal quality of actual experience. In both the novel and memory, time is "indefinitely compressible," that is, subject to "abrupt contractions, . . . followed by long expansions" (*WL*, 137). A novel, like memory, can linger to describe a decisive event in great depth and detail, or it can skip over large chunks of time. Writing about the novelistic technique of Dos Passos, Sartre says, "There is no narrative, but rather the jerky unreeling of a rough and uneven memory, which sums up a period of several years in a few words only to dwell languidly over a minute fact. Like our real memories, it is a jumble of miniatures and frescoes" (*LPE*, 96). In addition, the novel, like memory, can explain the importance of a seemingly insignificant present act by reference to its subsequent consequences. While the future may not be known to the reader, it has already been fixed by the author and its shadow falls over the present. In other words, a present act in the novel acquires significance in relation to a future situation. This process violates the normal irreversibility of time as it unfolds in present experience. I cannot appeal to the future to understand what is happening to me now, since the future is as yet indeterminate and must be awaited. In novels and in memory, time is not irreversible. "One can cross it backward and forward" (*WL*, 138). I understand the past by the future and the future by the past. In short, by comparing reflective interpretation and memory with the structure of a novel, Sartre establishes the idea that the self is neither static nor fixed but is constituted by a story in which events are continuously ordered and evaluated, and time is manipulated.

LANGUAGE AND THE SELF

To a great extent, the meaning and structure of a person's life are molded by the linguistic and symbolic descriptions which we use to isolate specific aspects of our dreams, emotions, desires, and past experiences. Sartre regards the use of language as an important form of action. Using words to name objects, feelings, or events is not a harmless form of contemplation, a "gentle breeze" on the surface of things that leaves them unchanged, or a mirror of preestablished qualities, relations, or dimensions. Rather, words represent a decision as to what aspect of the world to disclose (*WL*, 23). Our understanding of reality is constituted by the language we use to express it.[17] Consequently, the possibilities for multiple true descriptions of our lives are virtually inexhaustible.

Even Freud—whose archeological model of the psyche gives the impression that consciousness reproduces ideas, feelings, and memories in their original form—realized that the quality of an experience as it exists in consciousness is a function of the language in which it is expressed. In his essay on the unconscious, Freud admits that a conscious and an unconscious idea "are not, as we supposed, different records of the same content situated in different parts of the mind."[18] Rather, unconscious ideas or instincts are qualitatively and ontologically different from conscious ideas. Freud notes that certain thought processes are "so far remote from the original residues of perception that they no longer retained any of the qualities of these residues." Instead they acquire "new qualities" and become comprehensible only by being "linked up with words."[19] Roquentin, the fictional author of *Nausea*, notices how his images of the past have congealed into words that have replaced the original lively images. He laments that for much of his past life "nothing is left but words: I could still tell stories, tell them too well, . . . but these are only the skeletons" (*N*, 48).

Freud proposes that knowledge of "unconscious" memories and feelings occurs only when they have "undergone transformation or translation into something conscious,"[20] that is, linguistic. This "transformation" is not a simple shift from an "unconscious" language to a conscious one, as the metaphor of translation might imply. French psychoanalyst Serge Viderman points out that in psychoanalysis, "Only the interpretive word gives them [unconscious elements] form and concrete representation, thereby not limiting itself to *translating* one meaning by another, but creating a new representation of that which existed in a broken, fragmented, unrecognizable form. Speech gives it a denomination which unifies it and concretizes it in a totally original way and in a form which exists nowhere in the patient's unconscious, nowhere other than in the analytic space via the language which gives it form."[21]

Just as the archaic religious mentality understands naming as an act of creation and the establishment of a sacred order that endows objects with their qualities, so, too, for the modern person naming brings the reality of emotions, desires, and instincts into existence. There is no fixed object ("signified") in the unconscious for which words are the "signifiers." Rather, the signifier molds the signified in the moment of articulation. To put it otherwise, *an instinct is indistinct*. Prelinguistic thought is amorphous, formless, and chaotic. It is only symbolically represented as instincts. Freud says, "Instincts are mythical entities, magnificent in their indefiniteness. In our work we cannot for a moment disregard them, yet we are never sure that we are seeing them clearly."[22]

Language brings the mere virtuality of unconscious thoughts and desire into formulated existence. In psychoanalysis, interpretation is not a pure invention ex nihilo of instincts, of course. What the language of interpretation determines is an instinct's "mode of existence."[23] Because of this process in which language (including associations to dreams and phantasies) and interpretation shape what is unconscious, the "facts" of psychoanalysis tend to be as much created as discovered.[24] Philip Rieff notes that it is through associations to dreams and phantasies that a symbol is engendered which reveals an aspect of psychic structure. "The meaning is imposed, not exposed; to be precise, only after the meaning is imposed does it expose itself."[25]

In the area of emotions and desires, linguistic interpretations have a major constitutive function. Cognitive and linguistic labels are necessary to mediate emotional experience. A person's emotional life is formed by the subtle linguistic and cultural differentiations one makes.[26] A more sophisticated vocabulary of the emotions makes one's actual emotional life more sophisticated.[27]

Considering the central role of linguistic ability in interpreting experience, it is obvious that as this ability increases, so too does the sophistication of one's recall and understanding of past events. Freud notes that analysis of a small child is limited precisely because "too many words and thoughts have to be lent to the child."[28] Processes which are later discriminated may not be distinguished by a child. "In children, the conscious has not yet acquired all its characteristics; it is still in process of development, and it does not as yet fully possess the capacity for transposing itself into verbal images."[29] In other words, a child cannot yet define the significance of its life experiences in the same way that the adult can. The conceptual and linguistic sophistication that produces awareness of the significance of certain experiences is tantamount to experiencing these events or feelings for the first time. As Viderman puts it: "*To create* is to give a name to and to unify by interpretation that which is only vague desire, nameless, obscure, barely outlined. Between this state of instinct and the precise firmness of form given by the word, there is a *qualitative jump*, dialectical to be precise, which is equivalent to a creation."[30] Sartre would approve of Viderman's emphasis on "a radical heterogeneity between the unknowable of the instinct and the word which formulates its meaning."[31] It preserves the dialectical nature of the self that is so important to Sartre. In contrast to Lacan, who attributes the structure of a language to the unconscious, Viderman counters that the unconscious appears this way only because we must use language to become aware of it: as soon as we *talk* about the unconscious, we have introduced linguistic structure. Language is "a network of intelligibility"[32] that we throw over our experience to create a personal world of meaning, just as the mythical Babylonian god Marduk threw his net over the chaotic dragon Tiamat and cut her into pieces to establish the order of the world.

THE IMAGE OF ONE'S LIFE

In light of the issues presented thus far, especially those in *Nausea*, it is understandable that Sartre concerns himself with the philosophical analysis of the imagination.[33] Indeed, it is precisely the nature and role of the imagination that confuses Roquentin in his historical examination of Rollebon and his reflection on his own life. Roquentin wonders, for example, if his research will result in merely "a work of pure imagination" (N, 23). At one point he remarks about his subject, "I could *imagine* [italics mine] him so well if I let myself go. . . . But if this is where it all leads me, I'd be better off writing a novel." (N, 82). Roquentin does not want to admit that reflecting on a person's life and writing a novel are fundamentally similar in their structure. Yet in both novels and historical reflection, one must *imagine* the events depicted. Trying to recall the past Roquentin says: "I don't *see* anything any more: I can search the past in vain, I can only find these scraps of images and I am not sure what they represent, whether they are memories or just fiction" (N, 48). This shift from perception (seeing) to imagination that occurs in reflection is crucial to Sartre's discussion.

Sartre's analysis of imagination as well as the nature of the image is important for several reasons. First, the imagination is central to the reflective restructuring of experience. Second, the imagination is a theme that pervades Sartre's work and provides valuable access to his later studies in existential psychoanalysis, particularly his works on Genet and Flaubert, as well as his own autobiography. Third, the discussion of the imagination serves as a useful context in which to examine aspects of Sartre's attitude toward psychoanalysis. Sartre's conception of the image strongly influences his attitude toward the psychoanalytic theory of mind, particularly the issue of the unconscious. Although the basis of his reservations about the Freudian unconscious may be found here, a number of Sartre's characterizations of images are not at all antithetical to a certain psychoanalytic perspective. Finally, Sartre's discussion of the imagination offers further material for his overall view of interpretation and meaning. It amplifies his analysis of what it means to interpret one's past and to reconstruct events in memory.

Central to Sartre's analysis of imagination is his radical distinction between the nature of perception and the nature of imagination. Sartre opposes the inadequate theory of the image that has pervaded philosophy and psychology. His position is especially important in relation to the "image" a person maintains of his or her own past. It is common to treat our images of the past as things we *see* with the "mind's eye." For Sartre, it is problematic to apply this kind of perceptual metaphor to our mental images of the past, since images and memories are not simply revivifications of perception. Images are not fixed reproductions of past situations that we store *in* our minds.

Sartre insists that the nature of images has been persistently misconstrued and misunderstood. According to the traditional theory of the image, there is no qualitative distinction made between perception and imagination because the image is treated as a residue or resuscitation of perception. In the classical philosophical systems of Descartes, Hume, Leibniz, and others, the image is treated as a *thing in consciousness*, a weak duplicate of some perceptual object. Philosophers and psychologists alike have tended to uphold what Sartre calls "the naive ontology of the image" (*I*, 4) which attributes the same kind of existence to an image as to an object of perception. Sartre rejects this common view of the image, because he regards the image not as a passive object, but as a spontaneous, active, and creative product of consciousness.

The conflicting views of the nature of the image are central to my general discussion, since they have divergent epistemological consequences for interpreting various aspects of a person's life as well as for understanding the nature of his or her memories. Briefly, if an image is treated as a passive, thinglike residue of perception, it will present itself to reflection as an object, contained in the psyche, that has predetermined characteristics and meaning. Like an object of perception, certain aspects of the image will be hidden and will simply need to be uncovered. The process of interpretation, therefore, will be a process of discovering qualities of the image that may be hidden but are already established. Reflection on the past thus will become a search among memories as though they were objects in a drawer.

The view of the image as a thing *in* consciousness, what Sartre calls "the illusion of immanence," stems from the tendency to treat all modes of existence as essentially physical (*I*, 3). By mistakenly regarding the image as an actual thing in consciousness, one naturally attributes to it the properties of an actual object of perception. For example, if we assume that images are like physical objects, we must then conclude that images are present at all times, even when we are not explicitly aware of them. In short, the image becomes merely "a content for which memory is only a receptacle" (*I*, 44). Despite the variety of philosophical and psychological theories of imagination, Sartre finds that in all of them the image has an "inert" existence. "It no longer exists solely for consciousness, but exists in itself, appearing and disappearing of its own accord rather than at the beck and call of consciousness. When no longer perceived, it does not cease to exist, leading instead a thinglike existence outside of consciousness" (*I*, 4). If an image is merely a thing that appears to consciousness, it can only be hunted, discovered, and deciphered by consciousness. Any changes that occur in a particular image must be attributed to mechanical processes like association, condensation, or synthesis that are external to consciousness. The decision to treat an image like a thing, moreover, immediately raises the question of where the image is when it is not present to consciousness. One is forced to posit the unconscious as a place to store images "where inert contents exist like things, neither *aware* of themselves nor existing *for* anyone, and where opaque data are related only by contact or by resemblance" (*I*, 114).

Although Sartre's work on imagination only occasionally addresses psychoanalysis or Freud in particular, most of his criticisms of the "naive ontology of the image" can be applied to a certain aspect of Freud's thought as well. Freud often treats imagined objects or scenes as if they were simply pictures passing before the mind. Nevertheless, Sartre's criticism need not be taken as a condemnation of psychoanalysis as a whole but only of certain mechanistic consequences of an inadequate theory of the image.

Sartre's alternate theory of images and imagination emphasizes the active and creative role of consciousness in producing images. Just as the self is not a material presence contained in the psyche, neither is the image a thing to be passively regarded. The existence and attributes of an image are established by an act of consciousness. Sartre says: "This imaginative consciousness . . . is spontaneous and creative: it maintains and sustains the sensible qualities of its object by a continuous creation. In perception the actual representative element corresponds to a passivity of consciousness. In the image, this element . . . is the product of a conscious activity, is shot through and through with a flow of creative will" (*PI*, 18). Imagination is the way consciousness represents an object or situation to itself. It epitomizes the creative power of consciousness to organize experience and endow it with meaning.

The radical distinction between perception and imagination may be juxtaposed with the distinction found in *Nausea* between living and narrating. Neither the story nor the image offers a passive duplication of experience. On the one hand, Sartre associates perception and immediate "living" with the infinite diversity of reality that confronts an individual. On the other hand, imagination, like the story or adventure emerging from reflection, represents a creative transformation and organization of reality. We organize situations when we imagine them, just as we organize our lives when we retell them.

When our image of a person or situation changes, the change is not the result of mechanical processes outside consciousness that present a new image to consciousness. It is the result of a new act of imaginative consciousness. Images change because there are "internal assimilations and disintegrations at the heart of an intentional synthesis" (*PI*, 33). In other words, Sartre wishes to preserve the idea that our ability to imagine or represent objects and situations to ourselves is always an activity of consciousness, not of mysterious unconscious mechanisms. This does not mean that we are explicitly aware of creating images for ourselves or endowing them with particular qualities. On the contrary, Sartre allows for varying types of consciousness and levels of reflective awareness.

In short, Sartre resists the notion of the unconscious only insofar as it refers to a nonpsychological sphere external to consciousness (in its broadest sense) where thinglike images are stored and shuffled according to mechanical laws. Sartre finds this kind of spatial concept of the unconscious ontologically false if intended literally, and seriously misleading if intended metaphorically, since it sets up an internal "world" of images analogous to the external world of perception. In either case, the fundamental difference between the characteristics of imagination and those of perception is overlooked.

Sartre's theory is that an image is a synthesis performed by human consciousness out of feelings, knowledge, and inner sensations; that is, an "affective, cognitive synthesis" (*PI*, 93). To form an image of a person or a situation, one needs a certain amount of knowledge about the object and its qualities. An image is always "charged" with one's own knowledge (*PI*, 73). Sartre says, "it is only what we know in some sort of way that we represent to ourselves as an image. . . . An image could not exist without a knowledge that constitutes it" (*PI*, 73).

Sartre emphasizes that feelings also form an intrinsic part of the image. Feelings represent one's sense of an object, the "affective structure" (*PI*, 89), which permeates the entire object. Sartre insists that an image itself does not arouse feelings such as love or indignation. Rather, an image is itself the spontaneous product of certain feelings of love or indignation in concert with knowledge about the object's qualities. Therefore the image of a certain person in my memory is the "strict correlative of my feelings for her" (*PI*, 186).

My image of another person or even of myself has certain phenomenological characteristics that clearly distinguish it from ordinary perception. First, my image of a person may draw together and synthesize differing and even contradictory aspects of a person. It does not necessarily correspond to that person at a specific moment. Rather, the various moods a person has displayed at different times may be condensed and synthesized in my present image of that person. Furthermore, images often appear in a form they could not have in perception. Thus one can imagine all aspects of an object at once, not just one side at a time as in perception. "What we try to recover in the image is not this or that aspect of a person, but the person himself, as a synthesis of all his aspects. . . . What is successive in perception is simultaneous in the image" (*PI*, 119).

Sartre's analysis of the imagination seems to have obvious applications to the recollections of the autobiographer and the historical reflections of the biographer. Each must deal with the reality of images and imagination. His or her interpretations aim at developing adequate images of events, people, and ultimately of one person's whole life. The examples of images that Sartre uses in his study of imagination suggest that events of the past are imaginatively reworked in memory or reflection, rather than passively recalled. In his most recent work Sartre calls memory "the crossroads of the real and the imaginary" (*IF*, 2.1526). Images represent our efforts to transform and rework reality in accordance with our cognitive and affective assumptions. Memory is not a collective of psychic traces, but rather something we do with our lives.

The overall direction of Sartre's work throughout his life generally supports the connection between the imagination and memory that I have just offered. Nevertheless, it is necessary to note a divergent and inconsistent description of memory that Sartre mentions in passing at the end of his book on imagination (*PI*, 236–37).[34] Despite his recognition that memories are helpful in clarifying the nature of the image, Sartre argues briefly (and unconvincingly) for "an essential difference between the theme of recollection and that of the image." The problem arises from Sartre's association of perception with reality and imagination with unreality. Sartre denies that a "real" incident of one's life becomes "unreal" simply by becoming a memory of the past. Rather, he says that the incident "simply *went into retirement;* it is always real but *past.*"

To acknowledge an element of reality in an image would blur the ontological polarity Sartre wishes to maintain between perception and imagination, or between being and nothingness. Instead, Sartre reifies the past as an ontological mode of reality where perception still obtains: "when I recall this or that memory I do not *call it forth,* but I betake myself where it is, I direct my consciousness to the past where it awaits me as a real event in retirement" (*PI*, 237). Sartre does not elaborate this idea of a retirement home where memory can go to interrogate past events. Frankly, it would be difficult for Sartre to do so, since this idea violates many of his other ideas about the operation of consciousness.

[2] STRUCTURES OF HUMAN MEANING AND THEIR INTERPRETATION

In his best known philosophical work, *Being and Nothingness*, Sartre offers an extended treatment of his theory of the nature of human existence and his method of interpreting it. Since Sartre's philosophical position has been continually discussed, analyzed, and frequently attacked, it is not necessary to offer yet another detailed exposition of *Being and Nothingness*. But it is important to correct a number of misleading impressions regarding Sartre's view of the nature of consciousness, choice, and motivation, and the relation of these ideas to traditional psychoanalysis. An inattentive or inaccurate reading of Sartre coupled with a narrowly deterministic understanding of psychoanalysis leads easily to the impression of a fundamental tension between Sartre and Freud that many interpreters have emphasized. This is not to say that there is no conflict between Sartre at his most voluntaristic and Freud at his most deterministic. A more moderate (and more adequate) reading of Sartre, however, is not inconsistent with a "higher" understanding of psychoanalytic interpretation.[1]

"CHOOSING" THE MEANING OF ONE'S LIFE

Sartre's position has frequently been seen as a radical rejection of determinism and unconscious functioning, and an effort to ground all human
existence in conscious decisions. It is true that Sartre rejects determinism in the realm of psychological phenomena, if by determinism one
means the operation of rigid causal laws like those in the physical world,
but it is not true that Sartre considers all psychological events or human
acts to be the results of deliberate self-conscious decisions in any ordinary sense. One easily distorts Sartre's position if his idiosyncratic understanding of terms such as "conscious," "unconscious," "choice," and
"project" is not carefully considered.[2] For example, the failure to appreciate Sartre's distinction between "consciousness" and "knowledge" makes
his theory appear more radical than it really is. Of course, Sartre does
deny that feelings, desires, or memories can exist *in* the mind in an
unconscious state. He contends that the very nature of such mental
phenomena implies that one is "conscious" of them at the moment they
come into existence.

Sartre's critics have attacked such claims which appear to contradict
the central discoveries of psychoanalysis. William Barrett complains that
because "Sartre's psychology recognizes only the conscious, it cannot
comprehend a form of freedom that operates in the zone of the human
personality where conscious and unconscious flow into each other. Being
limited to the conscious, it inevitably becomes an ego psychology; hence
freedom is understood only as the resolute project of the conscious ego."[3]
This appraisal, however, is not completely accurate. Indeed, if a "resolute project" of a "conscious ego" means a reflective deliberation and
decision about one's goals, it is a caricature of Sartre's psychology at best,
and a complete contradiction at worst.

By treating all psychological phenomena as "conscious," Sartre's purpose
is not to make an empirical claim in conflict with Freud but rather to
offer a conceptual clarification. Sartre does not dispute the validity of
Freud's discovery that insignificant acts have meanings of which people
are frequently unaware and that people's behavior often reveals desires,
feelings, or patterns which they do not realize. His point is simply that
psychological or mental events are qualitatively different from physical
objects and the interactions between physical objects. A psychological
phenomenon is never a direct *causal* result of an organic or physiological state, of particular environmental events, or of other psychological phenomena. None of these can completely determine psychological phenomena as though fixed laws were operating. The reason that
people respond differently to equivalent situations, physiological states,
and so forth is that these limiting factors are first mediated by each

person's system of meanings, goals, and values, *even* when the person is not explicitly aware of this system.

Similarly, when Sartre insists that one "chooses" the contingent facts about one's life (for example, one's race, class, physical disabilities, sex, etc.), he does not literally mean that a person actively decides to be white or black, male or female, born rich or poor, crippled or not, since that would be patently false. But I can "choose" to be a person who has any of these contingent qualities by attributing a particular personal meaning to that quality. "I choose the way in which I constitute my disability (as 'unbearable,' 'humiliating,' 'to be hidden,' 'to be revealed to all,' 'an object or pride,' 'the justification of my failure,' etc.)" (*BN*, 328). I "choose" pain by enduring it with resignation or patience, rejecting it, evaluating it as unjust, deserved, purifying, and so on. (*BN*, 330–31). Thus "choosing" my disabilities, or any of the accidental qualities that Sartre calls a person's "facticity," does not imply that I can decide *not* to be white, male, crippled or in pain if that is the case. It means only that the manner in which I live with such things reflects a personal system of meanings. This "choice," moreover, need not be considered a voluntary or reflective decision that is explicitly known. A person is not conscious of every one of his or her intentions, feelings, or desires in the ordinary sense of "conscious." Indeed, Sartre believes the most fundamental "choices" regarding a person's way of dealing with his or her world can only be known by means of an existential psychoanalysis that reconstructs the choices a person is expressing in his or her actions.

Thus Sartre's claim that all psychological phenomena are conscious or chosen is considerably weaker than, or at least different from, Barrett's understanding. Sartre equates "consciousness" with "choice" to distinguish it from genuine deterministic processes that operate in the physical world. Consciousness is discontinuous with deterministic mechanisms because they fail to account for the power of consciousness to transcend the conditioning factors of any situation. If mental phenomena are not mechanically determined, and Sartre insists no genuine "mechanisms" can be demonstrated, then they are necessarily "conscious" rather than nonconscious or unconscious. In a sense, the expression "conscious choice" is redundant in Sartre's vocabulary, since all consciousness is a choice and all choice is conscious. "Choice and consciousness are one and the same thing" (*BN*, 462).

CONSCIOUS VERSUS UNCONSCIOUS MEANING

To Sartre, all psychological phenomena must be understood as various ways of experiencing and relating to one's body, other people, and the world in general. As such, they are intrinsically phenomena of consciousness. The notion of unconscious feelings, if unconscious means "not of consciousness," is therefore illogical or absurd, since feelings and desires have been defined as types or modes of consciousness. Only if a feeling were a *thing* following mechanical laws and unrelated to one's personal mode of existence in the world could it be genuinely unconscious. For Sartre, the term "unconscious feeling" is a misnomer for a feeling that has been kept from explicit awareness or conceptualization, but is still an element of consciousness. Long and difficult analysis is usually necessary to attain explicit knowledge of the pattern of one's thinking and acting, that is, to understand the implicit form of consciousness one has been experiencing all along.

Sartre is presenting a much broader understanding of "consciousness" than is customary; it includes everything that Freud includes as part of the psyche and divides into conscious and unconscious. Consciousness simply refers to the whole psychological realm of subjectivity as distinct from purely physical relations between objects.[4] Within the realm of consciousness, there is a variety of modes, and not all of them include reflective knowledge. Sartre does not claim that consciousness is omniscient; a person does not always *know* all his feelings or the full significance of his behavior. Yet Sartre refuses to use the word "unconscious" to describe these aspects of personality, since they are not mere physiological mechanisms remote from the stream of consciousness.

In light of Sartre's broad understanding of consciousness, his refusal to admit unconscious mental phenomena is not so difficult to accept, for it does not require the view that one always knows what one is doing. His analysis of "bad faith" as an alternative to the idea of "the unconscious" acknowledges the reality of desires and feelings which are not explicitly known, yet it approaches them in terms of personal beliefs and purposes rather than psychic energy or quasi-physical mechanisms. Bad faith, that is, "hiding a displeasing truth, or presenting as truth a pleasing untruth" (*BN*, 49), is based on the view that "repressed" memories or desires must be understood as conscious *in some way.*[5] Moreover, while Sartre acknowledges that condensation, displacement, and transference occur in one's consciousness of images and memories, he sees these as the result of "inner dialectics" of meaning within consciousness rather than unconscious mechanisms.[6] Sartre's goal, therefore, is not to discredit psychoanalysis, but only to highlight what he believes is already implied in Freud's actual clinical discoveries.

Sartre appreciates psychoanalysis for recognizing that every state of consciousness points to a deeper level of meaning, to something beyond itself. One can understand an emotion or psychic fact only by looking for its "signification" (*E*, 41), the idea it symbolically satisfies. Sartre is willing to admit the validity of certain psychoanalytic interpretations of emotions and other actions. For example, psychoanalysis may be right to see a clumsy theft as a type of self-punishment for some "unconscious" complex. A phobia may express the refusal to relive a painful childhood incident associated with the feared object. What Sartre questions is the theoretical basis of psychoanalytic interpretations. While psychoanalysis may see conscious phenomena as a "symbolic realization" of repressed desires, it presents the meaning of the behavior as external to the behavior itself. "The *thing signified* is entirely cut off from the *thing signifying*" (E, 45); the manifest phenomenon becomes merely the passive effect of an external cause.

Sartre strongly resists the notion that conscious phenomena can signify something else without one's being conscious of it. Of course, the signification is not necessarily "explicit." "Many degrees of condensation and clarity are possible" (E, 46). Yet meaning is to be found "within" consciousness, not in an external cause: "consciousness is itself the fact, the signification, and the thing signified" (E, 46). In psychoanalytic terms, the symptom, the defense mechanism, and the traumatic or forbidden thought are all elements of consciousness.

The "profound contradiction" which Sartre finds in psychoanalysis is its juxtaposition of explanation based on causal links with explanation based on inner comprehension of the relation between symbolization and symbol. He notes that the psychoanalytic "practitioner" achieves results only "by seeking in a flexible way, the intraconscious relationship between symbolization and symbol," whereas the psychoanalytic "theoretician" establishes only "transcendent bonds of rigid causality" (E, 48). In other words, Sartre is sympathetic with psychoanalytic practice insofar as it tries to understand tensions within consciousness itself that involve personal meanings and goals. It is the mechanistic metapsychology of psychoanalysis that Sartre finds "coarse and suspect."[7]

Freud's initial acceptance of the Helmholtz School's program led him to formulate an instinct theory whereby a person could be reduced to the operation of quasi-physical-chemical processes. Under the influence of Newtonian scientific models, Freud postulated the operation of a "psychic apparatus" that operated on the analogy of the physical principles of inertia and conservation of energy. Impulses and wishes *cause* observable behavior by obeying these principles. At this level, Sartre's objection is that the physical metaphor or model is inappropriate for describing psychological functioning, since it ignores the structures of personal meaning and purpose which are essential to consciousness.[8] Speaking against materialism, Sartre says, "If the psychological fact is rigorously conditioned by the biological, and the biological fact is, in turn, conditioned by the physical state of the world, I quite see how the human mind can express the universal as an effect can express its cause, but not in the way a thought expresses its object. How could a captive reason, governed from without and maneuvered by a series of blind causes, still be reason?" (*LPE*, 202–3) Ironically, in his screenplay on Freud, Sartre has Freud respond to a reference to Helmholtz's program with the words: "there are forces in us which are not reducible to physical forces."[9] If consciousness were governed by blind causes, it could no longer be genuinely experienced as consciousness.

Sartre focuses on the fact of resistance to demonstrate the weakness of too literal an understanding of the unconscious. Resistance in psychoanalysis refers to the analysand's lack of cooperation and acceptance as the analyst approaches the inner meaning of his explicit behavior or feelings. Sartre wonders why a person would resist a particular interpretation of manifest behavior or thoughts if the meaning were genuinely "unconscious," that is, completely cut off from consciousness. If I were really unconscious of the "image" of myself that my psychoanalyst presents, I could not "recognize" it as something I already knew but was avoiding. I could only regard it as probable and believable (or not) because it explained a number of my behavior patterns (*BN*, 574).

When I "resist" a certain interpretation of myself, it may be because I do not "want" to see a particular aspect of myself. But this sort of self-deception implies that I am conscious in some sense of the aspect of myself or my past which I do not want to see or remember. "I must know the truth very exactly in order to conceal it more carefully" (*BN*, 49). The fact that certain feelings or memories are too threatening or too difficult for me to admit to myself suggests that an evaluation of them by consciousness has occurred at some level. Repression, therefore, is based on the inner desire not to see something about oneself rather than a real incapacity.[10] Of course, the desire may disguise itself as an apparent incapacity. What happens when resistance collapses is that I recognize the image of myself presented by the psychoanalyst as though I were looking in a mirror, that is, as a true reflection (*BN*, 573). I can then bring the ideas or feelings I have avoided to the level of self-reflection.

In short, Sartre's description of bad faith, imagination, and emotion emphasizes implicit beliefs within consciousness rather than mechanistic processes. The essential problem of bad faith is precisely "a problem of belief" (*BN*, 67). Bad faith occurs when a person believes in an image of himself for which the evidence is ambivalent or inadequate. Similarly, "true emotion," says Sartre, "is . . . accompanied by belief. The qualities conferred upon objects are taken as true qualities" (*E*, 73).[11] Emotion is a coloring of one's situation, an apprehension of the world in a certain light and a belief that these projected qualities are real ones. Emotional consciousness is a way consciousness tricks itself into believing that qualities which come from itself actually come from the world outside. One, therefore, suffers and sustains qualities of a situation (e.g., fearful, threatening) due to one's own evaluation and interpretation of it. Bad faith and emotion are not mechanistic discharges of blocked psychic energy, but strategies designed to "mask, substitute for, and reject behavior that one cannot or does not want to maintan" (*E*, 32); they deny the urgency of certain problems by substituting others (*E*, 66).[12] Psychoanalytic insight seeks to adjust the person's *beliefs* so that they are based on more adequate evidence and reason.

Sartre's rejection of determinism has sometimes created the misleading impression that a person decides upon actions in a vacuum without regard to his situation or past. However, Sartre's criticism of determinism as an explanatory principle for human action does not deny the influence of past events on present actions and feelings, or the relationship between a person's environment and his or her behavior. Sartre's position is simply that environment and past events are never "sufficiently effective" (*BN*, 31) to cause behavior in the same way that "a determined point of one given mass determines the courses followed by other masses" (*BN*, 31).

Sartre radically separates relations of motivation from relations of causation[13] (*BN*, 27). To say that every act has a motive is not the same as saying that every phenomenon has a cause, since motives are not an inherent quality of events or situations. No factual state, whether past or present, can in itself motivate behavior, since everything depends on the variety of ways in which consciousness defines a situation and picks out particular qualities about it. For that reason "under no circumstances can the past in any way by itself produce an act" (*BN*, 436). Any "determining" factors of behavior acquire their "determining" quality only as a consequence of being evaluated as such by consciousness. When Sartre refers to a "permanent rapture in determinism" (*BN*, 33), he is referring to the fact that motives for behavior do not exist as independent (or unconscious) entities or forces capable of producing behavior in the same way that a physical cause produces an effect. It is the task of consciousness to confer on a motive "its meaning and its importance" within a larger project (*BN*, 34). When past events serve as the grounds for repeated action over a period of time, it is because their meaning is continually "rediscovered" and "re-created." To this extent, the situation that motivates me is of my own making, since my interpretation has constituted and molded its characteristics and meaning. There is no way to ascertain the "facts of a situation" in any final form. My actions are limited by my understanding and description of both my situation and my possibilities for response.[14]

A "situation," for Sartre, is a specific apprehension of the "environment." It is neither an absolute creation of one's freedom nor a constraint passively submitted to. The environment is ambiguous and explains nothing until an individual's values and perceptions transform it into a personal situation. "The environment can act on a subject only to the exact extent that he comprehends it; that is, transforms it into a situation" (*BN*, 572). Of course, Sartre does not believe this personal comprehension of one's situation is always reflectively known or "thematically conceived and made explicit as in the case of deliberation" (*BN*, 437). Sartre is only emphasizing the intrinsic lack of motivating power in events themselves until they are incorporated into human projects.

Sartre sometimes describes the perception of a situation in terms of figure/ground relations from gestalt theory. Consciousness selects and organizes objects around it in patterns. "No one object, no group of objects is especially designed to be organized as specifically either ground or figure; all depends on the direction of my attention" (*BN*, 98). One's selective attention to the characteristics of a particular situation, moreover, depends on one's specific goals. "The world gives counsel only if one questions it, and one can question it only for a well determined end" (*BN*, 448).

SARTRE AND FREUD ON THE NATURE OF MEMORY

The evaluative function of consciousness in relation to any situation is especially evident in Sartre's characterization of the operation of memory. In memory, everyone becomes his or her own historian and "remakes" the past according to his or her own values and goals. One's character, for example, is not a hidden force from which behavior emanates, but rather "a free interpretation of certain ambiguous details in [the] past. In this sense there is no character, there is only a project of oneself" (*BN*, 552). Sartre insists, moreover, that "we continually preserve the possibility of changing the meaning of the past" (*BN*, 116). The only way to control or reappropriate the past is to interpret it. Even forgetting is a way of giving the past meaning. Memory, like imagination, is an active process of consciousness, not a passive and neutral recording of all that happens. The past has no ready-made meaning of its own. A person's memory is responsible for the sense of order and interrelationships among elements in his or her past. It selectively organizes the past in a coherent picture by emphasizing particular aspects. The result is an edited "image" of the past that contributes to the formation of a meaningful story.

Of course, memory must be concerned with the incontrovertible fact that certain events have occurred and certain acts have been performed in the past. Sartre, therefore, distinguishes between the "content" of one's past which is unchangeable, and the "meaning" of the past in relation to one's total life, which is "eminently variable" (*BN*, 497). Even if one can ascertain brute facts about one's past, these facts acquire meaning and significance in explaining present behavior only in terms of one's ongoing interpretation of the past from the perspective of present goals and values. The past, therefore, is in a "relation of interpretation" (*BN*, 28) with the present. This relation precludes any deterministic links between past and present. Any "compelling power" of the past to motivate present behavior is derived from a present choice or action that simultaneously "chooses" a specific view of the past. For example, a past disappointment does not compel one to feel sad subsequently. Rather, present feelings of sadness indicate a choice of a past as "disappointing."

The past acquires meaning only in relation to the unfolding sense of my life as a whole. Part of the significance of anything that happens to me rests on that which does not yet exist. To fully understand an episode in my story, I must wait for the "ending." An adolescent crisis, for example, may acquire meaning as a premonition for a person who subsequently experiences a conversion. Otherwise, its meaning might simply be that of an accident of childhood. As a person modifies the sense of his or her life as a whole, earlier values can lose their importance and significance. Sartre says "the future decides whether the past is living or dead" (*BN*, 449). For this reason, Sartre describes man as "a being whose meaning is always problematic" (*BN*, 129). The meaning of his past is always "in suspense" (*BN*, 501). The experience of "suspense" is the realization that the significance of what is happening will only become apparent later. A major characteristic of the human psyche is that "later determinations act upon earlier ones, envelop them and endow them with a new meaning" (*SG*, 78).

Obviously, the significance of past situations, traumatic or otherwise, does not persist from moment to moment like a quality of a thing; it is always possible to shift the way one construes the nature of an event. The lack of strict causal efficacy on the part of the past does not mean, however, that behavior is arbitrary or capricious, or "that I can make the meaning of my previous acts vary in any way I please" (*BN*, 498). Every person preserves his or her past "in the form of a tradition in the light of [his or her] future, instead of allowing it purely and simply to determine [the] present" (*BN*, 453). Accordingly, the past may not cause specific actions, but one's past supplies a context in terms of which one may react to a new situation differently from another person. Sartre's use of the word "tradition" points to a pattern in the cumulative development of one's actions or projects. Actions are loosely predictable when a traditional pattern of action has been established, though it is always possible to reinterpret or break with "traditional" ways of behaving.

Although Freud's archeological model of the psyche suggests that interpretation is necessary to rediscover lost, forgotten elements of the past, his actual practice revealed that memory operates along the same lines Sartre describes. For example, in many cases psychoanalytic interpretation simply marks a shift in the evaluation of the significance of an event or feeling that was *never* forgotten. A new way of seeing old material will often permit a more unified pattern to emerge. Interpretation *creates* the context in which the pattern can be *discovered*. It reassociates impressions that were isolated and establishes a new synthesis of meaning.[15] In the case of Rat-Man, for example, the "traumatic event" was never forgotten. He remembered it without trouble, although "he could not remember that he had ever attached any importance to the event."[16] Interpretation allows an unintelligible (dissociated) element to be placed within a new meaningful context.

Freud makes an important distinction between two kinds of "knowledge" of certain important events in life which is also consistent with Sartre's position. Freud says,

> . . . *it is just as reasonable to hold that the patient "knows" his traumas as that he does* not *"know" them. For he knows them in that he has not forgotten them, but he does not know them in that he is unaware of their significance. It is often the same in ordinary life. The waiters who used to serve Schopenhauer at his regular restaurant "knew" him in a certain sense, at a time when, apart from that, he was not known either in Frankfort or outside it; but they did not "know" him in the sense in which we speak today of "knowing" Schopenhauer.*[17]

Freud's analogy is particularly interesting, since it shows how an experience may be lived through naively, while its significance does not accrue until a later date. His example does not deal with two simultaneous forms of knowledge, with the subject aware of one and "unconscious" of the other. Rather, he describes two temporally separate moments. It would be foolish, of course, to say that the waiters in Freud's example had repressed the significance of Schopenhauer or were unconscious of it in a traditional psychoanalytic sense. His significance "today" is something that the waiters could have known only at a later point in time.

Similarly, one could claim that the traumatic significance of an event is not simply a knowledge that was unconscious, hidden, or forgotten. In many cases a person does not "remember" the special significance of an event, not because it was "forgotten," but because it lacked its full significance when it occurred. Only in the light of subsequent experience is the interpretation of its significance possible. Within this new context, many other remembered events may acquire new meaning, and new constellations of the past occur. Thus, to say a person does not "know" all the possible implications and significance of his or her actions does not mean that interpretation can uncover the "real" original meaning of these actions. Freud was aware that meaning is often retrospectively attributed to past events. He struggled to account for this fact while preserving his archeological picture of psychic functioning. Straining his metaphor to the limit, he noted that psychoanalysis, like archeology, cannot always date its findings reliably, since materials of a late origin may be carried down to earlier levels after certain disturbances.[18] In one case, Freud tries clumsily to preserve the archeological view while also acknowledging the transforming effect of new experience; the result is an ambiguous position. He insists that mental impressions are preserved *both* in their original form "and also in the forms that they have assumed in their further development"; memory contents can be restored "even though all original relations have long been replaced by newer ones."[19] Ironically, Sartre himself comes close to slipping into the same archeological metaphor that he rejects in Freud. When he tries to explain the order of the past within a person's memory, he says, "It would be wrong to think that when the present is past it becomes our closest memory. Its metamorphosis can cause it to sink to the bottom of our memory, just as it can leave it on the surface. Only its density and the dramatic meaning of our life can determine at what level it will remain" (*LPE*, 88). Memories floating or sinking to different levels in the "ocean" of memory is not so different from Freud's image of archeological relics at different levels of the mind.

While Sartre justifiably criticizes the lack of dialectical development in Freud's notion of a linear determinism of the present by the past, he fails to note clear elements of a dialectic of meaning present in Freud's work. From the very start Freud was aware of the effect of *Nachträglichkeit* or "deferred action." This is the process by which initial experiences and impressions are revised at later times to fit in with new experiences or new stages of development.[20] This phenomenon implicitly destroys the possibility of a linear determinism from past to present. In the course of analysis, and more generally in the course of life, the "same event" may at different times vary in relation to the details emphasized, the conceptual framework of understanding employed, the emotional response evoked, and so on. Although Freud never gave up his problematic trace theory of memory, he admitted to Fliess in 1896 that the material of memories is subject at different times to "a rearrangement in accordance with fresh circumstances—. . . Memory is present not once but several times over."[21]

The retrospective investment of past material by later experience is what Sartre described as the determining of the past by the future.

Psychologist Erik Erikson remarks that the past "is part of a present mastery which employs a convenient mixture of forgetting, falsifying and idealizing to fit the past to the present."[22] He notes that therapy is not concerned with actual events, but with "certain retrospective moods of the patient."[23] In short, autobiographical memory is a dynamic, selective process in which the past and present dialectically interact to produce a unified account of one's life. Autobiographical interpretation, therefore, is not a simple reexperiencing of a forgotten event, but a particular appropriation of past experience according to current interests and needs.[24] Memory simultaneously compresses and expands the story of one's life.

THE FUNDAMENTAL PROJECT AND THE TOTALITY OF THE SELF

According to Sartre, the minor everyday acts in my life as well as the most important ones "derive their meaning from an original projection of myself" (BN, 39). The "original projection of myself" or my "fundamental project" is an extremely complex and ambiguous notion in Sartre's thought. Much confusion exists regarding its nature and its role within existential psychoanalysis. By examining the notion of the fundamental project in relation to the other aspects of Sartre's thought that have already been discussed, it is possible to establish a consistent understanding of the fundamental project which amplifies and develops the notion of the self as a retrospective and imaginative reconstruction embodied in a narrative structure. Furthermore, it is at the level of the fundamental project that the mythic quality of an individual's personal narrative becomes apparent. When understood in this way, the fundamental project or original choice is something far more profound than a simple decision to lead a certain kind of life, to embark on a certain career, or to aspire to specific goals.

The goal of existential psychoanalysis is "hermeneutic" (BN, 569): to decipher, elaborate, and conceptualize the unifying theme, pattern, or meaning that is expressed by the whole variety of specific activities in a person's life. In other words, the goal is to describe the person's fundamental project. Although Sartre is not systematic in his use of the term "fundamental project," in general he uses it to refer to the total sense of a person's life, the context within which every detail in that life has significance.

Sartre assumes that every life is a unified whole or "organized unity of conduct patterns" (BN, 476) rather than a simple flux of phenomena where each is externally conditioned by the preceding one. In analyzing this unity of personality, Sartre deliberately avoids a clear distinction between discovery and invention. On the one hand, the fundamental project is not something hidden that has been discovered. On the other hand, it is not a complete fabrication of interpretation. In a certain sense, one must invent it in order to discover it.[25] Interpretation simultaneously "invents" the unifying theme of a life in order to "discover" how that theme permeates every individual fact.

Sartre sees his method of "existential psychoanalysis" as a *reverse* psychoanalysis. Unlike classical psychoanalysis he does not interpret present phenomena as merely the result of the past. Rather, he analyzes them from the point of view of an emerging gestalt or future totality that develops as a person pursues his or her future projects. This unifying, evolving structure of meaning—the fundamental project—should not be confused with unconscious complexes or aspects of a systematic unconscious à la Freud. Sartre criticizes psychoanalysis for trying to reduce the complexity of human experience and behavior to several basic drives that take a particular form in each individual due to the deterministic effects of such things as personal history or family situation. He believes the interpretation of human lives is more than a simple matter of analyzing behavior into basic drives as though one were a chemist analyzing a compound. It must attend to the particularity of a person's behavior, not appeal to dubious reified concepts or abstractions such as universal instincts. Accordingly, Sartre calls psychology "the most abstract of the sciences because it studies the workings of our passions without plunging them back into their true human surroundings, without their background of religious and moral values, the taboos and commandments of society, the conflicts of nations and classes, of rights, of wills, of actions. . . . We do not reject psychology, that would be absurd; we integrate life."[26]

Sartre's method of interpretation takes an individual's tastes, lifestyle, profession, etc. and tries to establish a "thematic organization and an inherent *meaning*[27] in this totality" (*BN*, 468). He compares empirical desires in order to locate elements common to them all. The resulting interpretation reflects what Sartre describes as three identical elements: "the fundamental project, the person, the free realization of human truth" (*BN*, 567). The overall goal of interpretation is "to disengage the meanings of an act by proceeding from the principle that every choice, no matter how insignificant, is not the simple effect of the prior psychic state and does not result from a linear determinism but rather is integrated [s'integre] as a secondary structure in global structures and finally in the totality which I am" (*BN*, 459). The reflexive verb *s'integrer* is significant in this passage, since it suggests that each act in a person's life integrates itself into a larger structure that is always developing as an organic whole. An individual act is not simply an isolated item to be collected with others and inventoried. Every act becomes part of "richer and more profound meanings" (*BN*, 457) as the future unfolds. Ultimately, interpretation may arrive at a total Weltanschauung or "hierarchy of interpretations" (*BN,* 457) within which every gesture and action occupies a place.

"Totality" is the key notion that emerges from all Sartre's discussions of the fundamental project. When he describes the fundamental project, Sartre is not concerned with some abstract principle or drive behind the concrete behavior of an individual, nor does he see the fundamental project as a kind of superchoice a person makes in addition to his individual acts. Rather, it is only by first looking at the specific behavior of a person that one can find a unique and individual expression of "the totality of his impulse toward being, his original relation to himself, to the world, and to the Other, in the unity of internal relations and of a fundamental project" (*BN,* 563). In short, the fundamental project is not an abstract desire or goal, but the concrete totality of the individual. Specific attitudes and behavior both "express" and "are" that "total relation to the world by which one constitutes oneself as a self" (*BN,* 563). Each act expresses that totality from a specific angle. Just as Husserl treats an object of perception as the ideal or transcendent unification of all its aspects, the fundamental project is "the transcendent meaning of each concrete, empirical desire," "a center of reference for an infinity of polyvalent meanings" and "the totality of the individual human being" (*BN,* 563, 570).

If one recognizes its transcendent quality, it is obvious that the fundamental project is not a choice of specific goals. When Sartre refers to the fundamental project as a person's "choice of being," he is primarily referring to the person's general style of experiencing and acting in the world. One might call it the "way of life" or "manière d'être" (*BN,* 567) that is revealed in a person's individual tastes, opinions, and gestures. Individual acts are thus never just what they seem to be, since they are "symbolic" of a more inclusive sense of a life as a whole in which the past and future are integrated.[28]

Since Sartre considers the fundamental project to be the sense of a human life's "totality in progress," it is wrong to think of a fundamental project as "first conceived and then realized" (*BN,* 463) in the way we would understand an ordinary project. As Sartre says, "we shall be able to apprehend it only by living it" (*BN,* 463). Although we are "conscious" (in Sartre's sense) of all our feelings and desires, we do not experience their unity as something additional. The fundamental project is not ontologically prior to each of our empirical choices in some unconscious or noumenal realm.

The "secondary structures" of the fundamental project, that is, a person's actual concrete behavior, in no way *emanate* from the fundamental project. Although the meaning of specific acts always depends on "the total meaning which I am" (*BN*, 470), there is no *necessary* connection between this totality and any particular action. The fundamental project cannot by itself account for one particular act rather than another. It is neither a force animating the course of life nor a fixed character or temperament that motivates behavior. It is not a general principle to be applied to specific situations in order to logically deduce particular responses.

Each act is merely a mode of the fundamental project within a particular situation. Specific actions may be interpreted as part of a fundamental project, but they themselves are what serve to "enrich," "articulate," and "make concrete" (*BN*, 470) that fundamental project. They are its "expression and symbolic satisfaction" (*BN*, 565). It is "beyond" them as the "transcendent" aspect of every empirical choice one makes. It is the whole that is coming into existence through each of its parts. Each concrete act in a life is a potential symbol of the person's total mode of being. The fundamental project "exists and manifests itself only *in* and *through* specific feelings of greed, courage, and a host of other empirical expressions" (*BN*, 565). Sartre calls this relation "the connection between a totality and a partial structure. The view of the total project enables one to 'understand' the particular structure considered" (*BN*, 469). In short, the relation of act to fundamental project is that of part to whole.

The dialectical development of this totality reveals the powerful influence of Hegel on Sartre. Sartre's treatment of the fundamental project reflects the dialectical notion

> *that a whole governs its parts, that an idea tends of itself to complete and enrich itself, that the forward movement of consciousness is not linear, like that which proceeds from cause to effect, but synthetic and multi-dimensional, since every idea retains within itself and assimilates to itself the totality of antecedent ideas, that the structure . . . is not the simple juxtaposition of invariable elements which might, if necessary, combine with other elements to produce other combinations, but rather an organization whose unity is such that its secondary structures cannot be considered apart from the whole without becoming "abstract" and losing their essential character* (*LPE*, 204).

If the fundamental project is a dialectical totality, then individual acts are never isolated but are bound together by inner relations in the unity of a whole such that "the presence of one modifies the other in its inner nature" (*LPE*, 204). This dialectical dimension is embodied in Sartre's claim that "man is a totality and not a collection" (*BN*, 568). Dialectical relations, unlike causal ones in which an effect is an inert reflection of what preceded it, involve a progressive or cumulative enrichment of the totality. Each new dialectical movement turns back on the past synthesis, absorbs it, and adds new layers of significance.

The dialectical relation between the meaning of individual details in a life and the meaning of the whole life rests on an evident circularity. On the one hand, an individual act is meaningful only in relation to the fundamental project of which it is a partial expression. On the other hand, the fundamental project can be deciphered and understood only in terms of the meaning of individual acts. In other words, one must recognize the fundamental project in order to understand the significance of a specific choice, and one must apprehend the nature of the specific choice to understand the fundamental project it expresses. This hermeneutical circularity means one must interpret an individual act in relation to one's sense of the whole path of a life even though the whole is partially formed by that individual act.

Some critics have questioned the basis of Sartre's commitment to "totality" as a model for human life. Joseph Fell wonders whether a person really is "a tightly knit totality all of whose behavior is ultimately traceable to some single originative source,"[29] and whether the idea of fundamental project can account for the randomness and lack of direction of much human experience.[30] Phyllis Sutton Morris similarly doubts whether menial and mundane acts really express any global project at all. These concerns, however, are misplaced. Fell overlooks the dynamic nature of the project. Sartre does not claim a single originative source from which all subsequent action derives. Unfortunately, both Fell and Morris imply that the fundamental project is a kind of discernible goal against which actions can be judged by how they contribute to fulfilling it. If the fundamental project is understood as a mode of being, however, even the most mundane activities—walking the dog, brushing one's teeth—could contribute in a small way to the total sense of a person's life. When sufficiently probed, even seemingly random experiences may express basic attitudes toward one's existence.[31]

The major consequence of Sartre's approach is that the fundamental project is known only as the product of retrospective construction. A person never has immediate awareness of some distinct choice which determines every specific attitude and desire he or she has. Only by looking back over an individual's life can one reconstruct the path it has followed and the choice this person has made for his or her life. At the beginning of *Being and Nothingness* Sartre rejects the idea that human beings have an essence or nature which is the source or cause of their behavior. The meaning of their behavior stems from freely chosen projects oriented toward the future. The theory of the fundamental project at the end of *Being and Nothingness* is meant to replace the deterministic concept of essence. As an alternative to traditional definitions of human nature, Sartre maintains "the overflow of our consciousness progressively constitutes [our] nature, but it remains always behind us and it dwells in us as the permanent object of our retrospective comprehension" (*BN*, 35).

THE ORIGINAL CHOICE AS MYTHIC EVENT

It is important to address a contrary understanding of the fundamental project for which there is some support in Sartre's thought. At some points in his theoretical discussions and especially in his actual case studies in existential psychoanalysis the "fundamental project" or "original choice" seems to refer specifically to a critical period in childhood when a "choice" is made that establishes the basic attitude one will have toward his life and its goals. For example, Baudelaire is six years old when his father dies and his basic values and perspectives are allegedly established. Sartre says he himself was about seven when he made his basic choice to be a writer. Sartre's specification of such childhood events or choices has resulted in the problematic view that the fundamental project is something which "radiates like the ripple from a stone through the whole life that follows."[32] Sartre's use of the word "choice" is unfortunate since, while preserving his emphasis on noncausal attribution of meaning, it gives the impression of a discrete event. It leads William Barrett to treat the fundamental project as a literal decision made in childhood, which is sustained throughout life. Barrett contends, moreover, that since this choice cannot be established in all cases as a resolute, self-conscious, decision, Sartre is indirectly admitting the presence of an unconscious, where the hidden meaning of all one's actions and attitudes can be found. Barrett concludes that the project is hidden in the child in the form of an unconscious idea or complex. Even those who *know* their project are still unaware of the meanings being manifest in each of their acts. Anthony Manser, likewise, wonders if the child is really aware or responsible for his original choice and whether the original choice is not "only an eccentric name for the Freudian complex [which] . . . might just as well be relegated to the unconscious."[33]

One way to respond to these criticisms is to clarify the kind of "choice" Sartre sees in every person's life. The ways I am conscious of the world, the meanings I find in it, my tastes, interests, and values, all comprise a certain "image" or "choice" of myself (*BN*, 463). All of these elements help me to "sculpt my figure in the world" (*BN*, 464). This unifying image that I live and choose (but do not explicity *know*) cannot be considered unconscious in a traditional psychoanalytic sense. Before the analysis of my fundamental project, there is nothing hidden to be discovered, but simply a lack of conceptualization. Before analysis, everything exists "without shading, without relief, without connections . . . —not that these shades, these values, these reliefs exist somewhere and are hidden from it, but rather because they must be established by another human attitude and because they can exist only *by means of* and *for* knowledge" (*BN*, 571). Analysis isolates, condenses, and conceptualizes the sense of a life as a whole. It provides reflective knowledge of what was lived or understood in a state of prereflective consciousness. Although Sartre rejects unconscious determinism, he claims that a person cannot know the total significance of what he or she is doing at the moment it occurs. Continual analysis would be necessary to understand the total meaning of one's life. If the fundamental project is a choice, it is an incomplete one, a "choice in the making" ("un choix en train de se faire") (*BN*, 479). At any particular moment, the fundamental project is only an *emergent* choice which develops through time. It must be constantly renewed: "I choose myself perpetually" (*BN*, 480). This temporal dimension of the self is essential to Sartre's position.

But these considerations cannot escape the fact that Sartre does discuss pivotal moments of crucial significance for the lives of the people he analyzes. Here especially one must keep in mind John Mack's warning to all psychoanalytic biographers to avoid the temptation to find some important event in a person's life which is *the* turning point from which all subsequent developments are derived. There is the danger of providing artistic grace and unnatural direction to "the often rather amorphous nature and fitful course of human life, even that of a great man."[34]

In the final analysis, it is probably more valuable and more consistent with his total discussion not to regard the critical childhood events or "original choices" in Sartre's studies as genuine historically datable acts, decisions, or events. The crucial childhood events that he describes cannot be regarded as determinative of subsequent experience in the lives of his subjects without radically contradicting Sartre's analysis of the meaning of the past as something that develops throughout life. The critical childhood events and choices that Sartre mentions are in a similar position to the traumatic scenes that Freud reconstructs in psychoanalysis. In neither case does the theoretical importance of the event rest on its historicity. The childhood event and choice may be real or imagined, or perhaps a mixture in which the event remembered is either a condensation of several events or an elaboration of a real event.

For Sartre's psychoanalyses, *the childhood event is primarily important as a symbol, paradigm, or mythic structure of later layers of significance.* Sartre's attitude toward the past suggests that the traumatic significance of a childhood experience and the unifying function of a fundamental childhood choice are not so important as actual psychological experiences of the child; rather they reflect subsequent reconstructions and elaborations of the meaning of the event and the choice.

Past events remain traumatic or pivotal only insofar as they are given continuing significance by present consciousness. The *appearance* of a necessary connection between the past and the present arises when "nonsignificant accidents of being are surpassed toward a significance they did not possess at the beginning" (*BEM*, 158). In other words, when one interprets a situation or action in terms of an earlier event, it is often the later event that establishes new qualities or implications as the significance of the earlier event. For Sartre, these new meanings were not necessarily hidden within the original event, but rather represent dialectical accretions of significance to it. By placing a later event in the context of an earlier one, both events are enriched and grasped in a new light.

Accordingly, one way to understand the nature of the crucial childhood event and the "original choice" that arises in response to it is as a *mythic paradigm*, symbolic of a basic orientation toward the world. When Sartre focuses on a specific childhood event within an existential analysis, he is dealing with a dramatic crystallization of a series of events. It is very likely that the childhood dramas Sartre recounts did not occur all at once, but they serve as images in which other events or feelings are condensed and unified. A crucial childhood event can "symbolize" my psychic evolution when it is described in a way that relates to the total sense of my life at a particular moment. Although every event in my life is a factor in my psychic evolution and the unfolding of my fundamental project (insofar as it is integrated within the totality of my personality), there is also a distinct "psychic crystallization" around each event (*BN*, 569). As each event is preserved within my life as an image in my memory, it is colored by various cognitive-affective assumptions. My image of a past situation is strictly correlative to the significance I presently attribute to it. Since it is the crystallization of meaning around my past that ultimately constitutes my project, the past "in itself" is only of secondary importance for me or my analyst.

Freud also recognized that many memories are nuclei around which meaning has thematically crystallized. Particularly in the case of early childhood memories, there is considerable evidence that we are dealing more with imaginative constructions than with actual reproductions of past experience. Often, when we remember our childhood, we envision ourselves from the outside, as a spectator would. The genuine perspective of the child, whose attention was directed toward outside impressions, not toward himself, is thus distorted. Freud says: "Whenever in a memory the subject himself appears in this way as an object among other objects, this contrast between the acting and the recollecting ego may be taken as evidence that the original impression has been worked over. . . . But no reproduction of the original impression has ever entered the subject's consciousness. . . . The raw material of memory-traces . . . remains unknown to us in its original form."[35]

Freud notes that childhood memories, unlike adult memories, are not fixed at the moment events occur. Only at a later period are they "elicited," "formed," "consolidated," "molded," "remodeled," "altered," "refurbished," and "elaborated" according to later needs and projects.[36] For this reason, memories have symbolic importance that may be either "retrogressive" or "progressive." That is, they may represent other things that came before, after, or simultaneous with the actual remembered event. Memories thus are symbols of accumulated meaning in which the memory of earlier events may reflect the influence of later concerns, interests, and attitudes, and the memory of later experience may reflect the influence of earlier events. Freud compares childhood memories to the legends and traditions of a nation's prehistory, because both have been gathered and interpreted to fit later ideas. He goes so far as to wonder

> . . . whether we have any memories at all from our childhood: memories relating to our childhood may be all that we possess. Our childhood memories show us our earliest years not as they were but as they appeared at the later periods when the memories were revived. In these periods of revival, the childhood memories did not, as people are accustomed to say, emerge; they were formed at that time. And a number of motives, which had no concern with historical accuracy, had their part in thus forming them as well as in the selection of the memories themselves.[37]

Similarly, Alfred Adler points out that early memories are particularly important as indices of the fundamental attitudes and goals of a person's life as a whole. Early moments epitomize the entire mode of being of a person. Adler notes that

> . . . early recollections are found always to have a bearing on the central interests of that person's life. Early recollections give us hints and clues which are most valuable to follow when attempting the task of finding the direction of a person's striving. They are most helpful in revealing what one regards as values to be aimed for and what one senses as dangers to be avoided. They help us to see the kind of world which a particular person feels he is living in, and the ways he really found of meeting that world. They illuminate the origins of the style of

life. The basic attitudes which have guided an individual throughout his life and which prevail, likewise, in his present situation, are reflected in those fragments which he has selected to epitomize his feelings about life, and to cherish in his memory as reminders. He has preserved these as his early recollections.[38]

Memories may also be especially vivid because they epitomize best the various aspects of a conflict that extends over a long period of time and involves other events. Thus a so-called traumatic event is most often paradigmatic of a pattern. Freud discovered that symptoms are usually "not the precipitate of a single such traumatic scene, but the result of a summation of a number of similar situations."[39] Accordingly, interpretation and reconstruction deal more with patterns within the personality structure than single events. Ernst Kris found that certain of his patients developed (without explicitly knowing it) a consistent and idealized "autobiographical self-image" or "personal myth" whose pattern they reenacted in their actions.[40] This personal myth has a paradigmatic function even though it was often based on factual and chronological inaccuracies. The psychoanalytic interpretation must deal primarily with this symbolic world of personal myth, and not with objective events.

The emphasis on symbolic importance over historical accuracy can be correlated in some ways with the psychoanalytic distinction between psychic reality and material reality. Freud discovered that "the neurotic symptoms are not related directly to actual events but to phantasies embodying wishes, and that as far as the neurosis was concerned psychical reality was of more importance than material reality."[41] Freud's realization that the primal scenes he reconstructed in analysis were of a psychic or imaginary nature rather than datable historical events was a major development for psychoanalytic theory. Ultimately, Freud regarded it as a matter of little importance therapeutically or epistemologically whether a primal scene or reconstructed childhood memory was a phantasy (an "emotionally charged fiction")[42] or a real experience. This theoretical position raises a further question, however, since it is easy to historicize psychic reality by treating reconstructed primal phantasies as *datable psychic events* from the past. When this happens, Freud's archeological model can still be maintained in relation to past mental "events." The distinction between material and psychic reality merely shifts the focus from the *discovery* of discrete material events in the past to the *discovery* of a discrete moment of past mental life inscribed in memory.

It is better, perhaps, to regard reconstructed primal scenes as for the most part *neither* hidden material events in the past *nor* hidden phantasies in the past. In a certain sense, the phantasy or scene acquires its structure only at the moment it is interpreted. As Serge Viderman puts it, a psychoanalysis is only superficially the reconstruction of an ideal objective history ("*the* past"). At the deepest level it is "a mythical prehistory" ("*his* past").[43] The primal or original event is important insofar as it acquires the status of a transhistorical model that symbolically embodies the fundamental structures of a person's life. This is why Sartre is indifferent to the historical accuracy of his reconstructions. In this sense, the reconstruction may be treated as a way of understanding a life in terms of a "mythic" model that is "ritually" reenacted in the subsequent course of life. Freud, too, found himself reconstructing for his patients crucial early events and feelings that were never actually remembered. They "have to be divined—constructed—gradually and laboriously from an aggregate of indications."[44] In describing the components of one particular phantasy, Freud admits that "the most important and most momentous" phase of it "in a certain sense . . . has never had a real existence. It is never remembered; it has never succeeded in becoming conscious. It is a construction of analysis, but no less a certainty on that account."[45]

Dominick La Capra criticizes Sartre's discourse for being overwhelmingly "mythomorphic," thereby undermining the distinction between truth and fiction and throwing in question the whole project of totalizing the meaning of a person's life. He observes "the concept of original choice has at best the status of a heuristic fiction or even a myth designating a virtual object that is required for a unified or totalizing understanding of a life."[46] La Capra sees Sartre slipping into the option which likewise tempted Roquentin: using art, fiction, or stories to salvage the absurdity of real existence. La Capra is right to point out the mythic quality of the original choice, but his misgivings about it are largely unwarranted. Sartre deliberately uses this technique in his analysis to reflect the very process of mythicizing that every person must employ to create meaning out of his or her past. Again, Sartre is trying to achieve in relation to others what we normally regard as the privileged domain of autobiographers. The achievement of autobiography, says Roy Pascal, is "to give us events that are symbolic of the personality as an entity unfolding not solely according to its own laws, but also in response to the world it lives in. . . . It is not necessarily or primarily an intellectual or scientific knowledge, but a knowing through the imagination, . . . an understanding of the feel of life, the feel of living."[47] Sartre would like to present the same kind of understanding in telling the story of a person's fundamental project.

CHANGING ONE'S FUNDAMENTAL PROJECT

If a fundamental project refers to the total path of a person's life and the meaning it reflects back on each step along that path, the implications of changing one's fundamental project must be carefully considered. Sartre does refer to the "perpetual modifiability of our initial project" (*BN*, 464). The possibility of such a change can easily be misunderstood, however, if the fundamental project is confused with a specific project, or if its essential characteristic of being a *totality* is ignored. This prospect of change cannot refer to a specific new decision from which new acts will emerge, since the fundamental project does not precede specific acts. To change fundamental projects would require that I literally become a different person with a different past. Of course, as my life unfolds, its history as a whole takes on new forms and meanings. In this sense, my past is always changing and my sense of my life as a whole is always open to revision. Nevertheless, if I claim to be a "new person" as a result of some conversion, I have not completely left one fundamental project behind and begun another. Although people may radically alter specific projects in their lives, it would be misleading to think of an individual's life as a sequence of fundamental projects wherein each new fundamental project takes up where the prior one leaves off. If the fundamental project is a genuine evolving totality, then every person has only *one* fundamental project extending throughout his or her life.

A mid-life crisis or major change in career attitudes or beliefs is not the end of one fundamental project and the beginning of another. Such changes, however radical, do not represent distinct fundamental projects but rather aspects of a single, continually modified, fundamental project. Despite the impact of "radical modifications," "metamorphoses," and "conversions" in my fundamental project, my life is but a single totality within which complex stages of reevaluation and reintegration occur.[48] Sartre notes that "a converted atheist is not simply a believer; he is a believer who has for himself rejected atheism" (*BN*, 467). In other words, even my rejected interpretations and my old image of the totality of my life are preserved within my new interpretation and sense of the whole. A conversion of my fundamental project encompasses all that preceded it, albeit in a new light. The most radical conversion maintains a continuity with the past even if the past is only the rejected and despised foundation on which a new edifice stands.

A radical modification of the fundamental plan is thus not a matter of tearing oneself up by the roots[49] but a reinterpretation or reidentification of those roots. Such reinterpretation is inevitable since the fundamental project is in a state of "continuous temporalization" (*BN*, 467). Rather than an impetus behind action, the fundamental project is the continuously recovered sense of a whole developing in time, constantly synthesizing past, present, and future. This sense of the whole, the story I tell about my life, develops in (what Sartre later calls) a dialectical state of "totalization." This means that every new act, choice, and situation is integrated with all previous ones into a total structure. Each element in the developing totality is comprehensible only in relation to the rest of the changing whole. In the development of a totality, new factors emerge as significant. Their meaning is not a new discovery of something present from the start which was hidden or latent, but virtually a new creation. This dialectical movement means that the significance of any part of a life is tentative and awaiting further development. The extreme challenge of psychotherapy is that it must push a stalled dialectic to a new mode of being and new system of interpretation.

THE FUNDAMENTAL PROJECT AS A LITERARY WORK

Since literature is the paradigmatic art for Sartre, it is not surprising that he construes the fundamental project on a more or less literary model. The fundamental project resembles a work of art insofar as it represents a systematic structure of interrelated meanings. Sartre says, "A living past, a half-dead past, survivals, ambiguities, discrepancies: the ensemble of these layers of pastness is organized by the unity of my project. It is by means of this project that there is installed the complex system of reference which causes any fragment of the past to enter into an hierarchical, plurivalent organization in which, *as in a work of art* [italics mine], each partial structure indicates in different ways various other partial structures and total structure" (BN, 500).[50] Although this structure of meanings is lived on an intuitive level, its form only becomes explicit when the fundamental project becomes a retrospective narrative. In fact, the fundamental project cannot really be separated from the *story* of the fundamental project in a particular person. In a sense, the project is consubstantial with the story of the individual life up to the moment of narration. Those who mistakenly try to identify one specific goal as the fundamental project are looking for the hidden "point" of the story. But as Stanley Hauerwas accurately puts it, one's life is inseparable from one's life story and the story *is* the point: "the mysterious thing that we call a self is best understood exactly as a story—a story that has no point but the display of itself for others but especially for ourselves."[51]

The ability to modify perpetually the fundamental project is the ability to change the tone or direction of one's life story. Sartre describes human existence as "a perpetual, searching *historization*" and psychoanalysis as an interpretation of "the meaning, orientation, and adventures of this *history*." [italics mine] (BN, 569). "Historization" represents the fundamental project in its implicit state of becoming a story. "History" represents the fundamental project as a realized story *(histoire)*. Historization leaves a history in its wake just as living leaves behind the story of the totality of a person's life. The fundamental project signifies the coming into being of a choice, a style, a self, a history, and a story. Unlike Roquentin, we do not have to choose between living and telling. Realizing our fundamental projects requires that we do both. Montaigne aptly points to the interpenetration of living and telling in a well-known passage: "In modeling this figure upon myself, I have had to fashion and compose myself so often to bring myself out, that the model itself has to some extent grown firm and taken shape. . . . I have no more made my book than my book has made me—a book consubstantial with its author, concerned with my own self, an integral part of my life."[52]

An even more direct link can be made between Sartre's theory of language and literature, and his analysis of the fundamental project. To be more specific, the meaning and interpretation of a person's life shares certain common characteristics with the meaning and interpretation of a literary text. Every person is the "author" of his life; his acts, like the words of a writer, combine to constitute a unique view of the world. Sartre explicitly compares individual acts in a life with words in a sentence. He says, "To understand the word in the light of the sentence is very *exactly* to understand any given whatsoever in terms of the situation, and to understand the situation in light of the original ends" (*BN*, 515).

The meaning of a word is determined by the context in which it appears. Sartre insists that the sentence and not the word is the elementary structure of speech (*BN*, 514), since the sentence is the necessary condition for the meaning of words (*BN*, 36). Similarly, the sentence finds meaning only within the context of the work as a whole. "The sentence which I write is the meaning of the letters which I trace, but the whole work which I wish to produce is the meaning of the sentences" (*BN*, 37). In writing a book, one is never totally immersed in spelling each word or constructing each sentence. Writing is always an anticipation of the not yet existing context of the chapter and ultimately of the book.

A sentence, therefore, is Sartre's paradigm of a "project" because it is a totality in the process of making itself. The meaning of individual words as they are spoken or written is cumulative, resting on the unfolding order of the sentence. It is not fixed prior to the use one makes of them. A sentence is defined by "the order of words which become *these words* only by means of their new order" (*BN*, 518). In short, the words in a sentence establish an overall order, but the meaning of the words is not determined until the order is set. The word has only a "virtual existence outside of complex and active organizations which integrate it" (*BN*, 514).

More generally, the meaning of what exists is constantly placed in suspense by a totality that does not yet completely exist. But the totality that does not yet exist relies on the individual things that do exist. The meaning of the part and whole of a sentence, therefore, is defined within the same hermeneutical circle as the meaning of an individual act in relation to the fundamental project. A sentence does not preexist the words which comprise it anymore than a fundamental project preexists the specific acts that "express" it. Sartre's insistence on the indefinite nature of the meaning of past events is easy to understand as analogous to this relation between the meaning of word and sentence. In one sense, acts are like words since they have a "virtual" significance that becomes specified only in light of the subsequent totality of events.

Sartre has emphasized that the fundamental project is a "totality in the making" which is manifest in a person's life but which could never be permanently achieved. His dialectical characterization of the fundamental project is partly derived from Hegel, but another more interesting source for it is the dialectic between writing and reading that Sartre presents in *What Is Literature?* The relation of his literary theory to the theory of existential psychoanalysis is never made explicit in Sartre's own work and consequently has been completely overlooked. This connection is not at all fortuitous when one considers that all the major examples of existential psychoanalysis which Sartre offers are studies of writers. His interest in the nature of literature and the writer has been a lifelong concern. His own autobiography, which may be considered an example of existential psychoanalysis, is called *The Words* and is divided into sections on "Reading" and "Writing." Thus, Sartre considers the way literary texts are produced and understood a model for the way in which any life can be understood or interpreted.

By linking the theory of consciousness with the theory of art, the fundamental project with the literary work, and lifestyle with literary style we can highlight the similarity between the ordinary life of a person and the activity of a writer. Despite the fact that an author is essential to the interrelationships of the various elements in his work (WL, 33), Sartre makes the unusual claim that the creative act of an author is "only an incomplete and abstract moment in the production of the work" (WL, 36). In order for a work to exist as a "work," that is, as a unified object, the joint effort of the writer and the reader is required. The reader is conscious of the work as an object that slowly discloses itself. Certain expectations or anticipations develop in the reader, and he or she waits to see if they are confirmed or disappointed. To the author, however, there is no object that discloses itself. The author "projects" (WL, 35) the successive elements of his work. He does not wait to see what happens to his hero; he decides it. For the author the future is a "blank page" (WL, 36) that is not preestablished, as it is for the reader. The work never seems fixed, necessary, or definitive for the author but is constantly in a "state of suspension" (WL, 33), since he can always change or add a line to his work. While an author is in the midst of writing a book, its meaning as a whole is always in doubt; the author never knows his work as a totality.

Reading, says Sartre, is a "synthesis of perception and creation" (WL, 37). To the reader, the work is an object that gradually reveals its structure. The reader synthesizes the various aspects and enables the work to exist as a whole. Understanding a text is not a mechanical process in which words leave an impression on a passive reader. Without the reader, there is only a string of words. The reader enables the work to exist as a transcendent object, as a "synthetic form" beyond the individual words and phrases. Reading is thus a creative act, since it constitutes the words as a work which did not exist as such until that moment. What Sartre is trying to say is that the meaning of a literary object is not contained in individual words but is expressed "through" them, just as the fundamental project is expressed through specific projects. The reader perceives individual words, but he must create the work as a whole by both uniting and going beyond them. The real meaning of a text, therefore, lies not in the sum of its words, but in their organic totality (WL, 37–38). A literary text, like a human being, is a totality and not a collection.

Sartre refers to the total meaning of a text as a "silence" and an "opponent of the word" (WL, 38). It is not to be found in any of the individual words. The reader must "invent" this silence which is beyond the words in order to "awaken" the sense of individual words and sentences. Sartre emphasizes that the meaning or organic whole of the work that results from reading is neither a reinvention nor a discovery, but a new and original act. The meaning does not come at a definite moment in the reading. It is "everywhere and nowhere" (WL, 39). It is something that never existed before. The silence or meaning which the reader invents is different from that which guided the author. The author has been guided by a silence which is "subjective and anterior to language. It is the absence of words, the undifferentiated and lived silence of inspiration, which the word will then particularize" (WL, 38). The reader's "silence," however, is a transcendent object that did not exist before the work was created. It is simultaneously disclosed and created through the individual words and phrases. Reading involves Sartre's version of a hermeneutical circle since the reader must "disclose in creating, create by disclosing" (WL, 37). By creating the total meaning, the reader discloses the meaning of individual words within a network of relations, but the total meaning emerges only out of what the individual words create.

Sartre says that a work exists only at the level of the reader's capacity.

The paradox of the work of art is that "tout est à faire, et tout est déjà fait." For the reader, everything is "to do . . . and already done," "to make . . . and already made" (WL, 40). The reader can always create more profoundly; consequently, a work is inexhaustible, capable of being interpreted by the reader in multiple ways. Sartre believes the total meaning of a sentence may escape the writer, though eventually it will be grasped by the reader. The reader may see something in the text that the author did not put there or understand when he wrote it, but which later appears as the veritable meaning of the text and conditions the author's view of what he wrote.[53]

There are striking similarities between Sartre's descriptions of the reader's creation of an overarching meaning that is disclosed in the individual words of a text and the interpretation of a fundamental project as the total meaning of a life in terms of which individual acts become significant. An author requires a reader to realize his work as a totality just as every individual requires existential analysis to specify his fundamental project. Every individual is the "author" of his life in the sense of "projecting" future acts, just as the writer projects what his hero will do, but the meaning of his life as a whole is out of reach. The interpretation of the fundamental project is always tentative because the project is, to use a literary metaphor, a "work in progress." First, it is analogous to the process by which the meaning of a book unfolds as it is being written. And, on another level, it resembles the unfolding of an author's total *oeuvre* or "life work." These metaphors suggest how a person might modify a given project or "work" yet still be contributing to the total *oeuvre* of his or her life. Furthermore, Sartre's insistence that the meaning of a literary work exists at the level of the reader's ability parallels his idea that the meaning of events in a person's life can vary within the context of his or her life work. This is the reason why everything remains "to make" while being "already made." Events have already occurred, words have already been written. But their meaning is not fixed and depends on how they are "read."

In examining the peculiar nature of the fundamental project and its relation to actual empirical actions and feelings, Sartre employs the literary model as an explanatory device; he compares the hierarchy of meanings implicit in a person's life to the hierarchy involved in the creation of a literary work (word, sentence, paragraph, chapter, book), and the relation of living versus analyzing a fundamental project to the relation of writing versus reading a text. To use another metaphor, Sartre believes that the total meaning, or fundamental project, of a person's life is expressed in the totality of his actions in the same way that the genius or significance of an artist is expressed by the totality of his work. The genius of Proust, says Sartre, is not his work itself nor a subjective ability which produced it. "It is the work considered as the totality of the manifestation of the person" (*BN*, xlvi). Thus we might say that a person's life is a total work which expresses that person as a whole. The fundamental project is neither the person's acts themselves, nor some decision that prompted them, but his or her actions as a whole seen as an expression of a way of apprehending the world.

If the structure of a person's life resembles a literary text in some important way, then general hermeneutical theories about interpreting texts may offer insight into the process of interpreting lives.[54] Literary interpretation, for example, is often defined as a search for the hidden intentions of the author of a text.[55] This approach likewise has represented the dominant tendency of the psychoanalytic interpretation of lives. In psychoanalysis, the "intentionalist" approach to interpretation aims at retrieving hidden or lost intentions from moments in the past in a way that is analogous to finding an author's original intention in a text. The interpretation must discover what the subject's past feelings and actions meant to him or her at the time they occurred. If the subject does not seem to know what he or she meant by a particular action, or offers an improbable reason for it, the interpreter will try to discover the unconscious or disguised intention. Within this model of interpretation, the subject is treated as a forgetful and/or dishonest "author" who must be confronted by what he or she really meant by some part of his or her "text." When interpretation is construed as looking for something hidden in a text, the result is a process of *discovery*.

Literary interpretation and the interpretation of lives can also be conceived of as process of imaginative creation. When an interpretation provides a narrative account that introduces order into a chaotic field of material and thereby contributes to a cumulative sense of the whole, it is an active process of imagination which enables compelling connections to be discovered. This is not to suggest that there is an ideal point toward which all interpretations converge. Any interpretation may be transcended by a new interpretation that forms a more comprehensive and plausible context.

Insight into the pattern of a person's life resembles the creative "reading" of a poem. It establishes a unifying schema for an array of data, but in no way does it correspond with a single correct meaning that is hidden. Psychoanalyst Roy Schafer, for example, insists that psychoanalysis does not show what a person is "really" thinking or wishing. There are always a number of ways to understand a person's actions. This perspective, he adds, "corresponds to a well-accepted principle of text analysis: there are more ways than one to understand a text; more than one view may be required; and the author's view of it counts as only one among others, and is a view whose authority cannot be taken for granted."[56]

There is an important difference, however, between interpreting literary texts and interpreting lives. In one sense, at least, a literary text is relatively fixed and unchanging. Ordinarily, there is an *authoritative* version of it with which all interpreters must contend. For this reason, the historical shift from oral "texts" to written texts represents a fundamental cultural development. Stories that are transmitted orally lack the fixity of a written text. There tend to be multiple versions of the same story as well as embellishments and elaboration in progressive retellings of the story. It may therefore be inappropriate to treat an individual's life per se as the text of interpretation. This gives the impression of a fixed, unique text. While it is true on one level that a person has but one life and one past, it is not so obvious that there is only one authoritative story of his or her life. There can be different "versions" of the story of one's life, each presenting a different text for interpretation. Since there is no one "true" description of the past, there is no one "true text." Indeed, a dialectical relation exists in which a text presents itself for interpretation, but the text may be subsequently changed by the interpretation.

Freud's archeological model sees the textual quality of a person's life as something which has been lost or corrupted by defenses but which can be recovered through analytic interpretation. However, to lose or to corrupt a text implies the preexistence of an original text. French psychoanalyst Serge Viderman rejects the archeological metaphor of reconstructing a lost text. "The text was never lost because a text, i.e., a formal unity with a preexistent structure, has never existed."[57] The interpretation of dreams, symptoms, transference, etc., is not a matter of recovering an original text, but of assembling a unified text for the first time.

Textuality implies a sense of the work as a whole and how each detail contributes to that whole. This sense is not always present in every act as it is lived, but only in reflection on one's life. The coherence, interdependence, and significance of past events can only be fully seen when they are reconstructed in the present. Thus, to be the author of one's life means to form a convincing story by which one reassumes it.

One of the most suggestive, albeit speculative, applications of a literary model of interpretation to the study of lives is David Bakan's association of psychoanalysis with the hermeneutic principles of Jewish mysticism.[58] From this point of view, not only is every individual's life like a text, but it is like a *sacred* text. In Jewish mysticism, the Hasidic holy man or Zaddik was regarded as the embodiment of Torah, the sacred text. His every act and word, like every letter and word of the Torah, was sacred and full of profound meaning. Even his most mundane act was regarded as revelatory of Torah. For Freud, says Bakan, everyone is interpreted like a Torah.[59] In psychoanalysis, therefore, we find "a transfer of subject matter from the text of Torah to the text of human behavior, a point not even very novel in Jewish tradition."[60] When Jewish mystical tradition compared the Holy Man's life to the Torah, it understood the Torah as more than simply a book. It was the sacred blueprint of the cosmos itself. According to Jewish tradition, the Torah was God's guide in establishing structure and order out of chaos. In this sense, the entire structure of the universe is that of a text.

In his autobiography, *The Words*, Sartre notes his childhood illusions about the sacred power of the writer. As a writer, Sartre felt he could redeem his superfluous existence by identifying with the structured world of the text he created. The world of the text has a pure existence beyond anything in this world; it exists outside ordinary time or space. Roquentin's decision at the end of *Nausea* to write a novel is precisely based on a view of literary creation as a cosmogonic act. Of course, Sartre gradually realized the illusory nature of literary salvation. Yet if he gave up the idea of personal embodiment in a literary text, his understanding of the meaning of a person's life, like Freud's, is increasingly based on a textual approach. If modern men and women live in a chaotic world without the comfort of cosmic order as it appears embodied in Torah, their fundamental task is the creation of a personal cosmos. The literary nature of the fundamental project gives it the qualities of a personal Torah, that is, the overarching order which establishes the world of an individual. Just as every act of the Zaddik is revelatory of Torah, every act of a person is revelatory of his fundamental project. Thus for Freud and Sartre, human life must be examined as a sacred text.

[3] *DIALECTIC AND TOTALIZATION: NEW THEORETICAL DEVELOPMENTS*

In the first part of this book, I examined the implications of certain aspects of Sartre's early thought for an overall system of interpretation of human reality. Sartre calls this system *existential* psychoanalysis. Although a number of Sartre's thoughts regarding the interpretation of an individual's life are in harmony with dimensions of classical psychoanalytic interpretation, one cannot overlook the stubborn resistance to psychoanalysis permeating Sartre's early works.[1] Sartre himself confesses that in his youth he had "a deep repugnance for psychoanalysis" and was "deeply shocked by the idea of the unconscious" (*BEM*, 36–37). It is in the context of this early opposition that Sartre's subsequent reevaluation of psychoanalysis and its increasing role in his work becomes important. Although Sartre's mid-life "conversion" to Marxism is well known, his concomitant change of heart toward psychoanalysis has not received adequate attention. The nature of Sartre's revised opinion of psychoanalysis and several other aspects of his later thought contribute new elements to his overall theory of interpretation. By incorporating the new methodological and ideological concerns into Sartre's developing existential psychoanalysis, we will also find a very interesting parallel to the theories and psychobiographical applications of psychoanalytic ego-psychologist Erik Erikson.

SARTRE'S REEVALUATION OF PSYCHOANALYSIS AND THE UNCONSCIOUS

Much of Sartre's early opposition to psychoanalysis was the result of a fairly superficial acquaintance with it. Simone de Beauvoir, for example, notes that during the early days of their careers in the 1930s, she and Sartre had only "the most rudimentary knowledge" of psychoanalysis, and a blindness regarding the conditioning effects of their own childhoods.[2] She recalls,

> We looked favorably on the notion that psychoses, neuroses, and their various symptoms had a meaning, and that this meaning must be sought in the patient's childhood. But we stopped short at this point; we rejected psychoanalysis as a tool for exploring a normal human being. We had hardly read any Freud apart from his books The Interpretation of Dreams and The Psychopathology of Everyday Life. We had absorbed the letter rather than the spirit of these works: we were put off by their dogmatic symbolism and the technique of association which vitiated them for us. Freud's pansexualism struck us as having an element of madness about it, besides offending our puritanical instincts. Above all, the importance it attached to the unconscious, and the rigidity of its mechanistic theories, meant that Freudianism, as we conceived it, [italics mine] was bound to eradicate human free will. No one showed us how the two might be reconciled, and we were incapable of finding out for ourselves. We remained frozen in our rationalist-voluntarist position: in a clear-minded individual, we thought, freedom would win out over complexes, memories, influences or any traumatic experience. It was a long time before we realized that our emotional detachment from, and indifference to, our respective childhoods was to be explained by what we had experienced as children.[3]

This passage shows clearly that de Beauvoir retrospectively recognizes the inadequacy of Sartre's and her attitude. It was only psychoanalysis "as we conceived it" that they opposed, and their conception of it represented a fairly narrow view. Accordingly, de Beauvoir and Sartre had "a very limited faith in psychoanalysis."[4] They construed it as "a form of energetics," which gave causal explanations of people by a mechanical application of its concepts but did not really "understand" them. Sartre tended to ignore Freud's genuine concern for the origin of symptoms or symbols in the intentionality of the subject perhaps, as Christina Howells suggests, to make his own position more dramatic and in sharper relief.[5]

De Beauvoir has since acknowledged that she and Sartre failed to distinguish the serious research of Freud from the vulgar application of his theories by amateurs. They had been particularly scandalized by those people who felt obliged to consult psychoanalysts about every plan and action in their private lives.[6] They found it impossible, however, to reconcile the existence of free will with the existence of the unconscious determinations of action. Only after many years would Sartre attempt to achieve this reconciliation in the development of his own work.[7]

Although Sartre's first two efforts at existential psychoanalysis—*Baudelaire* (1947) and *Saint Genet* (1952)—reveal an increasing appreciation for psychoanalysis, there is a more appropriate time to date the dramatic shift in his attitude. In 1958, film producer John Huston asked Sartre to write a screenplay for a movie dealing with the early career of Freud. Since he had spent considerable energy denying that the unconscious exists, Sartre understandably found it amusing that he was asked to write about Freud, the pioneer in the exploration of the unconscious. Sartre claims he agreed to the project only because he was broke and needed the $25,000 that Huston had offered. Regardless of his motives, Sartre read or reread many of Freud's works during this period as well as commentaries and criticism.[8]

Although the screenplay concentrated on Freud before he had developed his most famous theories, working on this film offered Sartre the opportunity to deepen his entire appraisal of psychoanalysis and to base it on a firmer knowledge of Freud. Sartre says this project "led me to rethink what I had thought about the unconscious,"[9] and enabled him to acquire "an average, satisfactory knowledge of Freud."[10] It is no accident that Sartre's renewed awareness of psychoanalysis corresponds with a period of renewed concern with two of his own major studies in existential psychoanalysis—his autobiography and his work on Flaubert. These two works reveal a much closer relation to Freudian psychoanalysis than his earlier studies had shown. Here and elsewhere one finds a new appreciation for the idea of the "unconscious" and the effects of childhood experiences on the adult personality.

More recently, Sartre has characterized himself as "a critical fellow traveller" of psychoanalysis rather than an opponent or detractor (*BEM*, 199). He has no doubts about the permanent value of Freud's discoveries, and, like many others, he is more concerned with clarifying theoretical difficulties than refuting psychoanalysis. To be sure, Sartre retains his earlier misgivings about psychoanalysis on certain points. For example, he remains troubled by Freud's biological and physiological metaphors that tend to make psychoanalytic explanation too mechanistic

(*BEM*, 37). Whether this mechanistic tendency in Freud is essential to psychoanalytic theory is what contemporary psychoanalysts have likewise wondered.

Despite Sartre's continued opposition to mechanistic accounts of human beings, his position on the unconscious reveals substantial modification. No longer is the unconscious the point of bitter contention it was in some of Sartre's early work. The concept of "bad faith" in *Being and Nothingness* had specifically been developed as an alternative explanation for alleged "unconscious" phenomena. The notion of the "unconscious" had originally shocked Sartre's rationalism. Yet even in Sartre's early thought, there was a sense in which his resistance to the idea of the unconscious was illogical, since he had accepted other ideas resembling the unconscious. As Simone de Beauvoir reflects, "One of our inconsistencies was our refusal to accept the idea of the subconscious. Yet Gide, the surrealists, and despite our resistance, Freud himself had all convinced us that in every person there lurks what André Breton called *un infracassable noyau de nuit*, an indestructible kernel of darkness, something that . . . now and then, bursts out in a peculiarly scandalous fashion."[11]

This "kernel of darkness" at the core of consciousness has become increasingly important in Sartre's understanding of human psychological functioning. Sartre's references to the "darkness," "night," and "obscurity" within consciousness in more recent work represent a recognition that the meaning of one's life is not completely transparent or lucid, but includes a certain opacity, accessible only indirectly through interpretation. Sartre has come to recognize the limitations of ordinary consciousness. Given his original position, it is rather ironic that Sartre broke off his work with Huston on the Freud film "precisely because Huston did not understand what the unconscious was. . . . He wanted to suppress it, to replace it with the preconscious. He did not want the unconscious at any price" (*BEM*, 36).[12] For Sartre to defend the unconscious against misunderstanding is unusual indeed.

What Sartre realizes in his 1969 interview on the development of his thought is that the unconscious can be acknowledged without at the same time treating its operation mechanistically. He therefore, distinguishes Freud's "*mythology* of the unconscious" from the "*facts* of disguise and repression" (*BEM*, 37). Sartre insists that Freud often slips into a mechanistic fiction when describing unconscious processes. As a result, Sartre finds that it is not possible to "believe in the unconscious in the form in which psychoanalysis presents it to us" (*BEM*, 37). While Freud sometimes transcends mechanistic explanations and focuses on the teleological purposes of unconscious mental functioning, his refusal to renounce causal explanation produces a curious mélange. Sartre calls the result "a strange representation of the unconscious as a set of rigorous mechanistic determinations, in any event a causality, and at the same time as a mysterious finality, such that there are "ruses" of the unconscious, as there are "ruses" of history; yet it is impossible to reunite the two in the work of many analysts—at least early analysts" (*BEM*, 37–38). For example, argues Sartre, the psychoanalytic concept of condensation can be seen as an example of associationist psychology whereby two images are brought together externally and condensed into a third. In this case the unconscious becomes a mechanism operating outside of consciousness. However, condensation can also be an intentional combination of images that unconsciously satisfies a specific desire or need. Sartre readily acknowledges the latter aspect of unconscious thought. He is willing to accept the unconscious as a dimension of the psyche, but he is not willing to treat it as a mechanism that is completely removed from purposive psychological activity (*BEM*, 38).

"LIVED EXPERIENCE" VERSUS "THE UNCONSCIOUS"

In recent years Sartre clearly became more comfortable discussing the reality of unconscious psychological functioning than he had been before. Nevertheless, Sartre preferred to introduce his own terminology to deal with this aspect of psychic life. The central concept in Sartre's revised understanding of consciousness is *le vécu*—"lived experience." Sartre uses this concept to deal with the "facts" of unconscious phenomena without presenting these facts mechanically. At the same time, Sartre now speaks of *le vécu* where he formerly referred to "consciousness." *Le vécu* represents

> . . . *the equivalent of conscious-unconscious, which is to say that I no longer believe in certain forms of the unconscious even though Lacan's conception of the unconscious is more interesting. . . . I want to give the idea of a whole whose surface is completely conscious, while the rest is opaque to this consciousness and, without being part of the unconscious, is hidden from you. When I show how Flaubert did not know himself and how at the same time he understood himself admirably, I am indicating what I call experience* [le vécu]—*that is to say, life aware of itself, without implying any thetic knowledge or consciousness. This notion of experience* [le vécu] *is a tool I use, but one which I have not yet theorized* (LS, 127–28).

Sartre calls lived experience "a compression of consciousness" containing a richness that is undeveloped.[13]

Sartre further explains, "Understanding is a mute accompaniment of lived experience, a familiarity of the subjective enterprise with itself, a putting in perspective of components and movements but without explanation; it is an obscure grasp of the meaning of a process beyond its significations" (*IF*, 2:1546). It would not distort Sartre's position to call this "obscure understanding" unconscious.[14] Sartre insists that there is always a kind of silent understanding of the important elements of lived experience, a "spontaneous appreciation without intellection" (*IF*, 2:1546). In short, the unconscious does exist for Sartre, but not as a mechanical process. Rather it is the depth of nonrational intuitions within a person's experience of which he has only a tenuous grasp, "a total absence of knowledge, but a real comprehension" (*BEM*, 41).

Sartre acknowledges that his position in *Being and Nothingness* was too rationalistic and failed to account for such processes that are lived irrationally "below consciousness" (*BEM*, 42). These processes have meaning at the level of lived experience even though this meaning eludes ordinary reflective consciousness. Our awareness of what Flaubert called "the terrifying and tedious depths" within ourselves is not an intellectual process (*BEM*, 40). In addition, since language is intrinsically inadequate to express fully the ever-changing nature of lived experience, "comprehension of the unconscious in most cases never achieves explicit expression" (*BEM*, 41).

Le vécu involves the prelinguistic, prerational "silence" or "meaning" that Sartre first mentioned as the source of literary creation. The initial "silent meaning" that inspires the author cannot be grasped as such and can be analyzed only as it is expressed in linguistic terms. This "nonsignifying silence enclosed by words" (*BEM*, 272), what Flaubert called the "unsayable" core of lived experience, is the stylistic flavor that is condensed and particularized by each part of a literary work. Sartre makes the cryptic statement that what a writer has to say is "nothing *sayable*, nothing conceptual or conceptualizable, nothing that signifies" (*BEM*, 272). The explicit content of a literary text is surrounded by a "silent knowledge," which it communicates to the reader. By this, Sartre seems to be suggesting that what is distinctive about an author and his text is no specific content which can be stated in simple facts of knowledge. I have already compared this "silence" at the heart of the author's style to the meaning of a person's fundamental project, which likewise is expressed through specific acts but never is witnessed in itself. The meaning of a literary work or of a fundamental project is in one sense "everywhere and nowhere" (*WL*, 39). It is "everywhere," shining through each word or act. But it is also "nowhere," somehow beyond each of these same words or acts. In the same way, Flaubert's flashes of insight into his unconscious or "lived" depths simultaneously reveal to him "nothing and everything" (*BEM*, 40).

By introducing the category of "lived experience," Sartre has built upon the idea of the "fundamental project" developed in *Being and Nothingness*. The fundamental project referred to the cumulative development of a mode of being rather than a primordial choice from which subsequent acts emanate. Similarly, lived experience, which in some ways is coextensive with the prereflective fundamental project, develops within a process of "dialectical totalization." Lived experience, says Sartre, is "the ensemble of the dialectical process of psychic life, insofar as this process is obscure to itself because it is a constant totalization" (*BEM*, 41).

THE DIALECTICAL DEVELOPMENT OF THE SELF

Sartre's major criticism of psychoanalysis no longer lies in the notion of the unconscious. He accepts it in a modified way. The object of his attack is elsewhere. He complains that traditional psychoanalytic theory lacks "dialectical irreducibility" (*BEM*, 39). According to Sartre, the key issue of *his* psychoanalysis is *dépassement*, which refers to the fact that psychic life is a "perpetual process of integration and reintegration on a base prior to it."[15] The fundamental error of both orthodox Freudians and Marxists lies in trying to prove that what has happened had to happen just as it did because of the interaction of certain prior conditions and mechanistic principles.[16] This assumption destroys the dialectical dimension of all human phenomena. Psychoanalysis recognizes pathological experiences that may have occurred in childhood, but it ignores "the acting itself, which interiorizes, surpasses and preserves the morbid motivations within the unity of a tactic, the act which gives meaning to the meaning conferred on us" (*BEM*, 204). Of course, Sartre admits to the existence of structured "complexes" or psychic configurations that are conditioned by the past. The feeling or passion between two people, for example, may be "highly conditioned by their relationship to the 'primal object' and one can locate this object within it and explain the new relationship by it; but the relationship itself remains irreducible" (*BEM*, 39).

The dialectical nature of psychic development causes Sartre to reconsider the place of freedom in this process. Although his original doctrine of freedom was not as radical as it has sometimes been portrayed, by the 1960s Sartre recognizes far greater limitations on the power of freedom than he formerly had. He admits to what he calls "some basic change in the concept of freedom. I still remain faithful to the notion of freedom, but I can see what can modify its results in any given person."[17] Sartre expresses regret that in *Being and Nothingness* he had a total lack of awareness of the dialectical process by which an individual internalizes both his or her family relations and the values of society and then reexternalizes these factors in action.

In 1969, Sartre confesses that he is "scandalized" when he rereads his earlier claim that whatever the circumstances, a person is always free to choose. He notes, "it's incredible; I actually believed that!" (*BEM*, 34). Sartre now openly rejects that position as false, and insists that a person is "totally conditioned" (*BEM*, 34) by his situation, particularly his childhood situation within a given family. Of course, the phrase "totally conditioned" means considerably less to Sartre than it might to a radical determinist, owing to Sartre's dialectical perspective. Each stage of development, while "conditioned" by its past, is not reducible to past conditions.

The fact of an individual's pervasive conditioning by his environment does not, therefore, eliminate the reality of human responsibility. On this issue, Sartre retains his original attitude. "The idea which I never ceased to develop is that in the end one is always responsible for what is made of one. Even if one can do nothing else besides assume this responsibility. For I believe that a man can always make something out of what is made of him. This is the limit I would today accord to freedom: the small movement which makes of a totally conditioned social being someone who does not render back completely what his conditioning has given him" (*BEM*, 34–35). There are options open to every person, but their range has been narrowly circumscribed by early parent-child relations, methods of education, and the prevalent cultural ideologies. Each person internalizes these external factors. Sartre explains that when he speaks of "a free singular project" he merely means that "there is spontaneity but stemming from a prefabricated essence" (*IF*, 1:351). Options remain available, but they are always conditioned options. Sartre contends, "historical conditioning exists every minute of our lives. We can fight it, but that doesn't mean it isn't there. Even people who try to deny their roots and background, as many do today, are nonetheless victims of both. And that background will assert itself in the very manner by which they try to deny it."[18] Although every one of us internalizes the external conditions of our situation, we express our uniqueness in the way we externalize our internal conditions. The result is something new and irreducible.

In *Being and Nothingness*, Sartre dismissed the idea that character is an essence or force hidden in individual acts. He described it as a retrospective summation of a pattern of behavior, the "synthetic unity" of a series or succession of acts. In *Search for a Method*, however, it is a person's first human relations that establish the general structure or style through which he or she will experience the world. Here Sartre describes character as "traces" that have been "inscribed" by early experience.

Childhood leaves its mark in learned gestures and roles. Consciousness does not merely float above the world unaffected by its past. One's character or style of living includes "the traces left by our first revolts, our desperate attempts to go beyond a stifling reality, and the resulting deviations and distortions. To surpass all that is also to preserve it. We shall think *with* these original deviations, we shall act *with* these gestures which we have learned and which we want to reject" (SM, 101).

This process of internalizing the conditions of one's family relations, even if it is in the form of rejection, represents Sartre's equivalent for the process of superego formation that Freud described. The values of adults are not arbitrary exercises of will or even rational decisions, but are grounded in experiences initially lived "in the depth and opaqueness of childhood" (SM, 62). The tenacity and irrationality of our present prejudices, beliefs, and passions have "their true density, their roots" (SM, 65), in childhood. In Sartre's analysis of Flaubert, for example, Flaubert sets up certain of his father's values within himself, but without being aware of so doing; rather, he "lived all this through in darkness—that is, without gaining any real awareness" (SM, 59). Psychoanalysis, as Sartre conceives it, permits one to examine the process by which a child works through the relations and values imposed by his or her family, whether they are rejected or assimilated, and how they are preserved in the adult. In his earlier thought, Sartre often seemed to picture children as autonomous moral agents. Now, however, he recognizes childhood as "radically distinct from the adult condition" and the source of "unsurpassable prejudices" (SM, 60). This shift has produced major changes in Sartre's theories.

THE NATURE OF "TOTALIZATION"

The idea of "totalization" is a modification of the claim in *Being and Nothingness* that a person is a *totality* rather than an unrelated collection of actions. Sartre believes there is a unity expressed by the variety of elements which comprise a person's life, or fundamental project. The original term "totality," however, sounds static and could imply the possibility of analyzing a whole into its component parts. This static understanding is remedied by the more dynamic concept of totalization. Totalization is never a "simple inventory followed by a statement of totality, but an intentional oriented enterprise of reunification" (IF, 1:653). Sartre wishes to convey the dynamic movement and development at the heart of an individual's project. He wants to focus on the progression by which the past constantly acquires new layers of meaning in relation to future events. The process of totalization is something that consciousness does spontaneously and continuously in its assimilation of *new* experience. Sartre has not altered his view of human experience as basically unstable. Totalization implies that the fundamental Sartrean polarities of being and nothingness, essence and existence, in-itself and for-itself, are each unstable moments in a dialectical process, temporary moments of stasis rather than radical opposites.

Sartre often talks about the meaning of a person's life as a *developing* or *ongoing totalitization* ("totalisation en cours") which continues from birth until death (*CDR*, 51). A totalization is a process, a choice *in the making.* Like the idea of a project, it refers to a unified whole that is in the process of being formed. Critics who say that existential psychologies lack any sense of dynamic evolution of personality, of conflicting aims, and of developmental resolution have not considered the concept of totalization. Human development, says Sartre, consists of a cycle of totalizations, detotalizations, and retotalizations.

Initially, totalization takes the form of a child's internalization of his or her family situation and the reexternalization of it in a certain manner or style of existing.[19] Subsequent experiences can then threaten to rupture or "detotalize" this unified system. A stage of retotalization would vary according to the specific person, his or her stage of life, and the circumstances of the situation. Although strange new elements of experience can disrupt a temporary stage of totalization or cause its collapse, any new stage of retotalization will nevertheless be guided and limited by certain structures of previous totalizations that are still preserved within each new stage of consciousness. As we confront new stimuli and experiences, the integrative unity of our "lived experience" is like a snowball, rolling on itself and constantly increasing in volume, enveloping new determinations (*IF*, 1:654). It includes the affective presuppositions and structured options in terms of which we interpret and integrate any new dangers we encounter.[20]

In a totalizing process, each part contributes to a whole that is at any moment only a general orientation or framework. The whole is distinct from the sum of its parts, yet in some sense, the whole is present in each part. When Sartre says that each part of a totality "contains the whole as its fundamental meaning" (*CDR*, 92), he does not mean that the whole is already *determined* by its constituent parts, but that as the whole develops the meaning of individual parts develops as well.[21]

In other words, while a person's project of living is always based on certain primordial conditions, it is the movement of subsequent developments that reveals the meaning of the original conditioning. The general style of a project first established in childhood is only a framework, and its later content enriches the meaning of the whole. "The end is enriched in the course of the enterprise" (*SM*, 160). Consequently, the final expression of a project "infinitely surpasses" the richness of the project at any previous stage. A person's life can be understood only if one "interprets every partial totality in terms of the overall totalization, and all their internal relations in terms of their relations to the develop-ing unification" (CDR, 92).[22]

The process of totalization holds in tension two seemingly contradic-tory elements within the unfolding of an individual's life. On the one hand, childhood does not mechanically determine the subsequent course of life. The conditioning of the past is "surpassed." On the other hand, in a dialectical process, continuity exists with the past to the extent that the original conditions which were surpassed or transcended are simul-taneously preserved in the new stage of development. An individual's project is not a radical uprooting accomplished by a sheer act of will, but rather this gradual movement of surpassing while preserving the experiences of childhood. Sartre says that the early determining forces of a person are "sustained, internalized, and lived . . . by a personal project" (SM, 170).

Despite its continuity with the past, each stage of a process of totali-zation, however, is autonomous and irreducible to the previous stage. Consequently, the process of totalization is fundamentally unstable, since the meaning attributed to specific events is never fixed but merely rela-tive. Sartre says, "Particular facts do not signify anything; they are neither true nor false so long as they are not related, through the mediation of various partial totalities, to the totalization in process" (SM, 30–31). Sartre's dialectical approach makes it inaccurate to refer to either "discovering" the meaning of past events or "inventing" it (BEM, 231). Both processes interact.

Although Sartre's description of the process of totalization is fairly schematic, it is crucial to his understanding of the process of becoming a person, what he calls "personalization" (IF, 1:656) or "personalizing evolution" (IF, 1:657). Personalization is similar in a number of respects to what others might call identity formation. Of course, for Sartre an identity is not something that a person has or is. If anything, it is fundamentally "only the *surpassed* result of the unity of totalizing processes by which we try continually to assimilate the unassimilable, that is, in the first place our childhood" (IF, 1:656). Sartre wishes to steer clear of both radical determinism and radical voluntarism by focusing on the complex dialectical changes that occur in the course of a person's life. The intricate structure of a life is neither a completely new creation ex nihilo, nor is it identical with the original conditions of the person's past. Identity, says Sartre, "is neither completely suffered nor completely constructed" (IF, 1:656).

WORKING ON THE SPIRAL OF LIFE

Sartre sees the development of a direction or orientation to one's life as a personal task with which each individual must struggle throughout his or her life. The dialectical process of transcending one's past is "a long work; each moment of this work is at once the surpassing and, to the extent that it is posited for itself, the pure and simple subsistence of these deviations at a given level of integration. For this reason a life develops in spirals; it passes again and again by the same points at different levels of integration and complexity" (*SM*, 106). Each new problem in the external world offers a chance to build a larger unity on the foundation of those childhood factors still preserved within the totalization already accomplished. This is why Sartre imagines totalization as a three-dimensional *spiral*. This process consists of moving farther and higher from the original point of departure in childhood through an indefinite number of revolutions. One never leaves the childhood center of the spiral behind, yet the meaning and function of childhood characteristics are always developing, since "each revolution installs them in a richer, more differentiated and better integrated unity" (*IF*, 1:658).[23] One preserves one's origins while transcending them to higher irreducible levels.

Vladimir Nabokov likewise uses the image of the spiral to describe his life. The spiral, he says, is a "spiritualized circle. In the spiral form, the circle, uncoiled, unwound, has ceased to be vicious; it has been set free."[24] Nabokov sees the spiral as the essential nature of things in relation to time. In fact, the spiral is crucial to Sartre's sense of time since it mediates between two opposing models of time. One of the decisive changes marking the transition from traditional societies to modern societies was the shift from a cyclical view of time to a historical view of time. *Cyclical time* emphasizes the periodic repetition of timeless archetypes. History is devalued in favor of transhistorical models. *Historical time* breaks out of the vicious repetition of cyclical time. It introduces a linear movement away from the past and open toward the future. In this way, it affirms human freedom, autonomy, and the ability to make historical events that are irreducible.[25] This tension between cyclical and historical time has parallels to the attitudes about human development in Freud and Sartre. Freud sometimes seems to treat psychological experience as the eternal cyclical repetition of the archetypal events in childhood. Sartre's concern for human freedom can be read with a historical view of time. The spiral view of time, however, links Freud and Sartre. It recognizes both the repetition of archetypal events and the transcendence of the conditions of the past.

Eventually, however, a moment may come in a person's life when there is a hardening of the spiral or a "regressive involution." "In this case there is an indefinite repetition of the same revolution or even a collapse to a lower one" (*IF*, 1:657). The ambiguity in the word "revolution" is ironic, since it can express two diverse elements of Sartre's thought and two views of time. Earlier, Sartre sometimes depicted consciousness as an explosive "revolutionary" uprooting from the past and its influence. In the present context, however, the "revolutions" within experience represent the continuous preservation of past structures in a new unity, a spiral revolving around its inner core. A revolution of consciousness can be either cyclical (to revolve) or historical (to revolt).

Sartre's description of the totalizing spiral as "work" is also important in dispelling the fallacy that his approach to psychic life is overly cerebral; that is, the individual intellectually decides on the direction of his inner life. Nothing could be further from Sartre's position. Indeed, the dialectical work of lived experience is "directly opposed to intellectual knowing" (*SM*, 12). Sartre recognizes that human change and development is hard work: "ideas do not change men. Knowing the cause of a passion is not enough to overcome it; one must live it, one must oppose other passions to it, one must combat it tenaciously; in short one must 'work oneself over' " [se travailler] (*SM*, 12–13). Accordingly, psychoanalysis is *not* a question of knowledge, but "a movement, an *internal labor* that at one and the same time uncovers a neurosis and gradually makes the subject capable of supporting it" (*BEM*, 145). Freud emphasized the importance of "working through" the ideas that emerge in analysis. For Sartre psychoanalytic therapy is a long effort to enable a person to recover his "mislaid freedom to act" (*BEM*, 204).

The description of human totalization as a "long work" can also be used to suggest the artistic quality of an individual's life project as a "work of art." Sartre continues to use the idea of artistic style to describe the subtle quality of a project. In his later discussions of life projects, Sartre makes the crucial point that a project does not have any specific *content*, but rather has "an *internal coloration*" [italics mine] (*SM*, 105). The project is not a specific desire, need, choice, or passion, although all of these can express moments in the unfolding of a project (*SM*, 151). Like artistic style, the coloration of the project represents the flavor or "taste" of an individual's way of life.[26] An author's style is not a specific content of his work; it is an "invisible but *felt* presence" in his books (*BEM*, 274). The fundamental project, likewise, is more of an invisible presence than a content. It is a personal *style* of living that is expressed in every specific endeavor. An author's style of writing is only one indication of his larger "*style of living* (supple or hard, a devastating vivacity of attack or, on the contrary, a slow start, careful preparations, leading up to brusque compressions). . . . all those characteristics which conjure up so much of a man that we can virtually feel his breath, *without giving us any knowledge of him*" (*BEM*, 281). The fundamental project is thus similar to what Barrett and Yankelovich, building on the work of Erik Erikson, call a "mode of being."[27] Sartre prefers, however, the terminology of "style" to preserve the literary qualities of the project and to avoid the alternate mechanistic terminology that is often employed.

SARTRE AND EGO PSYCHOLOGY

Sartre's revised attitude toward psychoanalysis may have been influenced by the work of Jacques Lacan who, like Sartre, is especially concerned with the relationship of consciousness and language. Sartre acknowledges in a number of places some acquaintance with Lacan's work. Nevertheless, it is not French structuralist psychoanalysis that most resembles Sartre's position but rather American ego psychology. In an otherwise critical article, Benjamin Nelson describes Sartre's existential psychoanalysis as "a distinctive variant of what many American and British writers, alike, are now calling ego psychology on an object relations basis."[28] In particular, the theoretical framework and practice of psychohistory developed by Erik Erikson closely parallels the theory and practice of existential psychoanalysis. Ironically, neither Erikson nor Sartre have indicated any awareness or appreciation of the other's work. It is unfortunate, moreover, that many of those interested in revising psychoanalysis in the direction of psychoanalytic ego psychology have made questionable criticisms of Sartre and have overlooked the striking similarities that exist between Sartre's position and their own. The work of Erikson has often been endorsed as a necessary revision of Freud and a correction of the glaring excesses in Sartre's thought. In fact, however, Sartre's work might have been employed to support some of the central ideas in a reconstructed psychoanalytic theory.

In *Ego and Instinct* William Barrett and David Yankelovich criticize Freud's mechanistic reduction of adult characteristics to their childhood origins. They turn to ego psychology, especially as it has been developed by Erik Erikson, to reestablish the individual as the major source of *meaning* within psychological life. The fundamental search for ego identity in Erikson's scheme is essentially a search for meaningfulness. Barrett and Yankelovich note, "If we think of new and emergent human relations as structures of meanings, desires, and predispositions, instead of assemblages of forces held together by energy, we introduce the thought that there may be an element of indeterminacy in human experience."[29]

Acknowledging a similarity between ego identity and Sartre's notion of "self-definition," Barrett and Yankelovich nevertheless dismiss Sartre's formulation as inadequate for several reasons. They contend that Sartre does not account for the step-by-step development of identity as a process of "becoming."[30] They believe Sartre emphasizes abrupt, defiant changes of identity created in a void by absolute freedom. Don S. Browning likewise notes similarities between Erikson's concept of modes and modalities and the existentialist concept of being-in-the-world, but criticizes Sartre's "existentialist fallacy" that "man makes himself in all respects,"[31] "trusting only the lucidity of man's historical consciousness."[32] He claims that Erikson, unlike Sartre, has added a developmental dimension to his schema.

Such criticism is peculiar, since Sartre's dialectical model of the fundamental project comes closer to the reconstructive work of ego psychology than either Barrett and Yankelovich[33] or Browning realize. In many respects, the developmental approach that ego psychology adapts from biology resembles the dialectical approach that Sartre adapts from Hegelian philosophy. Indeed, Browning does note in passing a " 'dialectic' relationship within human development between internal and external, child and adult, nature and culture,"[34] yet his use of quotation marks around "dialectic" reveals some reluctance about this type of description. In any case, it seems rather unjustified to fault Sartre for ignoring human development. A dialectic is precisely a process of development.

Sartre presents the fundamental project of an individual as a process of dialectical totalization that continually transcends various experiences and conditions while at the same time preserving them within a higher level of development. Browning's description of the ego points to exactly the same process. The ego or self, he says, is not a thing within consciousness enduring through time, "but an active agency of synthesis. It forever seeks to coordinate the various fragments of one's experience into a meaningful *whole*."[35] Erikson himself describes the process of identity formation as "an *evolving configuration*—a configuration which is gradually established by successive ego syntheses and resyntheses throughout childhood."[36] Ego identity requires one to "test, select, and integrate the self-representations derived from the psychosocial crisis of childhood. It could be said to be characterized by the more or less *actually* attained but forever-to-be-revised sense of the reality of the self within social reality."[37] All these ideas are nothing other than descriptions of what Sartre has called totalization, the process of synthesizing past experiences to form new wholes. Erikson's "evolving configuration" is identical to Sartre's "fundamental project."

Drawing on Erikson, Barrett and Yankelovich stress the fact that human life is characterized by the emergence of "synergistic" structures that are not reducible to their origins or to the sum of their parts.[38] They insist that the formation of new wholes, structures, and gestalts is a fundamental characteristic of the self. Building on earlier structures established in infancy, synergistic structures add new layers of meaning and complexity. In this sense, the self is in a state of flux, "a meaning structure never finished but always open to the future."[39] A person is reconstituted many times in the course of his life and reaches new stages of integration that cannot be accounted for solely by antecedent causes. Erikson has most often used the metaphor of a "cycle" to describe human development. He says, "in each stage of life a given strength is added to a widening ensemble and reintegrated at each later stage in order to play its part in a full cycle—if and where fate and society permit."[40] Sartre's suggestion of a *dialectical spiral* that develops new irreducible structures within a general totalizing framework points to the same phenomenon.

Ego psychologists tend to emphasize the synthetic activity of the ego as the locus of human autonomy and freedom. They reject the old psychoanalytic view of the ego as a weak or passive victim of traumatic experiences or overwhelming drives. According to Browning, the ego is "always converting inner and outer influences into experiences either actively chosen, actively accepted, or actively rejected. The ego seems to have the inner need to turn the passivities of life into experiences which, if not actively chosen, are at least actively affirmed."[41] According to Erikson, the sense of adult identity requires a person "to see one's own life in a continuous perspective, both in retrospect and in prospect. . . . The adult is able to selectively reconstruct his past in such a way that, step for step, it seems to have planned him, or better, he seems to have planned *it*. In this sense, psychologically we *do* choose our parents, our family history, and the history of our kings, heroes, and gods. By making them our own, we maneuver ourselves into the inner position of proprietors, of creators."[42] Such processes are precisely what Sartre describes as the small movement of freedom in each person which makes something different out of the forces that condition him, or if nothing else, assumes responsibility for what they have made of him. A person needs to feel he or she is the creator of his or her own life. When Erikson says we choose our pasts and create the meaning of our lives he is discussing the fundamental quality of consciousness upon which Sartre has always insisted.

In Erikson's scheme, the culmination of human development is the emergence of individual "integrity," which simply means "the acceptance of the fact that one's life is one's own responsibility."[43] One accepts one's life as something that "had to be and that, by necessity, permitted of no substitutions."[44] Sartre offers an even more radical version of this kind of "integrity," for he insists on integrity at every moment of life, not just at life's end. Of course, Erikson does acknowledge that in the rare spiritual genius or *homo religiosus*, the "integrity crisis" is "lifelong" and "chronic."[45] For such a person, the youthful crisis of individual identity and the mature crisis of integrity in relation to existential identity merge into one. It could be argued that in his later thought Sartre develops a vision of existential man as a type of *homo religiosus* who struggles to attain authenticity within a situation conditioned by alienating social and ideological structures.

BIOLOGICAL AND BIOGRAPHICAL INSTINCTS

Despite the similarities between some of Sartre's later ideas and certain positions of psychoanalytic ego psychology, there remains one final area where the relation between them is more problematic. This concerns the importance of the biological or instinctual dimension within human development. Erikson's ego psychology is based on the premise that personality grows like an organism. Central to this perspective is the "epigenetic principle"; this refers to certain inborn potentials or structures of the human life cycle in general that develop in stages according to a maturational schedule when a favorable environment exists. Without going into this area of ego psychology in greater detail, it is necessary to clarify Sartre's attitude toward the organic or biological axis of human life.

It would be foolish, of course, to try to transform Sartre into a developmental psychologist. It is likely that Sartre would criticize the epigenetic principle for lacking a genuine dialectical basis, since the various stages are seen as fixed in the human organism from the start. To be sure, Sartre sees the fundamental project as a "framework" within which subsequent developments occur. In a response to structuralist critics, Sartre denies the charge of historicism, that is, history develops unfettered by any structural limitations. Sartre asserts that while every person is "the product of structures," he inevitably goes beyond them, "reconstituting that which conditions him."[46] Structures emerge out of childhood, but they are transformed by the process of historical totalization. As this happens, "The 'qualities' of the child pass from the *structural* to the *historical*" (*IF*, 1:51). Therefore, while Sartre admits a structural core to a person, he would likely be averse to the establishing of a common framework for all people. At the level of the project, there can be no universal biological framework. Sartre's continued denial of a fixed human nature means that whatever natural potentials exist, they must enter into a unique historical dialectic within each individual.

Concerning the biological roots of human projects, Sartre has traditionally seen instincts and inborn tendencies as inadequate explanatory principles in themselves.[47] Although he never developed his thoughts on the subject of instinct in great detail, Sartre does not seem to reject instinct per se. He only denies that it is an irreducible force behind action. For example, Sartre does not deny the existence of sexual instinct; he simply expresses doubt that "this substructure of sexual need reappears intact in the superstructure of personality. It may appear but on a completely new level and in a completely different form, as any believer in a dialectical process must agree. It can no longer be reduced to itself."[48] Sartre explains that sexuality is not really either a cause or an effect (*IF*, 1:686). Sexual instincts are always expressed within a complex situation where they provide sexual form for all the structures that characterize a person. At a particular moment, a person's entire mode of being can be "totalized" within his or her sexual behavior. Conversely, every totalization of experience preserves, qualifies, and transcends the structure of sexual instincts as it moves toward new goals. There is a reciprocity among the structures in a person's life. Political, economic, or social alienation may be experienced as sexual alienation. A person's political ideology may reflect underlying sexual impulses, but sexual impulses also may reflect a person's political ideology. Sartre admits the primacy of sexual instinct within an "objective hierarchy of structures" (*IF*, 1:686) but this does not mean that complex organic structures can be reduced into simple ones. As Marx has shown, superstructures react upon the infrastructures from which they have emerged.

According to Sartre, the major contribution of Freud was demonstrating the *meaning* which instinctual and environmental forces acquire within an individual's project. Freud showed that "sexual desire is not simply sexual desire, but something which encroaches upon a man's whole personality, even affecting the way he plays the piano or violin."[49] Here we are not dealing with a simple biological drive but with a global style of living that has dialectically evolved.

In his *Critique of Dialectical Reason*, Sartre points to a more biologically rooted view of human existence, which takes greater account of the interaction of the natural and the cultural within each person. He describes people as "practical organisms" with biological as well as social natures. In particular, the origin of an individual's dialectical development is organismic "need." Need represents a person's first relation to the world around him or her. The environment reveals itself as a field of possibilities for gratifying one's primal needs. Biological need forces the individual to act, to explore the environment, and to construe it in meaningful patterns.

Marjorie Grene has criticized Sartre's treatment of the biological aspect of man as inadequate, since she claims it treats only animal needs and not the uniquely human needs for meaning and culture which are "built into our very ontogeny."[50] While it is true that Sartre has emphasized social and historical conditions more than biological ones, his brief suggestions regarding biological forces, though rudimentary, do not rule out an understanding of biological need in the direction Grene suggests. In this context, it is necessary to return to the literary axis in Sartre's understanding of the person.

The centrality of this literary model makes Sartre treat the interpretation of fundamental projects as a *biographical* endeavor, i.e., transforming one's life *(bio)* into writing *(graph)*, rather than as a question of biological roots. What Grene finds lacking is precisely this biographical rather than biological approach to human life. What mediates the two, however, is Sartre's understanding of the *biographical need* as a fundamental need of the human organism. Despite giving up certain earlier illusions about the power of literature, [51] Sartre remains convinced of one unshakable fact: "Writing is a need felt by everyone. It's the highest form of the basic need to communicate" *(BEM, 31)*. There is a universal human need to write and communicate, to give expression to the chaotic stream of experience.

Of course, this claim must be seen as largely metaphorical in importance. To be sure, Sartre regards the *vocation* of writing as no more significant than any other job. He does not believe that everyone literally wants to be a writer. Rather, the universal human need to write symbolizes the fact that "every person is always faced in his own lifetime with the task of wresting his own life from the various forms of night" *(BEM, 31)*. [52] Sartre no longer presents the radical choice between "living" and "telling" discussed in *Nausea*. Both aspects are intrinsic parts of human life. The desire to write represents a process of focusing, discovering, and creating the meaning of feelings and experiences that are otherwise ambiguous and confused. Sartre says, "something inside us obstructs their development, or interferes with them like crackle on a radio. Tragedy is not lived tragically, nor pleasure pleasurably. The need to write is fundamentally a quest for purification" *(BEM, 32)*.

The "biographical instinct," if it may be so called, reflects the universal human need to be meaningful, and reveals the cathartic effect of meaning. In this context one can appreciate Sartre's provocative comment that "there is no such thing as the psychological. Let us say that one can improve the biography of the person." [53] Psychoanalytic interpretation enables a person to communicate his life more meaningfully. With it, one can "improve" his biography, that is, the "text" of his life, the story of his fundamental project.

[4] EXISTENTIAL PSYCHOANALYSIS AND "TRUE NOVELS"

Sartre has prepared four major studies in existential psychoanalysis. These include his interpretations of Baudelaire (1947), Genet (1952), Flaubert (1971, 1973), and himself (1964). To call these studies existential psychoanalyses should distinguish them from more familiar forms of biography or literary criticism. Sartre is not concerned with simply recounting the events in the lives of his subjects. Nor is his main interest in dissecting their literary works as such. Existential psychoanalysis goes beneath the surface of a subject's life and works to deal with the underlying existential principle which radiates from everything that particular person does. Accordingly, Sartre sees his studies in relation to Freudian case histories, though modified by the theoretical positions I have already discussed.

TRANSFERENCE AND THE CLINICAL SITUATION

Before proceeding any further, I must note one major difference between Sartre's studies and Freud's case histories. For Freud, the interpretive

work that culminates in the case history is usually part of a larger process
of psychotherapy. For Sartre, however, understanding the overall meaning of a person's life is an end in itself. He had neither interest nor
expertise in the clinical treatment of living persons. Moreover, Sartre
explicitly disavows any intent to judge a given person as normal or
pathological.

To be sure, there are those who believe psychoanalytic interpretation
can be legitimately undertaken only within a therapeutic situation. The
majority of Freud's interpretations do occur in the course of his clinical
work. Nevertheless, Freud himself clearly regards psychoanalytic interpretation as a useful and valid tool in understanding people *even* where
there are *neither* symptoms to cure *nor* changes sought in the subject's
behavior. Freud notes that dreams are not just pathological, but normal
and healthy as well. Consequently, the principles of psychoanalysis are
useful not only in psychotherapy, but also as "the foundation for a new
and deeper science of the mind which would be equally indispensable
for the understanding of the normal."[1]

This concern with understanding the *meaning* of human lives is the
dominant force behind the life work of both Freud and Sartre. It is
guided by principles of interpretation that transcend clinical application
and that are related to the activities of historians, biographers, and literary critics. While acknowledging certain unique factors at work in a
clinical situation, we can still, *mutatis mutandis*, accept Sartre's decision to treat a writer's work, correspondence, and other writings as material
for interpretation that is roughly equivalent to psychoanalytic discourse.

In the past, the focus on the clinical setting of psychoanalysis has
sometimes skewed perspectives on interpretation by emphasizing the
importance of therapeutic outcome. Discussions of the validity of clinical interpretations or reconstructions by both Freud and his followers
invariably place great importance on the ability of such interpretations
to further the course of the analysis by stimulating new material and to
produce an alleviation of anxiety and symptomatic behavior. This focus
frequently introduces the complicating issues of suggestion on the part
of the analyst and the therapeutic efficacy of inexact interpretations.[2] By
widening the context in which we approach psychoanalytic interpretation, we can avoid becoming diverted into these therapeutic issues.
There is an obvious need to develop interpretive systems to understand
people whose lives are deeply meaningful but who either do not need or
do not seek therapeutic help.

The phenomenon of transference will facilitate the transition from
Freud's clinical to Sartre's nonclinical interpretations. For Freud, the
phenomenon of transference transforms the analytic situation into a
virtual microcosm of a patient's life. Freud says, "The patient reproduces
instead of remembering; . . . we may now ask what it is exactly that he

reproduces or expresses in action. The answer is that he reproduces everything in the reservoirs of repressed material that has already permeated his general character—his inhibitions and disadvantageous attitudes of mind, his pathological traits of character."[3] In other words, the transference means that the way in which the patient experiences the meaning of his or her past is expressed completely in the analytic relation to the therapist. For Freud, it is not the "real" past (whatever that might mean) which is interpreted in analysis, but rather the accumulated meaning which has accrued to various real and phantasied events. This meaning is expressed in the transference relation to the therapist, without the subject's actually knowing it. Transference is not, therefore, a simple reproduction or "reliving" of the past, nor is it a pure construction. It is a matter of working out and reworking the past. Thus, the past is not a fixed entity to which one returns in transference. Roy Schafer describes transference behavior as a way of *creating* a version of the past in the present based on certain childhood experiences. It is like a "creative work of art," making something new out of past elements.[4]

If we generalize the phenomenon of transference beyond the constraints of pathology and its treatment, we discover a phenomenon present in all lives. Indeed, what is "transferred" from the past to new situations is everything that has "permeated [one's] general character," that is, one's patterns of behavior; types of relations; bodily, verbal, cognitive, and emotional style—in short, the entire style of one's existence, neurotic or otherwise. Freud himself recognizes that the phenomenon of transference is not limited to the analytic relation but occurs "in all other matters occupying and interesting the patient at the time."[5] In other words, everything we do expresses our fundamental style or character in symbolic terms. Whatever situation we are in, we cannot help symbolizing ourselves, whether we realize it or not. Thus Freud notes, "no mortal can keep a secret. If his lips are silent, he chatters from his fingertips; betrayal oozes out of him at every pore."[6] When the phenomenon of transference is seen in its widest sense, it begins to resemble what Sartre calls the constant symbolization of a person's fundamental project in new contexts. This fundamental project, the origins of which lie in early childhood, is expressed in the pattern and style of behavior that one presents in any situation. Transference is a way of "remembering" childhood traits and conflicts by reproducing them in one's present character or action, rather than actually recollecting them. Sartre would describe such "remembering" as the way "lived experience" preserves the past within itself. The psychoanalytic patient's "compulsion to repeat" behavior that expresses childhood conflict resembles what Sartre describes as reenactments of the "liturgical dramas" of childhood in the dialectical spiral of personality development.

If the reenactment of these conflicts is, as Schafer suggests, similar to a creative work of art, we may also consider an actual work of art as a type of transference reenactment. In the case of those people whose main occupation and interest is literature, it may be appropriate to see transference at work in the writing of a book, as Sartre's analyses of Genet and Flaubert contend. Literature, no less than analytic behavior, may be a symbolic expression of preconceptual lived experience. Freud himself repeatedly shows that the principle of dream and symptom formation are also at work in imaginative writing and art. Works of art, like dreams and symptoms, embody deep-seated desires, wishes, conflicts, and (as Sartre would add) fundamental modes of being and relation to the world. Freud argued that Leonardo da Vinci's painting of the Virgin and Saint Anne, for example, symbolizes the way he appropriated the meaning of his childhood experience. Of course, like dreams, such works are not adequate by themselves to illuminate an individual's life and must be supplemented by his or her life history.

In his existential psychoanalyses, Sartre frequently shows little concern with distinguishing "genuine" biographical and autobiographical material from his subjects' poetic or novelistic production. Both sources of information are treated as equally valid for understanding the individual's sense of the world. Sartre treats Genet's literary work as an equivalent to the kind of dream work that Freud relied on so heavily. Behind both literary and dream work lies the operation of the basic dimension of consciousness—the imagination, the freedom of consciousness to create an image of the world and the self. Literature, says Sartre, is "a product of man: he projects himself into it; he recognizes himself in it; that critical mirror alone offers him his image" (W, 159). Whether Genet writes an autobiography or a novel or some mixture of both, the "world" of Genet, his fundamental project, is embodied within it and can be analyzed as such.

LIVING WITH STYLE

If the fundamental project is a "style" of existing, that style will be present in artistic or literary style as well. An author's style enables him to recreate the world according to his own values. In a more general sense, the nature of style reflects the fundamental characteristic of human consciousness, namely, the process by which a person "transforms his being into *meaning*, and through [which] *meaning* comes into the world" (BEM, 160). Our past experiences are merely "pretexts" for the "text" of meaning we weave of our lives; "facts" are molded into "arti-facts" by the stylistic work of memory and imagination.

The literary and imaginative quality of consciousness is evident not only in how a person remembers the past and makes sense of his or her life but also in the kind of narrative that existential psychoanalysis produces. Once again, it is useful to examine what Sartre says about literature as a key to the epistemological status of existential psychoanalysis.

Sartre distinguishes the use of language in scientific communication and philosophy from that of literature. He suggests that in science and philosophy, language should try to be completely unambiguous; each sentence should be univocal in its meaning. However, what is characteristic of the literary way of presenting a reality is *style*. Unlike scientific discourse, stylistic work, *le travail du style*, involves utilizing the plurivalence of language, "saying three or four things in one. There is the simple sentence, with its immediate meaning, and then at the same time, below this immediate meaning, other meanings are organized. . . . The artist of language arranges words in such a way that, depending on how he emphasizes or gives weight to them, they will have one meaning, and another, and yet another, each time at different levels." (*LS*, 7). Literary discourse thus produces an overall meaning, not by adding individual points in logical progression, but by superimposing various meanings in each sentence. The "work of meaning" ("travail du sens") is accomplished by the "work of style" ("travail du style") (*LS*, 9). The work of style, moreover, requires that the author treat the meaning of a particular detail in relation to the rest of the scene, the chapter, and ultimately the whole book. The implicit form of the whole must be contained within each part. Sartre says, "If this totality is present you write a good sentence. If it is not present, the sentence will jar and seem gratuitous" (*LS*, 8). Each sentence must project the meaning of the whole work.

The stylistic aspect of literary discourse closely resembles the kind of meaning present in "lived experience" where one also finds layers of meanings superimposed on various events. Sartre treats each act of a person's life as a moment of totalization in which a hierarchy of meanings is condensed. Although Sartre does not explicitly say so, he seems to believe that the study of a person's life ought to proceed in a similar fashion to the study of an author's stylistic work. To adequately appreciate and express a particular event in a person's life, one must analyze it in the context of the layers of meaning it acquires through time and in relation to the total meaning of the person's life. In this way each event will emerge with the full multidimensionality of its meaning and thus demonstrate its place within the fundamental project.

Sartre's description of the multiple layers of meaning that are essential to style is reminiscent of Freud's descriptions of the multiplicity of meaning in dreams. Indeed, Sartre insists that the language which describes lived experience will have the structure of a dream rather than that of explicit conceptual knowledge. Style expresses unconscious or lived experience in the same way that a dream may. Sartre inverts Lacan's notion that dreams are structured like a language to say that the language which expresses the desires of the unconscious is structured like a dream.

Sartre further suggests that if literary discourse is necessary for a person to express his or her lived experience, it is likewise the appropriate medium for existential psychoanalysis. By conceiving psychoanalysis on a literary model, rather than a scientific one, Sartre introduces standards of validity and truth more consistent with his overall view of human life than would otherwise be possible.[7] The epistemological consequences of construing a person's life and its meaning on the basis of a literary model, rather than a mechanical scientific model, are tremendous.

THE NATURE OF TRUTH IN EXISTENTIAL PSYCHOANALYSIS

The artistic, or more specifically the literary, dimension of existential psychoanalysis is evident in Sartre's description of his studies as "true novels." In examining the nature of this genre which Sartre calls the "true novel," one should not assume that his analyses are purely imaginative creations with no claim to validity. While some of Sartre's conclusions may be questionable, his approach to existential psychoanalysis nevertheless tells something important about the nature of any analysis of the meaning of any individual's life.[8]

Joseph Halpern has recognized the fact that Sartre's interpretation of literature has resulted in judgments which can claim little "scientific" validity. Halpern describes Sartre's work on literature as a series of "critical fictions" founded on a "network of personal myth" whose value depends, not on objectively demonstrable correctness or accuracy, but on its "creative genius and force."[9] While it is right to emphasize the fictional or novelistic element in Sartre's existential psychoanalyses, it is misleading to minimize their interpretive validity in proportion to their creative expression of Sartre's mythic vision. Indeed, Sartre's existential psychoanalysis requires one to reevaluate precisely the nature of validity in interpretation and to raise the question of the role of artistic imagination within this process. Jonas Barish, for example, contends that the validity of Sartre's analyses of Jean Genet lies in "the imaginative vigor of the construction, the degree to which it welds into an intelligible synthesis the bizarre career of its subject, and makes sense of his mystifying literary productions."[10]

In the simplest terms, the "true novel" produced by existential psychoanalysis is the story of an individual's fundamental project. Since the "truth" of a fundamental project is multidimensional, there is not an objective sense of the past with which one's description must correspond. A correspondence theory of truth is inappropriate for studying human beings. Rather the understanding of a person's life necessarily involves an interpretation of the real and the imaginary, the present and the past. The truth of one's description lies in a sense of the inner cohesion of the whole. Although Sartre believes he accurately analyzes himself in his partial autobiography *The Words*, he does not think self-analysis ever occurs, at a "scientific" level of discourse. Only when one recognizes the literary, and consequently imaginative, nature of all description of human experience can one understand how Sartre can describe his analysis in the seemingly paradoxical terms of a "true novel."

According to Sartre, Merleau-Ponty once discussed the possibility of writing an autobiography. Later, Merleau-Ponty is reported to have said it would be better if he wrote a novel "because in a novel I could give an imaginary meaning to the periods of my life that I don't understand" (*LS*, 121). For Sartre, there is no need to distinguish radically autobiography and novel, since self-analysis has much in common with novelistic works. He employs the multiple and superimposed meanings implicit in literary "style" to express the complex quality of his own past experience. In so doing he recognizes the novelistic structure he imparts to his life. He says: "I think that *The Words* is no truer than *Nausea* or *The Roads to Freedom*. Not that the facts I report are not true, but *The Words* is a kind of novel also—a novel that I believe in, but a novel nevertheless" (*LS*, 15). Sartre is not implying that *The Words* is only a personal fantasy without claim to truth. On the contrary, he is merely clarifying the nature of truth involved. That is to say, the truth of *The Words* does not rest ultimately on the truthfulness of particular "facts" contained within it. The "facts" of a life, like the sentences in a book, acquire meaning only in relation to a vision of the whole of which they are a part. Moreover, since the truth aimed at in existential psychoanalysis involves the project revealed by a certain style of existing, a work such as *Nausea*, as much as *The Words*, can demonstrate the truth of Sartre's understanding of his experience. Sartre admits, "I *was* Roquentin; I used him to show, without complacency, the texture of my life" (*W*, 158).[11]

Sartre's understanding of truth, moreover, is fundamentally dialectical and rests on his notion of totalization. The truth about a person is never fixed, but rather in a constant state of development. To analyze the truth about a person, to "totalize" him, means that the analysis of the past will always be open to revision from the perspective of the future. About ten years after writing *The Words* Sartre remarked that he "had to tell the truth" about himself. He considered extending his autobiography to show his own political evolution by means of a fiction where the main character would be himself. It was to be "a fiction which was not a fiction" (*LS*, 14). He was suggesting that a further level of totalization of his life was then possible. He later reflected:

> *It was above all a question of putting myself in a certain position in which a kind of truth that I had not known before would necessarily appear to me. By means of a true fiction—or a fictional truth—I would take up the actions and thoughts of my life again in order to make them into a whole. All the while I would be examining their apparent contradictions and their limits—to see if it was true that those limits were really there, to make sure that I had not been forced to consider such ideas as contradictory when in fact they were not, to confirm that my actions of a given moment had been interpreted correctly* (LS, 17).

Again, Sartre resorts to "true fiction" or "fictional truth" in order to recognize a previously unknown "truth."

"True fiction" is the process by which the imagination helps reveal new truths in the world. The detour of fiction is necessary to present the totality of an individual. Just as art or fiction does not seek an exact copy of the world, but creates a new way of seeing reality, existential psychoanalysis creates a new way of interrelating elements of an individual's life within a unifying structure.[12] Sartre acknowledges that the truth he attains from the perspective of his own system of thought may be valid only to a certain point and may not be the deepest truth ("la verité profonde") (*LS*, 17). There is no absolutely true account of a person's life. Yet simply because the total truth is infinite, it does not mean that one cannot attain some new truths at every stage of totalization. Sartre would have expected his true fiction to have presented some truths about himself and the historical epoch he lived in, even if he would not have obtained the entire truth (*LS*, 17).

When questioned about *The Family Idiot*, his most ambitious exercise in existential psychoanalysis, Sartre says that he would like readers to regard it as a novel describing the inevitable course of an individual's life.[13] Accordingly, though Sartre no longer is writing actual novels at the time, he feels writing about Flaubert has provided him with a kind of novelistic substitute (*BEM*, 49). Sartre says, "I try to achieve a certain level of comprehension of Flaubert by means of hypotheses. Thus I use fiction—guided and controlled, but nonetheless fiction—to explore why, let us say, Flaubert wrote one thing on the 15th March and the opposite on the 21st March, to the same correspondent, without worrying about contradiction. My hypotheses are in this sense a sort of invention of the personage" (*BEM*, 49). At the same time, Sartre insists that this fictional invention is *true*. One should read *The Family Idiot*, he says, "with the idea in mind that it is true, that it is a *true* novel [un roman *vrai*]. Throughout the book, Flaubert is presented the way I imagine him to have been, but since I have used what I think were rigorous methods, this should also be Flaubert as he really is, as he really was. At each moment in this study I had to use my imagination" (*LS*, 112).

At issue for Sartre is the fundamental relation between poetry and truth, what Goethe called "Dichtung und Wahrheit." Sartre insists "the intuition of essences can only be actualized by the free exercise of imagination. . . . The total truth is necessarily poetry." (*IF*, 3:337). When Proust created "a symbolic story of his life" he used his imagination to modify all the details. The purpose was not to disguise the truth but to speak "*truer* than true" (*plus vrai* que le vrai") (*IF*, 2:1530). The exercise of the imagination creates networks of meaning through which the unity of a person's life can be understood. Therefore, to establish relations between different aspects of Flaubert's life requires retrospective creation rather than discovery. For example, when Sartre juxtaposes two of Flaubert's letters written fifteen years apart, he emphasizes, "no connection was ever made between these documents by Flaubert, by the correspondents, or by the critics. At that time the connection did not exist. When I make it, I make it with my imagination. And once I have imagined it, this can give me a real connection" (*LS*, 112–13). In short, the connections Sartre makes depend on him to imagine them, but at the same time, once established they represent a genuine structure within Flaubert's life. Sartre's epistemology does not treat the truth of an interpretation in terms of its correspondence with established "facts" of the past. This is the reason why Sartre's interpretations often are novelistic inventions in one sense and at the same time are *true* in another sense. The truth cannot be "discovered" at some moment in the past when specific events occurred, since the meaning or truth of those events is simply a way of construing the whole life of which they are a part. This truth is cumulative and is not evident to an individual in the immediacy of his or her own experience.

The type of truth Sartre seeks in existential psychoanalysis is similar to the kind commonly associated with autobiographies. Interpreters of autobiography generally recognize that the truth of an autobiography is a unique sort and must be distinguished from the mere factuality of the events described. Georges Gusdorf, a well-known theorist of autobiography, contends that objective, historical accuracy is not the point of an autobiography. Errors in details, imagined memories, or distortions do not invalidate it and are peripheral to another kind of truth, namely, "the effort of a creator to give the meaning of his own mythic tale."[14] In autobiography, he adds, "the truth of facts is subordinate to the truth of the man."[15] The expression of this inner truth of the person is not something the autobiographer passively discovers. Rather it is something more often described in literary and artistic terms. Words like "fiction," "invention," "design," "symbol," "creation," "metaphor," "image," and "myth" recur in theoretical analyses of the life or self presented by an autobiography. Yet Gusdorf insists that the autobiographical account of a life is "truer" than the stream of experience itself, since it reconstructs a life as an essential unity and totality across time that is only visible to autobiographical reflection.[16]

The autobiographical truth of a person as a unified totality is precisely what Sartre means by the fundamental project of a person. However, Sartre does not believe access to this truth is limited to an autobiographer. Indeed, the existential biographer may be in a better position to present the unifying principle in a life than the person himself. Existential psychoanalysis aims at creating an artful orderly portrait of a person by imaginatively projecting oneself into the inner experience of the other. Errors in details do not affect the truth of this ideal structure of a person.

NOVELISTIC ELEMENTS IN FREUD'S CASE STUDIES

From the preceding discussion, it should be clear that Sartre's existential psychoanalysis does not reproduce the single true meaning of a person's life. Rather, the essential element of such psychoanalytic interpretation is the creation of a coherent story of a particular individual, a movement from unintelligibility to intelligibility. A brief look at Freudian case studies reveals the same approach.

Ordinarily, Freud begins an analysis by asking the patient to tell him "the whole story of his life."[17] One of the main indications of psychological illness is the patient's inability to give an adequate, complete, coherent story of himself. Patients usually cannot construct "followable" stories.[18] They lack a sense of the overall "plot" of their lives. Freud compares the initial account that a patient recounts to "an unnavigable river whose stream is at one moment choked by masses of rock and at another divided and lost among shallows and sandbanks."[19] Patients usually offer bowdlerized editions of their life stories.[20] They leave "gaps unfilled and riddles unanswered," "periods which remain totally obscure and unilluminated"; "the connections . . . are for the most part incoherent, and the sequence of different events is uncertain."[21] When Dora returns to Freud after leaving therapy prematurely, her goal is both "to finish her story and to ask for help."[22] Thus analysis begins with an "inability to give an ordered history" and ends with "an intelligible, consistent, and unbroken case history,"[23] and "a picture of the patient's forgotten years that shall be alike trustworthy and complete."[24] In this latter description one may take "complete" to mean an *unbroken narrative* and "trustworthy" to mean *worthy of belief or conviction*. These are two essential elements of interpretation; they constitute the core of its mythic dimension and the source of its creative and constructive qualities.

Thus the goal of self-understanding involves the creation of a narrative life history. The therapeutic task of "working through" requires learning how to be a good narrator, to establish the plot of one's life both as a pattern of the past and a course for the future. Michael McGuire explains: "In psychoanalytic case histories a story exists when a number of attributes (particular kinds of behavior, stages of mind, or typical responses) can be traced through enough novel situations for a long enough time . . . to convince the listener of the importance of the chosen set of attributes. Moreover, once this set of attributes is identified, each new situation serves to further define its characteristics."[25]

For Sartre, converting experiences of a person's life into a "true novel" is the primordial task of existential psychoanalysis because in so doing, one gives form and expression to the individual's fundamental project and its dialectical connections. Chronology is secondary in this narration.

In certain ways, Freud's case histories likewise have the characteristics of "true novels" following a dialectical logic of narration. The analysis of an individual is not, as we have seen, a reproduction of his or her past. Nor is the case history an exact copy of that analysis. In the case of Dora, Freud admits altering the order of his explanations "for the sake of presenting the case in a more connected form."[26] In the introduction to the case of the "Wolf-Man," Freud confesses to mixing together historical and thematic elements: "I am unable to give either a purely historical or a purely thematic account of my patient's story; I can write a consecutive history neither of the treatment nor of the disease, but I shall find myself obliged to combine the two methods of presentation."[27] Psychoanalytic biography thus has a nonlinear, nonchronological core. Freud's case histories offer a new attitude toward biographical narration. As Rieff describes the case of Dora, "A narrative account would have distorted the psychological reality that Freud wanted to portray; no linear style, however precise, could catch the eerie convergences of cause and effect sought by Freud."[28] Beneath the appearance of a simple, followable story, we find "a labyrinth into which the narrative thread soon disappears, replaced by a mode of presentation calculated to help us see events, remote and near, simultaneously—all having their effect upon Dora."[29] A literary critic calls the organization of this case "plastic, involuted, and heterogeneous, and follows spontaneously an inner logic that seems frequently to be at odds with itself; it often looks back around itself and is multidimensional in its representation of both its material and itself."[30] Such a description would be quite appropriate for Sartre's psychoanalyses as well.

For Sartre, the novelistic form of existential psychoanalyses is necessary to communicate the literary qualities of the fundamental project. Freud likewise notes that his case histories "read like short stories and . . . lack the serious stamp of science. . . . the nature of the subject is evidently responsible for this rather than any preference of my own. The fact is that local diagnosis and electrical reactions lead nowhere in the study of hysteria, whereas the detailed description of mental processes such as we are accustomed to find in the works of imaginative writers enables me, with the use of a few psychological formulas, to obtain at least some kind of insight into the course of that affection."[31] It is altogether fitting, therefore, that literary critic Stephen Marcus should characterize Freud's case of Dora as a "great work of literature," both an "outstanding creative and imaginative performance and an intellectual cognitive achievement of the highest order."[32] Marcus even demonstrates some significant resemblances between the Dora case and modern experimental novels. Freud, like Sartre, by utilizing all the sophisticated literary techniques of the modern novel, tends to blur one's ordinary discriminations of novels and truth. The psychoanalytic case history is thus a kind of poetic fiction that creates for its subject a unique story, plot, theme, and cosmos.[33] It is as much a work of creative imagination as of science. As James Hillman suggests, a diagnosis is "a gnosis: a mode of self-knowledge that creates a cosmos in its image."[34] Freud's reconstructions are not really homologous to an archeological discovery. Rather, Freud creates a reality in his own mind that is "heterogeneous, multidimensional and open-ended—novelistic in the fullest sense of the word."[35]

A MYTH TO BELIEVE IN

Commenting on Freud's *Moses and Monotheism,* which was originally subtitled "A Historical Novel," Robert Lifton suggests that Freud's concept of truth goes beyond ordinary historical description. What Freud presents is "a form of fictionalized truth, or perhaps fiction truer than truth."[36] The fiction that is truer than truth is what Sartre called the "true novel," and what I am describing as the mythic dimension of interpretation. While Sartre has admitted his own self-analysis is a sort of novel, it is also a novel that he *believes.* This may be taken to mean that the account has "mythic" power for him. It establishes the structures of meaning he experiences in his world. What distinguishes a myth in a religious society from a mere legend or story is that it is *believed* to embody primordial characteristics of reality.[37]

Similarly, psychoanalytic interpretation within clinical work requires more than simply constructing a coherent or plausible narrative. The element of conviction or belief is essential for a successful reconstruction, for it indicates that the individual has appropriated a particular way of looking at his or her life. Psychoanalytic insight, therefore, involves a combination of both intellectual and emotional acceptance of an interpretation. Intellectual acceptance demands a coherent narrative, whereas emotional acceptance implies the force of belief.

Conviction has been called "the *sine qua non* of the validity and effectiveness of reconstruction."[38] After one of Freud's interpretations, the Rat-Man "admitted that all of this sounded plausible, but he was naturally not in the very least *convinced* by it."[39] Such lack of conviction may be due to the fact that an analysand has not sufficiently "worked through" the interpretation. As one "works through" an interpretation, it accounts for more and more material, the present situation becomes more understandable, and the interpretation thereby becomes more convincing. One acquires a story to believe in. In Sartre's language, the process of "working through" an interpretation is part of the long "work" of totalization.[40] In any case, conviction must be the final point reached: "So long as he is not fully convinced the material must be considered as unexhausted."[41] The breakthrough for Rat-Man is winning the sense of conviction which he had lacked.

Consequently, clinical interpretation must concern itself with the way constructed narratives are transformed into the analysand's conviction. In an oft-quoted passage written near the end of his career, Freud says, "The path that starts from the analyst's construction ought to end in the patient's recollection; but it does not always lead so far. Quite often we do not succeed in bringing the patient to recollect what has been repressed. Instead of that, . . . we produce in him an assured conviction of the truth of the construction which achieves the same therapeutic result as a recaptured memory."[42] The goal of psychoanalytic interpretation is the creation of a coherent narrative account that is animated by the power of conviction. It is a response to the human need to introduce order and structure into the chaos of immediate experience.

By emphasizing the creative, constructive, and imaginative process by which meaning emerges, one can begin to appreciate the mythic dimension in the establishment of meaning within a person's life. To speak of the experience of meaning is to immediately invoke the realm of myth. The structures by which human experience acquires significance are essentially mythic. To describe them in these terms is not meant to disparage myth, but rather to celebrate it.[43] In premodern religious cultures the fundamental task of myth is to narrate the creation of cosmos out of chaos. As Eliade has shown, for such a religious person the world lacks true ontological reality until it has been religiously founded, named, and set in order. The myth of creation provides a transempirical paradigm, which establishes the structure of the world. Such a myth does not simply refer to a moment in the past but is regarded as an ever-present reality. Sacred time and sacred space are always accessible to religious societies as a means of maintaining and expanding the realm of reality.

In the same way, the task or project of every person is to create a personal myth that provides the foundation of his or her values and sense of the order of reality. In a religious society to build a house is to create a microcosm of reality, to establish an area of ordered space.[44] In the modern world, the individual must create and maintain the order of his lived world. Accordingly, psychologist Nicholas Hobbs says, "Man constantly engages in building and repairing and extending and modifying cognitive structures that help him make a personal sense of the world. The individual has got to have a cognitive house to live in and to protect himself from the incomprehensibilities of existence as well as to provide some architecture for daily experiencing. . . . He must adopt or invent a personal cosmology. When he invests this cosmology with passion, we may call it his personal mystique."[45] Psychoanalytic interpretation provides one means for making the movement from chaos to order. Preinterpreted experience that appears random, accidental, and unrelated is transformed into a meaningful orderly world. To establish "ego" where "id" was is therefore a fundamental act of cosmogony. Here one might find a new meaning to Sartre's characterization of man's fundamental urge as the desire to be God. Just as early religious societies identify with the power of the gods in creating the world, people in modern society also seek to create a necessary order in reality. What Sartre describes as totalization, the expanding spiral from a central axis of orientation, is simply the constant expansion of one's sense of cosmos or order.

The sacred space and sacred time established by a cosmogonic myth does not correspond to any specific moment in ordinary historical time. In a similar way, the concept of "analytic space" which Serge Viderman emphasizes, and which is the key to psychoanalysis, implies that the acts and interpretations (the transference) that emerge in that "space" do not really correspond to preexisting infantile space and time, but rather are creating a mythic space and time. The heart of analytic technique, therefore, is not so much a matter of discovering a historical account beneath a person's mythology,[46] but rather constructing a person's myth or mythology as it is expressed through his or her life history.[47]

[5] *TWO EARLY "TRUE NOVELS"*

BAUDELAIRE'S FALL FROM GRACE

Sartre's analysis of Baudelaire, his first major effort at existential psycho-analysis, was written in 1944 at a time before Sartre undertook a crucial reconsideration of Freud and Marx. Much of Sartre's study seems to be an undisguised moral polemic against Baudelaire's values, to the dismay of many critics.[1] Sartre has also been criticized for being so selective in his use of material that he has merely created a *"vie romancé*, a popular fictionalized biography."[2]

To a certain extent, Sartre's aim in *Baudelaire* is a response to the most deterministic elements in Freud. Sartre rejects the idea that the major conflict of early childhood stems from a literal drive for sexual possession of one's mother. Yet it is only partly accurate to call *Baudelaire* "a running debate with classical psychoanalysis."[3] In many ways, Sartre approaches Baudelaire as Freud would. He does not deny the ambivalences, compromises, and defenses in Baudelaire's personality that any psychoanalysis would consider. Of course, Sartre does redefine certain issues of human development in order to accentuate his own views about the emergence of personal meaning in every individual's life.

Sartre emphasizes that any child, and Baudelaire in particular, relates to his mother out of religious rather than biological instincts. Baudelaire's dilemma is not primarily the sexual desires of an unresolved Oedipal complex, but the existential desires of an unresolved "theological complex" (B, 55). The "sacred" dimension of the parent-child relationship refers to the transcendent level of meaning in human life, which lies beyond mere physical, biological existence. In this sense, a child's first experience of "the sacred" is the feeling of personal validation or justification that is received from his or her parents. Sartre insists that a child sees his or her parents as gods who incarnate the meaning and purpose of reality. They guarantee the child's permanent "sacred character" (B, 52). More simply, they offer a sense of belonging and importance to the child.

Like many children, Baudelaire "worshipped" his mother and felt "united body and soul to his mother in a primitive mystical relation" (B, 16). They comprised an "incestuous couple," who lived in "communal religious life" (B, 17). Sartre emphasizes the "sacred nature of their union." He observes,

> *The mother was an idol, the child* consecrated *by her affection for him. Far from feeling that his existence was vague, aimless, superfluous, he thought of himself as* son by divine right. *He was always living in her which meant that he had found a sanctuary. He himself was nothing and did not want to be anything but an emanation of the divinity, a little thought which was always present in her mind. It was precisely because he was completely absorbed in a being who appeared to be a necessary being, to exist as of right [exister par nécessité et par droit], that he was shielded from any feeling of disquiet, that he melted into the absolute and was* justified (B, 16–17).

Sartre emphasizes the fact that Baudelaire's father died when he was six. It is ambiguous, however, whether Sartre believes that Baudelaire's "sacred" relation with his mother existed from infancy on, or that it was largely the result of his father's early death. Since a child's relation to his mother is already firmly established by the age of six, it is unlikely that the death of Baudelaire's father alone could have been the primary factor in his relation to his mother. More likely, the emphasis on Baudelaire's fatherlessness serves as a symbolic confirmation of an already existing sacred relation with his mother, rather than a chronological description of causal connections.

Within this symbolic rendering of Baudelaire's childhood, Sartre's analysis introduces a fateful event that influences the entire course of Baudelaire's life. A year after his father dies, Baudelaire's mother remarries and he is sent off to school. As a result, Baudelaire suffers from what Sartre describes as "a profound sense of having fallen from grace" (*B*, 17). He discovers that he is an individual without justification for his existence. This is the dawn of genuine *self*-consciousness for him, and the beginning of his lifelong attempt to *recover* the sense of justified existence he has lost. For Sartre, this quest for justification is the fundamental task of all human beings. Baudelaire's sense of rejection represents his "original crisis." The fundamental project he pursues throughout the rest of his life is in large part a response to this crisis.

Ordinarily, as a child grows up, he experiences his own transcendence and freedom, and learns to accept the lack of justification for his existence. Baudelaire, however, refuses to grow up. Sartre criticizes him for failing to transcend the stable order and absolute security of childhood. He never challenges his mother's authority, and horrifies her with his poetry only to evoke her judgment. He will not accept his freedom to modify the meaning of the past with new acts. Instead, he views his life as already "frozen" from the point of view of death. He would like his present existence to have the characteristics of a memory (*B*, 184), that is, fixed and foreseen in advance.[4] In that way, he himself can replace the divine being (his mother) whose attention had justified his existence. Baudelaire attempts to become like God, to reach the impossible Sartrean synthesis of being-in-itself-for-itself (*BN*, 566). Such a state of permanent justification perpetually eludes human reality, since consciousness is like an infinite series, its meaning always transcended by a subsequent moment. The attempt to reach this state of permanent stability is doomed to failure, and Baudelaire's life is "simply the story of the failure of this attempt" (*B*, 28).

Although we need not be concerned with the specific details of Sartre's analysis of Baudelaire, the general structure of his study is important for understanding the nature of existential psychoanalysis. Sartre begins by noting Baudelaire's seemingly contradictory nature. For example, "The perverse individual deliberately chose the most banal and most rigid of moral codes. The refined man of the world went with the lowest harlots. . . . The recluse had a horror of solitude. . . . The apostle of effort . . . was incapable of settling down to regular work." (*B*, 15). As in his own self-analysis, Sartre endeavors to find a context in which such contradictions made sense. His underlying presupposition for this existential analysis comes only at the conclusion of the book. In retrospect, every event in Baudelaire's life must be regarded as "a reflection of the indecomposable totality which he was from the first to the last day of his life" (*B*, 192). Likewise, all of Baudelaire's different behavior and personality characteristics have interacted dialectically within an "indissoluable synthesis in which each of them expresses itself and all the others at the same time" (B, 185). The many "contradictions" in Baudelaire's life are "only modulations of a great primitive theme which they reproduce with different tonalities" (B, 191). Having conducted a performance of Baudelaire's life, Sartre now relaxes with the assurance that everyone can now recognize the "melody" of his life, to use Sartre's earliest metaphor for the self. The "indecomposable totality" and the "great primitive theme" of Baudelaire's life are both expressions for the *fundamental project*, the unfolding unity within a particular person's life.

In reading Sartre's statements about Baudelaire, it is easy to misinterpret the nature of this "totality" present in every moment of Baudelaire's life. In what sense is Baudelaire really a totality from the first day of his life? Certainly, if Sartre means that every detail in Baudelaire's life is predestined in the very first moments of infancy he has presented an absurd proposition. That Baudelaire's entire life is reducible to a single "original choice" he makes at the age of seven in response to his feeling of rejection is suggested by some of Sartre's statements. If taken literally, however, this position misrepresents Sartre's overall picture of Baudelaire's childhood. Sartre's shift in terminology from "totality" to "totalization" in *Search for a Method* and elsewhere clarifies the dynamic nature of development in an individual. His view is not that the last day of Baudelaire's life is determined by the first day any more than the last note of a melody is determined in advance by the first note, or the last word of a sentence by the first. Both the first day and the last day are linked within an emerging structure that becomes specified in the course of Baudelaire's life and conceptually grasped only in retrospective analysis.

In retrospect, a particular moment of childhood, like an individual word within a book, can only be understood in the context of the larger totality of which it is not only a constitutive *part* but also a *symbol* in a significant way. Sartre's reconstruction of Baudelaire's childhood as a key to the totality of Baudelaire's life has this symbolic, or better mythic, quality. In other words, Sartre constructs the childhood from the perspective of what Baudelaire is known to have become as an adult; but he simultaneously treats the world of childhood as a symbolic microcosm of that later adult development. Thus, the crucial event of childhood functions more as a mythic paradigm than as actual historical event. For this reason, while Sartre's analysis does employ a variety of Freudian themes, it likewise employs religious language to endow the account of Baudelaire's childhood with a mythic quality.

Sartre's analysis revolves around the idea that the advent of self-consciousness is the central event of childhood. Of course, one must use the word "event" in a symbolic sense, since the emergence of self-consciousness does not occur at a single datable moment. Moreover, the fundamental "choice" of Baudelaire is also a hypothetical and symbolic construction based on Sartre's general view of childhood and on the perspective of the type of man Baudelaire grew up to become. Sartre carefully interweaves his account of Baudelaire with his general account of the childhood drama by which every person discovers his self-consciousness. He makes the general point that "Each of us was able to observe in childhood the fortuitous and shattering advent of self-consciousness" (B, 19). The structure of Sartre's argument proceeds with a deceptive mixture of the general situation in childhood and the particular case of Baudelaire. In some ways, Baudelaire becomes a paradigmatic "Everychild." Sartre describes in general terms how the child who discovers his separateness with despair, rage, or jealousy may develop a narcissistic preoccupation as a "defense mechanism" (B, 20–21). Sartre constructs an imaginary monologue expressing the child's attitude toward his parents. " 'You threw me out,' he will say to his parents. 'You threw me out of the perfect whole of which I was part and condemned me to a separate existence. Well, now I'm going to turn this existence against you. If you ever wanted to get me back again, it would be impossible because I have become conscious of myself as separate from and against everyone else' " (B, 20). After several paragraphs describing the attitudes of this hypothetical child Sartre concludes that such a child "gradually becomes the man whom we call Charles Baudelaire" (B, 22). Sartre has not really presented a specific picture of Baudelaire's childhood so much as a general scenario appropriate to the kind of man Baudelaire became. As we find in his subsequent case studies, Sartre does not think a correlation of his picture of Baudelaire with literal historical events is absolutely essential.

Sartre's study of Baudelaire is not intended as the final or complete word on Baudelaire. Sartre has perhaps emphasized his own theoretical perspective too much, overextending the boundaries of the "true novel." Nevertheless, *Baudelaire* does reveal some new truth about Baudelaire's inner world and demonstrates the outline of Sartre's method of existential psychoanalysis. It emphasizes the presentation of a childhood event and an original choice, which together comprise a symbolic, sacred drama marking the emergence of self-consciousness and propelling the fundamental project of a person's life. Sartre's subsequent existential psychoanalyses employ this same rhetorical use of the crucial childhood event to symbolize the ensuing spiral of human development. In *The Family Idiot*, Sartre's construction of Flaubert's childhood will be a general description of the kind of child who gradually became Gustave Flaubert.

THE SACRED WORLD OF GENET

Following the publication of Sartre's study of Baudelaire in 1947, the next effort in existential psychoanalysis appears in 1952. In the cases of both Baudelaire and Genet, Sartre does not base his analysis on the historical accuracy of his reconstruction. The dialectical logic of a mythic structure overshadows the importance of actual chronological events. Sartre suggests this kind of analysis more closely reflects a person's psychological functioning.

The issue of historical truth in *Saint Genet* is further complicated by the sources of information on which Sartre must rely for his interpretation. Sartre depends almost exclusively on the testimony of Genet's novels to understand the personality of Genet. It is true, of course, that Genet's novels are highly autobiographical. Indeed, several are narrated in the first person and there can be little doubt that the "I" is Genet's. Consequently, it might reasonably be argued that in several instances Genet has completely obliterated any useful distinction between autobiography or history and fiction. Nevertheless, while there is much factual information within these novels, many of the memories are mainly significant for their symbolic value rather than as real incidents. [5]

In Sartre's view, Genet's literary efforts are a kind of waking dream life that can be explored for valuable information, in the same way that *Nausea* tells as much about Sartre's mode of being as his autobiography *The Words*. Writing represents Genet's way of "weaving a dream" around his experiences (SG, 453). Regarding Genet's novels, Sartre says, "The single subject of the single book Genet has written and rewritten five times is Genet himself" (SG, 519). Genet himself tells us that he does not write in order "to depict an event or its hero, but so that they may tell you something about myself." [6] All Genet's novels are part of a single effort of Genet to present an artistic vision of himself. Sartre calls them "false novels" (SG, 522), since all the novelistic techniques and characterizations are only thin disguises for Genet himself, his dreams, and his vision of the world.

Genet reflectively sees his life with the imaginative structure of a poem, or a myth. He openly acknowledges the artistic elements in this retrospective account of his life. What he seeks to convey "is not what I have lived, but the tone in which I tell of it. Not the anecdotes, but the work of art. Not my life, but the interpretation of it." [7] Consequently, the Genet discovered in these works and reconstructed by Sartre reflects the psychological or "imaginary" life of Genet, and only secondarily real facts and events. Genet calls the autobiographical *Thief's Journal* his "legend," his vision of himself. "My life must be a legend, in other words, legible, and the reading of it must give birth to a new emotion which I call poetry. I am no longer anything but a pretext" (Jean Genet quoted in *SG*, 519).

Genet's "project" is thus embodied in the textual creation he has made of his experience. He realizes the ambiguous status of his "legend." "Was what I wrote true? False? Only this book of love will be real. What of the facts which served as its pretext. I must be their repository. It is not they that I am restoring."[8] Sartre says that everything Genet tells us is "both true and false" (*SG*, 426). There are echoes of this same idea in Sartre's own autobiography, where he confesses, "What I have just written is false. True. Neither true nor false, like everything written about madmen, about men" (*W*, 43).

In any case, what is literally false may also be existentially and mythically true. Genet is important because he focuses upon the general process through which human experience is shaped by the imagination into a meaningful structure. His reference to the "facts" of his life as a "pretext" is significant. Sartre's earliest works demonstrate that the facts of experience are indeed "pretextual." They lack the structure of a "text" or story. To tell a story is to weave a text out of the experiences of one's life.

In the preface to Genet's *Thief's Journal*, Sartre insists that Genet does, in fact, provide us with a special kind of truth.

> *He does, to be sure, tell us everything. The whole truth, nothing but the truth, but it is the sacred truth. . . . His autobiography is not an autobiography; it merely seems like one; it is a sacred cosmogony. His stories are not stories. . . . You think he is relating facts and suddenly you realize he is describing rites. . . . His memories are not memories; they are exact but sacred; he speaks about his life like an evangelist, as a wonder-struck witness. . . . Thus there comes into being that new object: a mythology of the myth. . . . If, however, you are able to see at the seam the thin line separating the enveloping myth from the enveloped myth, you will discover the truth, which is terrifying.*[9]

Ironically, in existential psychoanalysis, Sartre himself is less interested in simple "truth," "autobiography," "stories," "facts," or "memories," than in "sacred truth," "sacred cosmogony," "sacred rites," and "sacred memories."

Sartre portrays Genet's early childhood as one of innocence and happiness. As a "good little boy" who worships his foster parents, Genet embodies what the adult world sees as the "original state of grace" (*SG*, 6). Nevertheless, Sartre posits an unnamed, unexpressed, undifferentiated anxiety lurking beneath this happy childhood; it slowly emerges as Genet becomes aware of his illegitimacy, his unnatural origin. Because his natural mother gave him up at birth, Genet's birth cannot express the intimate union of mother and child for him, but only his original rejection. Genet's natural mother acquires mythic proportions in Sartre's reconstruction as the one who makes Genet into an unloved, unwanted child. Since Genet later compares himself with filth and waste, Sartre suggests he sees himself as his mother's discarded excrement rather than as her beloved offspring. Genet's rejection of respectable society, therefore, is partly a response to his own primordial rejection.

As in the case of Baudelaire, the childhood of Genet that we receive from Sartre is a mythic reconstruction, which symbolizes the kind of man we know Genet to have become. According to Sartre, Genet's life is fundamentally influenced by the memory of a childhood event. Sartre's use of religious terminology to describe this event and the meaning of it is striking. This event and the meaning attributed to it provide the mythic structure through which Sartre understands the rest of Genet's life. Sartre begins his analysis:

> *An accident riveted him to a childhood memory, and this memory became sacred. In his early childhood, a liturgical drama was performed, a drama of which he was the officiant: he knew paradise, and lost it, he was a child and was driven from his childhood. No doubt this "break" is not easy to localize. It shifts back and forth, at the dictate of his moods and myths, between the ages of ten and fifteen. But that is unimportant. What matters is that it exists and that he believes in it. His life is divided into two heterogeneous parts: before and after the sacred drama.* Indeed it is not unusual for the memory to condense into a single mythical moment the contingencies and perpetual rebeginnings of an individual history [italics mine]. *What matters is that Genet lives and continues to relive this period of his life as if it had lasted only an instant* (SG, 1–2).

It does not disturb Sartre that the critical moment in Genet's life cannot be accurately determined. "What matters," he says, "is that it exists and that he believes in it." From the context of this passage, it is difficult to tell at first whether the "it" that exists and that Genet believes in is a real event of his life or just an imagined memory.

The "event" that forges the pattern of Genet's life occurs, asserts Sartre, when ten-year-old Genet is caught stealing from his foster parents. As Sartre constructs the scene, "A voice declares publicly: 'You're a thief' " (SG, 17). The unformed anxiety of Genet's childhood now becomes crystallized. But, Sartre makes no claims that his account accurately corresponds to an actual historical event. It quickly becomes clear that the sacred drama that bisects Genet's life in Sartre's version is a mythic or symbolic condensation rather than a datable historical event. Sartre repeats nonchalantly his indifference to historicity: "That was how it happened; in that way or some other way. In all probability there were offenses and then punishment, solemn oaths and then relapses. It does not matter. The important thing is that Genet lived and has not stopped reliving this period of his life as if it had lasted only an instant" (SG, 17). Does this then mean that Genet *remembers* an event which may not have occurred but which symbolizes his childhood dilemma for him? Yes and no. Sartre is not concerned with whether Genet has an actual reflective memory of this specific moment. Rather, he has what Sartre might call a "lived memory" of the event. Sartre here repeats what is important from his opening passage in almost identical words; namely, that Genet lived, lives, and relives his past *as if* he actually experienced and remembers this mythic event. Looking at what Genet says and does later, Sartre thinks it likely that he must have experienced (though not necessarily remembered) his childhood along the lines Sartre draws.

Thus the "event" or "instant" that Sartre locates at the core of Genet's development is primarily important as a hypothetical reconstruction of the "lived" psychical reality, which is preserved and totalized in Genet's life.[10] As in religious myths, the significance of narrated events lies not in their historical accuracy but in their function as a structure of meaning for present reality. The crucial "event" in Genet's childhood serves as a symbol for a period of his childhood that he must appropriate throughout the rest of his life.

Sartre's analysis of Genet also seems to be deeply influenced by the phenomenology of religion, particularly the categories of myth, ritual, and sacred time as they have been discussed by Mircea Eliade.[11] As in the case of classical religious myths described by Eliade, the "original crisis" in Genet's life exists outside of ordinary time as an eternal, sacred moment (SG, 2). Throughout his life, Genet preserves "a bygone instant which has lost none of its virulence, an infinitesimal and sacred void which concludes a death and begins a horrible metamorphosis" (SG, 2). For Sartre, Genet's crucial childhood event is a "liturgical drama," since it has the structure of an initiatory rite of passage. Genet, says Sartre, symbolically "dies" to his childhood existence and is "resurrected" into a new form of existence, though his rebirth is incomplete. Genet, the well-behaved child, is transformed into a thief. As an eternal "sacred" event, the original crisis is not simply in the past but is an ever-present reality, the repetition of which Genet both fears and desires, and continually reenacts in different forms.

Sartre describes Genet's response to the "original event" as a "conversion" experience, introducing another religious phenomenon as a metaphor for psychological development. Genet accepts his condemnation by actively willing to become what the label of others has made him—a thief. Yet it is clear that the specific moment of conversion from child to thief has no more historical reality than the traumatic condemnation which allegedly provoked it. The conversion is as much a mythic construction as is the original event to which it is a response. Sartre speculates:

> *This conversion can be situated between the ages of ten and fifteen. I imagine it kept beginning anew, over and over. Again and again the child pledged himself to evil in a state of rage, and then one of his judges had only to smile at him and the decision melted in the fire of love. I imagine, too, that he was afraid, afraid of himself and of the future. . . . And then one day he found himself converted. . . . The paradox of every conversion is that it spreads over years and gathers together in an instant. He decided to be what he was, or, to put it otherwise, the matter was decided within him. He seizes upon the curse which goes back to the depths of his past, of his mother's past, and which has continued to the very present, and he projects it before him: it will be this future (SG, 50).*

Sartre's description of conversion is his artistic way of expressing the developing style of existence that Genet creates in response to his situation. Sartre has merely presented a fictionalized or mythic scenario as he imagines it. (He repeats "I imagine" twice within the account just quoted.) The conversion itself should be understood in the same sense that the fundamental project represents an emergent choice, a "choice in the making" or an "ongoing totalization." This is why Sartre describes the original conversion or decision as beginning and dissolving again and again over a period of years until a level of dialectical development is finally achieved. Genet's "conversion" signifies a portion of the "dialectical spiral" by which his fundamental project develops.

"Conversion" has a dual connotation for Sartre. On the one hand, it represents a sacred or mythic moment where there is a break in ordinary time, which introduces a sense of before and after. On the other hand, Genet's conversion reflects the dialectical process by which he "converts" the constraints of his situation into his own action. Conversion is the movement that occurs between the internalization of external factors and the reexternalization of inner experience in the world. It is the individual's personal response to the challenge of his situation.

This conversion, of course, does not represent a single lucid decision that Genet makes at a specific moment in time. If this is what Sartre meant, the critics would be justified in their scepticism about the existence of such a choice. However, Sartre's analysis does not posit the existence of a choice that can be pinpointed at a specific moment. Rather, the "original choice" of an individual is "a protracted moment, covering a certain span of time in which one makes something of the self which so far has been made by others."[12] The "choice" is thus the first stage of developing a strategy for dealing with one's situation. It is a way of "surpassing and preserving the morbid motivations within the unity of a tactic . . . and gives meaning to the meaning conferred on us" (*BEM*, 204). Accordingly, Genet does not "decide" in any ordinary sense of the word; rather the "decision" gradually emerges from within him as a strategy for coping which unites his past with his present and his future. The conversion is a model that is seen repeated symbolically in the pattern of his life.

The original crisis of Genet—being caught stealing—has acquired an "aura of the sacred" (*SG*, 4); his activities as a homosexual and a thief exhibit a "meaning which transcends them" because they manifest the original metamorphosis of his childhood. Genet's life of crime, his poetry, and his homosexuality all reproduce the mythic moment of before and after, of rise and fall (*SG*, 4). The original childhood event is not the *cause* of his later behavior, but it provides a *symbolic model* or archetype in terms of which the structure of Genet's adult life can be understood. Genet's homosexuality and stealing as an adult are essentially ritual repetitions of a mythic model. Consequently, to understand Genet, one must reconstruct the "original event" behind his personal cosmogony; it is this to which his later activities and creations symbolically refer. Sartre says, "By analysis of the myths, we shall proceed to re-establish the facts in their true significance" (*SG*, 5).

Sartre describes Genet as living in sacred time. The details of his life are meaningful

> . . . *only insofar as they seem to repeat the original drama of the lost paradise. He is a man of repetition: the drab slack time of his daily life—a* profane *life in which everything is permissible—is shot through with blazing hierophanies which restore to him his original passion, as Holy Week restores to us that of Christ. Just as Jesus does not cease to die, so Genet does not cease to be metamorphosed into a foul insect: The same archetypal event is reproduced in the same symbolic and ritual form through the same ceremonies of transfiguration. To Genet, as to the faithful of a religious community, sacred time is cyclical: it is the time of Eternal Recurrence* (SG, 5).

Genet continually endows "profane" history with the "sacred" meaning of mythic categories. To a certain extent, Genet's refusal of profane history in favor of a sacred model represents the general process of giving meaning to the flux of experience by putting it into narrative form. Profane is to sacred as living is to telling. One of the major phenomenological differences between them is the quality of time. The time of ordinary experience is what Sartre calls "profane time" in Genet's case: "the drab slack time of his daily life." When life is remembered and interpreted, however, its temporal quality is altered. Time is no longer uniform. It clusters around certain critical events. Accordingly, "sacred" time is at once the time of myths and memory.

Sartre's analysis of Genet's earliest homosexuality reflects a kind of emergent choice that can only be understood from the perspective of Genet's adult behavior. Sartre rejects Genet's claim that his first homosexual feelings were at the age of ten. Whatever early childhood affections Genet felt toward his playmates, his homosexuality was not a passive complex already present in him as a child, or decided at the age of ten. The meaning of Genet's childhood activities does not emerge until later. When they first occurred they were merely "rehearsals, experiences, and experiments" (SG, 78). But later developments will act upon the earlier ones, endowing them with new meanings. Sartre explains, "It is only afterwards that these tentative efforts take on meaning. When the individual definitively takes one path rather than another, 'the retrospective illusion' then detects in them the premonitory signs of disorder or decides to regard them only as inconsequential deviations. Inversely, our inventions are mainly decisions and clarifications. What we think we discover in a moment of special insight is what we have been inventing for years, bit by bit, absent-mindedly as it were without being completely involved" (SG, 78). In other words, Genet's adult homosexuality retrospectively transforms his past into an anticipation of that subsequent behavior. Genet then discovers the meaning of his past and names it "pre-homosexual." At the same time, however, Genet's homosexuality is not a sudden decision simply projected onto the past. It has been gradually prepared for by the past.

In Sartre's analysis, Genet's tendency toward passive homosexuality is the physiological expression of his original crisis in which he was taken by surprise and "penetrated" from behind by the condemnatory gaze of the Other. Genet ritually relives his initial psychological "rape" as a sexual one. His passive homosexuality in which the Other pins him to the floor from behind is therefore a "religious ceremony" (SG, 108), a "willed and ceremonial repetition of the original crisis" (SG, 111). In this way, Sartre shows how sexuality reflects a person's fundamental relation to the world; its meaning is not purely instinctual. Each level of human experience expresses that fundamental relation in a different manner. The sexual act, therefore, has a sacred, symbolic quality for

Genet. It is not concerned with sensual pleasure, but rather is "his whole life condensed into a spasm, his whole past, his whole destiny" (SG, 111).

Genet's movement from child to thief to poet, regardless of its intrinsic importance, is extremely significant, since it reveals the principle of dialectical development implicit within his fundamental project. The following passage serves as a useful clarification of the dialectical nature of Genet's "original choice."

> One must will an act to the end. But the act is alive, it changes. The goal one sets at the beginning is abstract and consequently false. Little by little it is enriched by the means employed to attain it, and ulti-mately the concrete goal, the true goal, is what one wants at the finish. The interrupted act spoils and depreciates just as the truth that stops midway changes into error. In willing himself, unreservedly, to be a thief, Genet sinks into the dream; in willing his dream to the point of madness, he becomes a poet; in willing poetry until the final triumph of the word, he becomes a man; and the man has become the truth of the poet, as the poet was the truth of the thief (SG, 582). [13]

It is clear that Genet's fundamental project develops with a certain internal logic, yet the full meaning of that project and the symbolic importance of the original crisis are not yet established when Genet is ten years old. The "truth" of the project depends on which point in its trajectory that one examines. Any temporary moment of truth or stasis dissolves as the project continues to "totalize" itself. Only in relation to Genet the man, can the symbolic importance of his childhood experience be understood.

Sartre believes his study of Genet demonstrates "the limits of psycho-analytic interpretation" (SG, 124, 584). He admits that Genet may seem to exhibit "every possible complex," including feelings of inferiority, overcompensation, and so on. However, we should not explain any of these elements as the mechanics of a neurosis or psychosis. Rather, we must try to see Genet's behavior patterns as "the labor of a freedom relentlessly working out its salvation" (SG, 124). There is no denying the permanent effect of certain early experiences on the direction of Genet's life. Yet Genet cannot be explained without considering his constant struggle to transform the meaning of his situation. This enabled him to become ultimately a poet rather than a thief.

Sartre's claim for human autonomy is modest. "Freedom is not a triumph. For Genet, it simply marked out certain routes which were not initially given" (BEM, 35). Freedom simply refers to the emergent "choice" an individual's life reveals in its gradual development. Genet's move to literature eventually enabled him to master the original crisis. His books become an "equivalent to a psychoanalytic cure" (SG, 544) which had the cathartic effect of expressing his consciousness in words, and, in a sense, enabling him to recreate himself.

[6] EXISTENTIAL PSYCHOANALYSIS AS IDEOLOGY AND MYTH

THE STRUCTURE OF SARTRE'S AUTOBIOGRAPHY

In his analyses of Baudelaire and Genet, Sartre neither emphasized the historical accuracy of a reconstructed childhood event or period in childhood nor regarded it as essential for his purposes. A specific childhood event (e.g., Genet's "original crisis") acquires significance within the analysis of a person's life, not as a causal force for what follows but rather as a "sacred" symbol for the overall structure of that person's project. Since the full meaning of a childhood event can be understood only in light of later developments, the full analysis of such an event implicitly refers to the subsequent course of the person's life. When one "fully" understands the crucial childhood event, one likewise understands the meaning of the rest of that life, since the latter is what clarifies the general structure established in childhood. For this reason, although Sartre's self-analysis in *The Words* deals primarily with certain symbolic events of his childhood, the subsequent development of his life can be discerned within his presentation of those events.

In an incisive examination of the narrative structure in *The Words*, Philippe Lejeune convincingly argues that Sartre's account rests on a dialectical approach that is only thinly disguised by a semblance of chronological description.[1] Sartre goes beyond ordinary chronology as the organizing principle of his narrative. *The Words* does not provide a continuous account of Sartre's life from birthday to birthday. Rather, it offers a glimpse at various thematic patterns or structures. A person's memories of childhood are seldom preserved with accurate chronological relations in a continuous narrative. Owing to the imaginative quality of memory, temporal sequence is not a strict guide to the emergence of meaning.

In *The Words* one finds a seemingly chronological account of Sartre's passage from birth to the emergence of his "neurosis of literature" by the age of eleven. Although Sartre remarks in *The Words* that he will provide a sequel to the analysis of his childhood, he later decided not to; rather, he referred readers to Simone de Beauvoir's autobiography, which includes an account of the later events in his own life as well. Certainly, from a strictly chronological point of view, *The Words* is incomplete and seems to demand an account of Sartre's adolescence and young adulthood. However, if one penetrates the chronological surface and understands *The Words* as a dialectical analysis, a sequel is unnecessary, since the analysis is already complete. Embedded in the analysis of his childhood, the fundamental project of the author of *Nausea* as well as the rest of Sartre's "style" of existing can be found. In a sense, Sartre's view of his childhood establishes a "liturgical drama," which is reflected and reenacted in the twenty years that follow the events described in *The Words*. Obviously, existential psychoanalysis is not to be confused with simple factual, chronological reportage.

It is true, of course, that throughout *The Words* Sartre employs a number of chronological indications. The overall division of his analysis into two parts, "Reading" (W, 1–85) and "Writing" (W, 86–160), gives the impression of a temporal break separating a "before" and "after." A closer look, however, shows this chronological appearance to be misleading. As Lejeune argues, the events and acts in large sections of *The Words* are described as synchronous wholes, irrespective of their actual dates. Consequently, the structural relations linking the two parts of *The Words* are not those of history but of a "dialectical fable."[2] Specific events are described by Sartre where they serve a function within a dialectical structure and not because they fill in chronological gaps.

After a description of his family history and the circumstances of his birth, the remainder of the first part of *The Words* presents a variety of events that happen to Sartre mainly between the ages of four and nine. These events comprise little more than a collection of vignettes. The progress within *The Words* is one of dialectical unfolding, not temporal unfolding.[3] The events Sartre describes from his childhood function as symbolic or "mythic" illustrations of various attitudes, feelings, and conflicts, regardless of when they occurred.

The first stage in Sartre's reconstructed drama is his slip from freedom into "imposture" due to the circumstances of his family situation. Sartre illustrates this step with an incident involving his grandfather when he is nine (W, 13) but quickly moves to a general characterization of the whole period of his life until the age of nine as though it were a single timeless moment. On the one hand, it represents the happy paradise of childhood. Like his description of Genet's childhood, Sartre describes young Jean-Paul as a good little boy, content with his position. On the other hand, Sartre's description of this stage as one of "imposture" presupposes a critical outlook that transcends the childhood happiness, just like Genet's unexpressed, undifferentiated anxiety.

Therefore, Sartre next examines his growing awareness of this imposture, that is, the dialectical contradiction at the core of his childhood paradise. Sartre claims that he sensed his lack of genuine being and reality beneath his bourgeois play-acting. He offers a series of events that collectively signify his awakening to the nature of his existence and its contingency. For example, to illustrate his forlorness, Sartre describes his emerging consciousness of the reality of death in events occurring when he is five to seven years old (W, 59–61).

Sartre attributes great importance to his first haircut at the age of seven. Here, as elsewhere, an event is retold for its symbolic significance. It is like Genet's original crisis, which symbolized the destruction of his childhood illusions. The haircut incident signifies Sartre's discovery of his ugliness beneath his superficial appearance. The ugliness he finds beneath his long hair expresses the monstrous underside of existence. For a long time, says Sartre, ugliness was "my negative principle, the quicklime in which the wonderful child was dissolved" (W, 158).

There is reason to suspect, however, that the moment of Sartre's rupture with his prior "bad faith" is "purely mythical."[4] Sartre's fall from his childhood paradise must be examined at the same level as Genet's original crisis. As Sartre indicated in that case, Genet's break with childhood cannot be literally dated. "It shifts back and forth, at the dictate of his moods and myths" over a five-year period. In his own case, Sartre claims on the one hand a feeling of uneasiness during the period after his haircut as he found it more difficult to play his role. He admits, "I overplayed and sounded false. I knew the anguish of an aging actress" (W, 65). On the other hand, however, Sartre leads us to believe that his haircut may have acquired much of its importance *après-coup*, from the perspective of later events. His mother, for example, concealed her grief over Sartre's apparent ugliness following his haircut until he was twelve, three years later. It was at that time that he was "hit hard" (W, 66) by the realization. Thus, it took three years before one layer of the event's meaning fully emerged. Similarly, Sartre illustrates his awareness of the insincerity of his histrionics with "two striking memories," which "date from a little later" (W, 66) that is, age nine to ten, two to three years *after* the haircut.

In short, Sartre has superimposed two dialectical stages upon one another during the general period of his childhood from age five to ten. First there is Sartre's contented playing; *then* there is his uneasy awareness of deeper problems. But the word "then" in the last sentence does not necessarily signify temporal succession. Sartre's uneasiness is simply the implicit contradiction of the first dialectical stage as it gradually comes into consciousness. Both experiences coexist simultaneously in an undifferentiated state, though they can only be described successively.[5] Once aware of his imposture, Sartre can go back and find evidence of it in the early part of his childhood.

Because of the tension between the two dialectical stages, Sartre interrupts his analysis with an interesting confession. He says, "What I have just written is false. True. Neither true nor false, like everything written about madmen, about men. But to what extent did I believe in my delirium? That's the basic question, and yet I can't tell. I realized later that we can know everything about our attachments except their force, that is, their sincerity. Acts cannot themselves serve as a measuring-rod unless one has proved that they are not gestures, which is not always easy" (W, 43). The truth or falsity of the reconstruction of a person's past is highly problematic, since what he or she believed about it on one level may be contradicted by a successive stage of dialectical development and understanding.

The second part of *The Words* represents the next stage in the development of Sartre's project. From the age of six to nine, Sartre had tried to escape his anxiety about his life by taking refuge in heroic adventures of his imagination (W, 71). It is his initiation into literature, however, which marks the major "event" of the narrative. At the end of the first part of *The Words* Sartre sums up his life to the age of eight. "In any case, things weren't going right" (W, 85). This statement is immediately followed by a transition to Part II: "I was saved by my grandfather. He drove me, without meaning to, into a new imposture that changed my life" (W, 85). In other words, Sartre undergoes a virtual rite of passage which transforms his existence.

It would appear from this transition to Part II that Sartre's introduction to the vocation of writing is a chronologically later development than his earlier difficulties. What one finds, however, is that Sartre's acquisition of a vocation from his grandfather occurs when he is between seven and eight years old.[6] Sartre says he assumed responsibility for his mandate to write between the ages of eight and ten (W, 102) but had a "foreboding" of the sacred powers of the writer two years earlier (W, 104). In short, although Sartre presents the help his grandfather brings him as a response to the problems in the first half of *The Words*, it occurs chronologically in the midst of the period described in Part I. Similarly, when Sartre faces another dilemma further on, his grandfather once again "came to the rescue. Unwittingly of course. Two years before . . ." (W, 110). Sartre felt "rescued" by what his grandfather had said at a much earlier time. The solution may thus precede the problem; the rescue may precede the dilemma. Such is chronological nonsense, though dialectically it is possible.

Sartre believes the stages of dialectical development in a person's life do correspond with certain important periods of life—adolescence, early adulthood, maturity—when things fall into place (LS, 44). Self-analysis is most fruitfully undertaken at such a moment of transition. To be able to look with detachment at what one ordinarily lives without explanation it is necessary to reach "a crisis, a point of arrival, . . . or a starting point; when a changing situation suddenly uncovers one's life in a new perspective."[7] Of course, Sartre is quick to acknowledge that each new perspective is no more real or valid than the previous one. In studying oneself, "one only goes round in circles."[8]

A person's autobiographical self-image is constantly revised throughout the various stages of life. Especially in old age, temporal relations between events are subsumed by their personal significance within that self-image. Events separated by time may become contemporaneous in memory if this contributes to a feeling of personal continuity and consistency throughout one's life.

Although Sartre claims at the conclusion of *The Words* that he has changed (W, 158), there lingers a deep ambivalence in this attitude toward his past. On the one hand, he describes a distinct break with his past. In a later interview he asserts, "What I see most clearly in my life is a break dividing it into two almost completely distinct periods, two moments that are almost completely separated such that being in the second period, I can hardly recognize myself any more as I was in the first" (LS, 44, cf. LS, 75). He sees both his childhood and his young adulthood as a period of inauthenticity that is better left behind. "I loathe my past and whatever has survived of it" (W, 102). Sartre says he is quick to criticize his past and brush off praise for it, since he believes he has gone beyond that self. "The past has not made me . . . it was I who plucked my memory from nothingness by an act of creation which was always being repeated" (W, 148–49). On the other hand, Sartre recognizes that his desire and ability to keep his past at "a respectful distance" (W, 102) is merely the result of childhood illusions of self-creation. Consequently, when asked to explain how much he has changed throughout his life, he replied, "I have changed as everyone changes: within a permanency."[9] He emphasizes that certain facts in his childhood established within him "a predisposition toward a certain neurotic reaction" (BEM, 274).

In view of the link that exists between the development of a person's identity and the creation of a literary text, one of Sartre's observations has particular interest. He describes the experience of writing a new page only to find then a page he had written two years earlier with the same idea. Even if he believes he expresses his ideas better now, they—like his character—are not subject to abrupt change. It is simply a question of "fixing things up" (W, 151). He acknowledges that people, including himself, repeat themselves and fall into the patterns of acting that they may be unaware of or powerless to change.

Nevertheless, this realization does not mark a complete rejection of Sartre's old ideas of freedom and progress. It "undermines . . . old certainties without quite destroying them" (W, 151). Sartre assumes a moderate and somewhat ironic position. "Today's progress lies in my realizing that I've stopped progressing" (W, 151).[10] Sartre denies any desire or effort to break systematically with his past. "I want always to be accessible to change. I don't feel bound by anything I've written. Nevertheless, I don't disown a word of it either."[11] In short, a person is not confined in his past, yet he never can forget that it is his own.

While the "bad faith" of identifying completely with what one was in the past remains a valid concern for Sartre, he expresses respect and admiration for "the humble and tenacious faithfulness of certain people . . . to their tastes, their desires, their former plans . . . their will to remain the same amidst change" (W, 150). In the long run, says Sartre, people do not change much, since one can never repudiate one's past, one's childhood. "Even if you try to, you can never repudiate it completely because it's as much part of you as your skeleton" (BEM, 293–95). This may seem like a radical revision of classic existentialist dogma, yet Sartre's position here is still consistent with the dialectical understanding of the fundamental project he has presented throughout his life. Within the spiral of development, the investments of childhood remain at the core as both symbols of and factors in the style of being of the adult. In self-analysis, "one doesn't get cured of one's self. Though they are worn out, blurred, humiliated, thrust aside, ignored, all the child's traits are still to be found in the quinquagenarian. Most of the time they lie low, they bide their time; at the first moment of inattention, they rise up and emerge, disguised" (W, 159).

Sartre acknowledges that his life and work probably contain a unifying thread, though he has never looked for it nor tried to establish it.[12] He says, "There is an intellectual unity in my life from the start. . . . something like a system, which loses certain of its ideas and gains others; which is never completely the same, but which has a unity; which presupposes at each moment a kind of *lived idea* [*idée vécue*]."[13]

Sartre does not believe this system is linked together in some *logical* way that he is explicitly aware of, but it has a unity nonetheless. Rather it will be for those remaining after his death to piece together this system. Sartre concludes a recent interview by leaving a critical task of existential psychoanalysis to others. To those who will study his life work after his death Sartre says, "everything is there, everything appears in relation to what was before; everything can be reduced, different meanings can be subordinated one to another, linked horizontally or vertically: at that moment one can do a study of meaning, to see if I have been faithful to myself or not."[14]

THE "SINGULAR UNIVERSAL"

Sartre's existential psychoanalyses cannot be fully appreciated without considering his concern for the close relation between human development and the social, historical context within which it occurs and with which it interacts. The interrelationship between individual and culture is implied in Sartre's concept of the "singular universal" (*IF*, 1:7). By this, Sartre means that a person is never just an individual. Every person internalizes the universal or global values of his or her epoch, but these values become dialectically transcended by the singularity of the person's projects and experience. The process of human history in turn reabsorbs the singular projects of individuals to create new cultural values. An individual's life *contributes* to the total meaning of his or her epoch, but the epoch also *molds* the life of every person. It remains the task of existential psychoanalysis to analyze "the encounter between the development of the person, as psychoanalysis has shown it to us, and the development of history" (*BEM*, 44).

One of the major goals of existential psychoanalysis is to study this dialectical process from both directions. It is necessary to examine how the larger "universal" aspects of a cultural period are expressed in a particular person, and also how that person's "singular" experience contributes to new cultural syntheses and historical change. Describing his own self-analysis Sartre says, "I am not concerned with the particular meaning of one life. I want to recall the rather curious evolution of a generation."[15] Similarly, he tries to understand Flaubert's personality "totally as an individual, and yet totally as an expression of his time" (*BEM*, 43). Flaubert's idiosyncracies and "subjective neurosis" are his particular response to his family and culture. At the same time, his individual neurosis becomes "universalized" by the collective culture and contributes to what Sartre calls the "objective neurosis" of that period of history. Sartre thus focuses on Flaubert's family relations as a means of penetrating the ideological tensions of the bourgeois family in general. At times he attributes ideas and values to Flaubert's parents with as much concern for illustrating general ideological options of the period as with accurately depicting them as individuals. In Flaubert's case, Sartre sees the ideological conflict between religious faith and analytical, scientific skepticism; between the aristocracy and the bourgeoisie; between the monarchy and the revolution all crystallized in Gustave's mother and father.

Sartre further believes that the lives of certain important figures not only *express* larger cultural issues, but actually help *shape* those issues and bring them into focus for everyone else. Just as there are special events in a person's life that signify a conversion or new totalization of his fundamental project, within history there are certain special people whose lives symbolize a detotalization of the old structures and a retotalization into a new unified moment of cultural history. In this sense, there comes a moment when "an individual in his deepest and most intimate conditioning by the family, can fulfill a historical role" (*BEM*, 44).[16]

This *historical* role readily becomes a *mythic* one as well. As Mircea Eliade points out, the lives of certain historical figures become "mythic" when they are transformed into exemplary models of a whole culture or society. It is a basic human tendency "to hold up one life-history as a paradigm and turn a historical personage into an archetype. This tendency survives among the most eminent representatives of the modern mentality."[17]

In his autobiography, Sartre wants us to see a broad cultural tension distilled in the childhood of one small boy. In this way, while he has given up writing plays as a way of communicating ideological positions, Sartre's existential psychoanalysis has the same "mythic" element which he sees as characteristic of modern drama; that is, using concrete individuals to embody certain universal conflicts and attitudes in man.[18] Sartre concludes his autobiography by describing himself as a kind of Everyman, "a whole man, composed of all men and as good as all of them and no better than any" (*W*, 160).

Existential psychoanalysis provides Sartre with the opportunity to criticize various cultural models and values, and to offer his own image of authentic human existence. In short, *Sartre's existential psychoanalyses perform a role traditionally associated with religious biography.* They are concerned with the evolution of cultural models of the self. For this reason, Sartre's work may be of particular interest to students of religion. Surely, it must seem odd that hidden within the preeminent spokesman for atheistic, secular humanism in the twentieth century is a religious biographer. Nevertheless, this genre is the most appropriate for Sartre's ideological purposes. It is necessary to keep in mind Donald Capps's observation that "in the long tradition of historical scholarship, religious biography will continue to have its place. The problem in our own era is that religious biography is not easy to identify as such."[19]

ERIK ERIKSON AND RELIGIOUS BIOGRAPHY

While Sartre's existential psychoanalyses have received little attention with religious studies, their structure and goal is surprisingly similar to that found in the psychohistorical works of Erik Erikson, a figure well known to psychologists and historians of religion. Consequently, it will be useful to consider certain elements of Erikson's projects that relate them to religious narrative and religious biography before applying these categories to Sartre. Erikson and Sartre have pursued remarkably similar enterprises, despite, apparently, a mutual lack of acquaintance with the other's work. Erikson's psychohistory and Sartre's existential psychoanalysis are both concerned with the link between individual development and cultural development in a larger sense. This concern, moreover, leads both of them to adopt normative and quasi-theological positions that pervade both the form and tone of their analyses.

Erikson's studies of Martin Luther and Mahatma Gandhi demonstrate how a "great man" can achieve a breakthrough that solves both his own conflicts and identity crisis as well as the historical crisis of his epoch. Erikson says that "psychosocial identity . . . has a *psychohistorical* side, and suggests the study of how life histories are inextricably interwoven with history."[20] People like Luther, Gandhi, Freud, and (we may add) Sartre do what Erikson calls the "dirty work" of their respective ages at the same time that they deal with their own individual problems. As Erikson says of Luther, each of these men struggles to solve problems of human conscience and "to lift his individual patienthood to the level of a universal one and to try to solve for all what he could not solve for himself alone."[21] In other words, each one responds to a personal neurosis or crisis in a way which corresponds to a latent universal conflict and produces a new form of human awareness. Luther, for example, channelled his personal difficulties into a theological system that radically transformed the Western concept of the self by replacing excessive guilt with trust and self-reliance. Likewise, biographers of Freud have long noted that it is from analyzing his own relation to his father that Freud suggests the universality of the Oedipal complex. Marthe Robert observes that Freud's status as a Jew when creating psychoanalysis raises "the paradox of a localized particular giving rise to something universal."[22]

The psychohistorian's analysis of psychological difficulties in specific individuals as a means of investigating larger historical and cultural issues has been met with careful scrutiny and a fair amount of criticism by many historians. Much of the criticism involves the charge that a psychologist's historical conclusions remain spurious, since they too often rest on a structure of unverified conjectures or questionable data. Erikson's study of Luther, for example, is confounded by bad translations, questionable sources, and other errors.[23] To a certain extent, the historian's critique of psychobiography parallels the more general critique of the scientific status of psychoanalysis as a whole. Psychoanalysis is often accused of offering unverifiable theories on the basis of very ambiguous evidence. There is a certain irony in the fact that those supporters of psychoanalysis who recognize both the futility and error involved in defending the rigorous scientific status of psychoanalysis tend to retreat to the position that psychoanalysis is closer in methodology and nature to the work of the historian than to that of the scientist.[24] Yet historiographers seem to have as much skepticism about psychoanalytic interpretation as philosophers of science.

The historian's criticism, while valid on one level, overlooks an important dimension of the work of people like Erikson and Sartre. Erikson's psychohistories have received new attention from people in religious studies who find them a project implicitly related to the concerns of religious narratives. Roger Johnson has offered a suggestive interpretation of Erikson's work, which uncovers a normative vision of human history within it.[25] According to Johnson, *Young Man Luther* is "a story of the psycho-social, moral, and spiritual evolution of humanity—a story whose past—like the past of all religious stories—is informed directly by the perceived crisis of the present."[26]

Erikson's ideological concerns, says Johnson, lead him to reconstruct events and personality traits in the lives of his subjects that are supported by neither his psychological theory nor historical scholarship. The figures Erikson portrays, such as Martin Luther and his father Hans, Gandhi, and so forth, serve as *paradigmatic* figures in which the crucial issues of various historical periods converge. The objections of historians, however well-founded, fail to recognize Erikson's role as an *ideologist*. Specifically, Johnson argues that Erikson's depiction of Hans Luther is an "ideological construct" or ideal type that embodies the general characteristics of the emerging bourgeoisie. With scant evidence, Erikson presents a portrait of Hans as "ambitious," "brutal," and "suspicious." Hans appears less as a living person than as a one-sided villain who represents the dark side of personality that Martin Luther must overcome in himself. As such, Hans reminds us of the persistent psychological conflicts confronting modern persons and societies. Johnson says, "To read the story of Hans is not primarily to gain access to the life history of a sixteenth-century peasant turned miner, but to gain insight into the dilemmas of the corporate and individual histories of the present."[27]

Furthermore, Erikson admits that a lack of definitive information means that "anybody can sketch his own Martin. . . . Here is my version."[28] He openly conjectures on Luther's past on the basis of what Luther later thought and did. Thus, Erikson claims that Luther's early childhood relations can be inferred from his concept of God. He imagines, moreover, that Luther secretly hated his father because "in later life Luther displayed an extraordinary ability to hate quickly and persistently, justifiably and unjustifiably."[29] These inferences, in turn, are used to illuminate the meaning of Luther's theological position; early doubts about his father are linked to his doubts about God the Father. Erikson's strategy, of course, involves a danger of circularity, not unlike Sartre's progressive-regressive method. Yet, as Sartre insists in his own work, such an approach operates with a sort of dialectical progression. The fact that childhood and adulthood mutually illuminate each other is a necessary part of interpretive understanding.

When Erikson is seen as an ideologist and "lay theologian," his subjects obviously have more than historical interest. Luther and Gandhi are offered as *exemplary models*, whose conflicts are reminiscent of the mythic archetype of the hero. In Erikson's narrative, Luther's struggle with his father starts to resemble a cosmic struggle between good and evil. When biographical subjects become exemplary models whose main function is ideological or normative, the historical accuracy of events in their lives becomes subordinate to the mythic themes they illustrate.

Certain key events in Erikson's analyses clearly have mythic overtones. The crucial developmental events in the lives of his subjects, moreover, are emphasized not for their "factual occurrence" but for what Erikson calls their "intrinsic actuality." In *Young Man Luther*, for example, Erikson finds Luther's "fit in the choir" particularly important. As a young adult, Luther is said to have fallen to the ground and cried "it isn't me" or "I am not." Erikson interprets this event as part of a severe identity crisis. He recognizes, nevertheless, that the actual occurrence of the alleged event may be far from certain, but that is not important. Clearly, the primary value of the event is not as a cause of Luther's problems, but as a *mythic symbol* of pervasive psychological, ideological, and theological conflicts. Erikson is not concerned that the event may be legendary. It "could well have happened," he says, but "if some of it is legend, so be it."[30]

These crucial events in Erikson's studies closely resemble the original crises that appear in Sartre's analyses. Each is equivalent to what Sartre described as a "liturgical drama" from childhood which is repeated in various forms throughout a person's life. According to Erikson, such traumatic moments are "indicative of an aspect of childhood or youth which comes to represent an account that can never be settled and remains an existential debt all the rest of a life time. But it must be clear that one single episode cannot be the *cause* of such a curse, rather the curse is what we clinicians call a 'cover memory,' that is, a condensation and projection of a pervasive childhood conflict on one dramatized scene."[31] The great figures of history manage to transcend such childhood crises and reenact them in a form that resonates with certain universal conflicts of mankind.[32] Luther's crisis, therefore, represents a "crossroads of mental disease and religious creativity."[33] Luther sees his personal conflicts and family situation against the background of mankind's relation to God. Luther redefines this relationship for Western civilization as a way of coming to terms with his own oppressive and tyrannical father. Erikson's entire analysis finds Luther in the throes of pervasive Oedipal conflict with a father who is nothing less than a "jealous god."[34] The thematic centrality of Luther's oppressive father provides a striking contrast to the theme of fatherlessness that is at the heart of Sartre's normative vision.

Erikson's way of treating events and people has drawn him into what Donald Capps calls the tradition of religious biography, a genre with unique structural and moral purposes.[35] First, he has used particular persons as paradigms or models of various ideological alternatives. Second, he structures his narrative around events primarily to illustrate recurrent mythic themes. Finally, as Johnson and Capps both agree, his explanatory theories themselves contain a quasi-theological substructure with affinities to the mythic structure of classical theology. Johnson claims that Erikson's concern with the meaning of history as a whole is more theological than scientific. Similarly, Capps focuses on the "mythological trend" in Erikson's theory of the life cycle. He notes that despite the psychological framework of Erikson's studies, his narratives have "a peculiarly religious tonality that is not wholly attributable to the fact that his subjects are religious men."[36] In other words, Erikson's ostensibly psychological states of development sometimes function analogously to traditional categories and biographical formulas which he then illustrates with mythic dramas in the lives of particular persons. As a religious biographer, Erikson is ultimately concerned with analyzing his subjects as potentially exemplary models. Don Browning has shown how Erikson's psychology rests on a normative image of man and an ideology that supports it. [37]

The religious and theological elements in Erikson's psychohistory that have attracted recent attention raise pertinent issues for the interpretation of existential psychoanalysis. As in Erikson's case, historians have also criticized Sartre's existential psychoanalyses for often speculating without adequate evidence. There is another dimension, however, in terms of which Sartre's work must be considered. Implicit in Sartre's studies is also a normative vision of human nature and human history. The ideological purpose of existential psychoanalysis is to both condemn and endorse certain cultural models and images of human existence. Like Erikson, Sartre is concerned with the interrelationship between "identity and ideology,"[38] how each supports the other. Identity rests on the integration of personal needs and strengths with the dominant images and ideologies of a historical period.

SARTRE AS RELIGIOUS AUTOBIOGRAPHER

The mythic dimension of certain lives to which Eliade refers has always been a fundamental aspect of Sartre's existential psychoanalysis. It is particularly evident in Sartre's own self-analysis, *The Words,* which treats Sartre's life as the embodiment of the intellectual and cultural conflict of his age. Like Luther, Sartre finds a solution to his own psychological conflicts and identity crisis, which also provides a solution of larger cultural and historical significance. The extent to which Sartre's own life has acquired a mythic or paradigmatic status can be seen in the kind of eulogies that followed his recent death.

*Inadvertent Guru to an Age. (*Time 4/28/80*).*

To some, he embodied all the anarchic emptiness and despair of the modern spirit. . . . To others he was the last great apostle of freedom. . . . he was the rare individual who seemed to sense something central about the age in which he lived (Chicago Tribune, 4/16/80).

Some of us may not even know his name or have read any of his works. But most of us use his language, and feel his thoughts, every day of our lives. . . . Whether we like it or not, we—the three generations of this century—are all the children of Jean-Paul Sartre. . . . Sartre, more than any other writer of our century, best reaches the inner depths of the young. . . . He not only speaks to them directly, he lives inside them. Sartre is not just the century's greatest moralist. He is also its greatest prophet (Philadelphia Inquirer, 4/20/80).

When an entire people identifies for a moment with a man, in a privileged and suspended moment, when projected out of their class by ritual, the different components of the nation reunite this people, giving it thus its completeness, then the praise rendered becomes a discovered ceremonial. We witness the making of a myth. It is one of the manifestations of the sacred. The most irreligious monster of the French elite since Gide arouses at the moment of his departure the most irrational tremors.[39]

Looking back once more at Sartre's autobiography, we can now examine the extent to which the solution of one person's developmental problem may become a historically significant innovation. The resolution of a traumatic identity crisis can be the basis of a new ideological synthesis and may provide a paradigm for others. At the same time, Sartre self-consciously uses the story of his childhood as a kind of religious narrative to explore the cultural tension of his age as it is reflected in his own life.

The ideological purpose in Sartre's self-narrative has frustrated certain readers who would have preferred a more traditional autobiography. Lionel Abel complains that "*Words* is not an autobiography in any clear meaning of the term," since Sartre does not recount exactly what happened and how he felt as best as he can remember.[40] Abel finds "autobiographical description, properly understood" and "ideological construction" to be mutually exclusive. In another early review, Paul de Man says that *The Words* is an autobiography "in name only." He thinks it is really an ideological essay that "presents a composite, organized, symbolical entity as if it were part of one's own childhood."[41] Germaine Brée has called *The Words* "a genuinely mythical childhood."[42] Although Abel and de Man have measured *The Words* against a simplistic understanding of autobiography and found it lacking, it would be more useful to appreciate *The Words* for the type of narrative it is, rather than criticize it for what it is not.

Recent study of biographical interpretation has pointed to the interaction of historical elements and mythic images or formulas in what has been called the "biographical process."[43] Sartre's *Words* can only be fully understood when the events it describes are seen as symbolic of the crumbling of one cultural model and its replacement by another. At first, Sartre borrows from existing biographical formulas in writing *The Words*. Biographical formulas serve as models for conceptualizing a person's life. While Sartre initially sees his life in terms of such a model, he subsequently rejects it in order to form a new biographical image, a new paradigm for the self.

In *The Words*, Sartre emphasizes themes related to the "biographical image" of the artist as analyzed by Ernst Kris.[44] According to Kris, the biographical formula that has developed around the artist since the Renaissance offers a modern secular version of the myth of the hero that is found in most religious traditions. For example, the royal origin of the hero found in many religious legends is replaced by the notion of the divine origin of the artist's genius. The hero is often an abandoned child who is miraculously recovered; the ideal artist is a child of low origin who is socially elevated by a new father figure. The recognition of the hero's power and mission through his youthful accomplishments recurs in the life of the artist as the discovery of the child's talent at an early age. The artist's childhood activities are seen as premonitions of his future character, and the child-artist immediately senses his vocation. In many ways the biographical image of the child prodigy is a descendant of the image of the hero or savior's childhood.

Kris examines the transition from the model of the religious hero to the model of the artist in part to show how biographical images change and develop to reflect social needs. Once they are well known, these biographical patterns exert influence on the self-identity of large groups of people. People base their lives on them, "enact" the pattern, and detect their personal "vocation" or "destiny." In periods of rapid social change, those lives are most important that both repeat a preexisting paradigm and create a new pattern for their successors. It is this process with which all Sartre's existential psychoanalyses are concerned. What are the cultural origins of our images of the self and how do they change?

Many of the elements in the model of the artist are present in Sartre's account of his childhood. Sartre's grandfather, for example, represents an elevated father figure and symbol of culture. He was the "patriarch" and "resembled God the Father" (W, 13). He is the one who discovers Sartre's sacred vocation. Jean-Paul, moreover, sees himself treated as "a child of miracle," a gift from heaven, an infant prodigy. His grandfather regards him as "prophetic," finding wisdom in everything Jean-Paul says. Sartre remembers, "I pronounce true oracles, and each adult interprets them as he wishes. . . . My words and gestures happen to have a quality that escapes me and that is immediately apparent to grown-ups" (W, 19). Learning to read allowed Jean-Paul to identify with literary heroes. Learning to write enabled him to become one.[45]

For most of his life, Sartre accepted an "heroic" view of art or literature as a means of salvation. The creation of a work of art would justify his existence and provide immortality. Like other recent writers faced with the decline in the authority of traditional religious values, Sartre found his values in literature. Sartre admits, "I had found my religion: nothing seemed to me more important than a book. I regarded the library as a temple" (*W*, 37). "I palmed off on the writer the sacred powers of the hero" (*W*, 104).

Sartre claims that while the religious training of his childhood never took hold per se, he transposed the Christian ideals of obedience, chastity, and poverty into literature. Writing was a sacred vocation. He says, "I would be unknown all my life but I would merit immortality through my dedication to writing and by my professional integrity. . . . In my imagination, literary life was modeled on religious life. . . . I had transposed religious needs into literary longings" (*BEM*, 27). Literature provides salvation because it introduces order and necessity into a meaningless, gratuitous, contingent world. It offers salvation by literary works. This is the final view of *Nausea* where Roquentin, having recognized the superfluousness of his existence, seeks salvation in writing a novel. Man as artist becomes the creative force in a world without God. The artist transforms the world into an object of his own creation (*IF*, 2:1589).

By the time Sartre writes *The Words*, he has begun to question his motives for writing and has renounced what he calls his "neurosis of literature,"[46] as well as the mythic model of the writer on which it was based. He has begun to create a new model of the self to replace it. We are confronted with a process of demythologizing and remythologizing in which *The Words* takes the form of a quasi-religious drama. Sartre uses symbolic protagonists to present a moral and ideological argument. This dramatic action can be seen in the relationship between Jean-Paul and his grandfather, an embodiment of nineteenth-century bourgeois and literary idealism. Although some of Schweitzer's own writings may not support Sartre's picture of him,[47] that is not the point. Sartre uses him as an incarnation of the values of the bourgeois world, especially its respect for tradition and authority. Schweitzer becomes an "ideological construct" in the same way that Erikson uses Hans Luther. Sartre's grandfather represents the negative side of Sartre, and indeed of all bourgeois existence. The narrative takes the form of a struggle between the false values represented by Charles Schweitzer and the stifled private existence of Jean-Paul. Sartre describes a continuing conflict between the false public role he performs for his family and his own sense of himself. He shows his seduction by, and struggle against, the romantic myth of the artist and the hero.

Appreciated as a religious drama, Sartre's self-analysis signals the breakdown of certain dominant cultural models and the creation of new ones. The vast influence and appeal of Sartre's work stems from the way in which he captures the essence of a changing situation in the modern world. His own life becomes an exemplary model in which individual life history acquires cultural and historical importance.

LIFE WITHOUT FATHER: THE PROTEAN STYLE

Robert Jay Lifton has discussed a major cultural pattern of the contemporary world in terms of a style of life and a concept of the self that he calls "protean."[48] The modern protean person feels a sense of historical dislocation. This situation is due to the fact that traditional cultural values and symbols have broken down or been rejected; our rituals increasingly seem shallow, irrelevant, and lacking in power. Mass media offer a flood of new undigested images and values in their place. According to Lifton, the protean style is characterized by a continual shifting of identity and commitment. This involves a permanent process of ideological experimentation and exploration. The sense of a stable, lasting identity relies to some extent on a traditional society in which a person enjoys a stable relation to social institutions and symbols. In the contemporary situation, this stability has disappeared, leaving the modern sense of identity marked by frequent change and flux. The modern Proteus hungers for ideological commitment, yet seldom is a lasting one to be found. Freedom from the cultural values of the past has produced images and fantasies of rebirth and self-creation. These are necessary to cope with the competing imagery of loss, scarcity, and extinction, which has surfaced in the modern world.

There is an obvious relationship between the protean attitude and the popular existentialist notion of a person's absolute freedom to change himself and his commitments at any moment in his life. Indeed, Lifton remarks that Sartre's protean characteristics make him a perfect embodiment of human life in the twentieth century.

This protean style is symbolized for Sartre in the theme of fatherlessness and the related themes of the orphan and the bastard. The protean person asserts his or her freedom from the authority of the past and the values of the fathers. Sartre presents his life as a paradigmatic case of the tension between tradition and modernity. In responding to his own situation, Sartre becomes a model of a particular solution to the problem of identity in general.

Social psychologist Alexander Mitscherlich suggests that social processes in modern society have made paternalistic culture obsolete. This loss of the father's authority and power in the family has made the issue of identity even more problematic. He notes, "fatherlessness—meaning loss both of primary relationship and of a model that has to be outgrown—is a condition which will have to be borne and coped with by the societies of our time."[49] American identity in particular has been deeply influenced by a rejection of fathers, a sense of rootlessness, and a dream of rebirth.[50]

In Sartre's self-analysis, the freedom from paternal authority in its broadest sense is thematized around a single childhood event. The death of Sartre's father is more than just a significant childhood event with deep psychological effects. The fact that the event occurred when Sartre was less than two years old makes it difficult to believe that his narrative is based on authentically remembered experiences or feelings of that moment. Rather the death of his father is the *mythic* kernel around which are condensed an overall alienation from society, religion, and the traditional view of the self. When Sartre calls the death of his father the "big event of my life" (W, 11), he is using that event as a symbol of his freedom from imposed values.[51] Within this event is crystallized all that he associated with the condition of fatherlessness and the concomitant struggle for an authentic sense of self and identity.[52] His insistence that he lacks a "superego" reflects his sense of independence from the values of the past. This statement must be seen as more than psychological.

The theme of fatherlessness can be seen behind much of Sartre's existentialism. It reflects the central existentialist notion that there is no necessity or justification for a person's existence. Every person is utterly contingent, an ontological accident. Consequently, the existential person suffers a sense of rootlessness and dislocation. Sartre symbolizes this in terms of his situation in his grandfather's household. The move there was a direct consequence of his father's death. Sartre's mother reminded him that they were not in their own home and had to be careful. Thus, fatherlessness leads to homelessness (both literal and figurative) and exacerbates the feeling of superfluousness. Surrounded by things that did not belong to him, Jean-Paul felt unnecessary. Sartre explains,

> A *father would have weighted me with a certain stable obstinacy. Making his moods my principles, his ignorance my knowledge, his disappointments my pride, his quirks my law, he would have inhabited me. That respectable tenant would have given me self-respect, and on that respect I would have based my right to live. . . . Nobody, beginning with me, knew why the hell I had been born. Had he left me property, my childhood would have been changed. I would not be writing, since I would be someone else. House and field reflect back to their young heir a stable image of himself. He touches himself on his gravel, on the diamond-shaped panes of his veranda, and makes of their inertia the deathless substance of his soul. . . . Worldly possessions reflect to their owner what he is; they taught me what I was not.*

I was not *substantial or permanent*, I was not *the future continuer of my father's work*, I was not *necessary to the production of steel. In short, I had no soul (55.)*

It is significant that the title of *The Words* was originally to have been *Jean Sans Terre* (Groundless Jean). To be superfluous is to lack the weight to plant one's feet on the ground; in other words, to be "groundless."

The religious position of existentialism is likewise a variation of the theme of fatherlessness. Sartre has said that existentialism is the "attempt to draw all the consequences from a position of consistent atheism."[53] God, of course, is the figure of the father in the metaphysical realm. He is the source of a human being's purpose and justification. The existentialist is metaphysically fatherless; he is a spiritual orphan. The result is that each person must create his own values, become his own God and his own "father." The response to one's sense of contingency is a dream of self-apotheosis. Theologically, God is the being responsible for his own being, the *causa causans*. The fatherless person seeks to usurp that role. According to *Being and Nothingness*, the fundamental human passion is "the desire to be God." Sartre says "I was a fatherless orphan. Being nobody's son, I was my own cause" (W, 70).

Politically and socially, fatherlessness means an antiauthoritarian attitude. The desire to dissociate oneself from the past leads to a revolutionary political stance, a distancing between the bourgeoisie and their victims. Sartre idealizes all the outcasts and victims of society. These are society's orphans: the Jew, the black, the homosexual, the thief, the revolutionary. This is why Jean Genet is presented as Sartre's ideological model of existential man. Genet the orphan, homosexual, and thief pits himself against bourgeois respectability. He is the pariah of society.

While Sartre's description of his personal childhood conflicts sheds light on some of his major philosophical concepts, it would be wrong to evaluate his mature ideas simply on the basis of their possible roots in his childhood. To assume from reading *The Words* that the themes of *Being and Nothingness* are only "disguised pieces of an autobiography"[54] would be an inadequately dialectical position, as fallacious as assuming that *The Words* is only a disguised piece of philosophy. It is true that Sartre describes his childhood in terms that are familiar from his philosophy. He continually mentions his early feelings of being superfluous, insubstantial, and unjustified. The lack of a solid sense of being which haunts him reflects the major ontological quest of *Being and Nothingness*. To be sure, Sartre's philosophy, like Freud's psychology, does reflect in a significant way the unique circumstances of his life; but in an equally significant way Sartre tends to recall his life in terms congenial to and supportive of his philosophy.[55] It is essential always to keep sight of both poles of this dialectic. As Sartre has always maintained, what interests him is what a man makes of the circumstances that make him. Not only is the philosophy the product of the childhood, but the childhood is in an important sense the product of the philosophy. The philosophy which grows out of Sartre's childhood guides the retrospective reconstruction of that childhood.

It may be that the description of one's childhood more naturally assumes a mythic or fictional structure than the description of later periods of life. Obviously, to an adult, his childhood is the most vague and confused time of life. Childhood memories are distorted both by their distance from the present and the child's incompletely developed intellect at the time childhood events are recorded. The magical or religious sense the child has of his world is difficult for the rational adult to appreciate fully. Consequently, when adult rationality is projected back into childhood events, the events are seen with new eyes. For this reason, the biography of childhood takes on a mythic or ideological flavor to a much greater extent than accounts of later life. Sartre's ideological bias in presenting his childhood can perhaps explain the shock of his mother on reading his portrait of her father Charles Schweitzer, and her failure to recognize her son in his descriptions. "He understood nothing about his own childhood," she said. [56]

In the case of Sartre, the idiosyncrasies of the individual are intended to reflect the dilemmas of the collectivity. Sartre's existential self-analysis reveals the decay and development of certain cultural models. The bourgeoisie is Sartre's antimodel which embodies all that is false, alienating, and inauthentic. Sartre first seeks to find truth and authenticity in the myth of the writer-hero, but he becomes disenchanted with that model when he realizes its bourgeois origin. Consequently, Sartre offers a new mythic paradigm focused on the theme of fatherlessness. The death of his father is a symbolic event, which is expanded to epic proportions with important ethical and metaphysical implications. Ultimately, Sartre's description of a Brecht play applies best to his own self-analysis: "an anti-myth that despite itself becomes a myth" (*BEM*, 50).

THE RETROSPECTIVE ILLUSION

Sartre's entire idea of justifying or saving himself through literature was, he admits, the result of a mistake, which he calls the "retrospective illusion." Once little Jean-Paul decided that he had a vocation to write, a mandate of destiny, his whole view of his life was altered. Sartre claims his fundamental error was to allow himself to view his life as an "epic" (*W*, 74). He began to regard his present life as an insignificant path leading to his ultimate immortality in the future masterpiece of literature that he would write. Only by fantasying himself dead, could he imagine his future eternality. At that time the metamorphosis would be complete. He would be resurrected and reincarnated in the word. "My bones are made of leather and cardboard, my parchment-skinned flesh smells of glue and mushrooms. . . . I am reborn, I at last become a whole man. . . . Hands take me down, open me, spread me flat on the table, smooth me, and sometimes make me creak" (W, 121). By regarding himself as answering the call of future greatness, Jean-Paul escaped his present feeling of worthlessness.[57] He could redeem his life by looking at it as a thing of the past. In this way he could cherish a life that he found otherwise unbearable. "I looked at it through future eyes and it appeared to me as a touching and wonderful story that I had lived for all mankind. . . . I chose as my future the past of a great immortal and I tried to live backwards. I became completely posthumous" (W, 124).

Jean-Paul read *The Childhood of Famous Men* and saw himself in it. Although men like Bach, Rousseau, and Molière seemed uninteresting and dull as children, not unlike Jean-Paul, they were described with constant allusion to their future greatness. Thus casual or trivial childhood details were artfully contrived so as to be automatically related to subsequent events (W, 127). In this way the author "introduced into the tumult of everyday life a great, fabulous silence which transfigured everything: the future" (W, 127). Jean-Paul felt that like Jean-Jacques or Johann Sebastian, everything he did or said was an augur or premonition of something to come, his destined greatness; Jean-Paul was "enacting" his biography. He viewed himself from the point of view of his death and the great masterpiece he would leave humanity. Since Jean-Paul decided his future success and glory in advance any unforeseen events that happened to him were treated only as signs that would be understood later. A sense of order was always preserved; there was no chance. Adversity, trouble, defeat were all steps toward ultimate posthumous victory. "I was often told that the past drives us forward but I was convinced that I was being drawn by the future. I would have hated to feel quiet forces at work within me, the slow development of my natural aptitudes. . . . I subordinated the past to the present and the present to the future" (W, 149).

While Sartre's childhood attitude toward his future is distorted by this inversion of temporal perspective, there is another sense of the "retrospective illusion" that is of major epistemological importance for Sartre's work in existential psychoanalysis. Sartre claims he first discovered the retrospective illusion in the attitude fostered by culture toward great men. However, Sartre fails to distinguish two different contexts in which he speaks of retrospection. When the child envisions his future as a destiny pulling him toward it and justifying the present, this future is as yet indeterminate and open to change. To predict the outcome of one's life as a means of justifying one's present is indeed based on an illusory faith in a not yet existent future as a fixed standard of evaluation. Although Sartre has emphasized that the meaning of the present rests on projects extending into the future, the future never has the fixed quality of a destiny or fate, as if some future idea forces a child to be born, and conditions and educates him until the moment when the idea is ready to appear (W, 126).

But it is quite a different situation when, in examining the complete life of a person, one uses the outcome of the person's life as a key to the meaning implicit in earlier events leading up to that outcome. Sartre notes that when a person dies, the experiential sense of time that life had is gone forever. The person's life takes on the appearance of an "unfolding." Every event, utterance, and act is then seen as a sign, not a chance occurrence. One cannot evalute any of his behavior without taking into account results that were not forseeable at the time, information he did not have, or "giving particular weight to events whose effects left their mark on him at a later time but which he lived through casually. That's the mirage: the future more real than the present" (W, 125). Sartre's other analyses have consistently maintained that when interpreting a life as a whole "the end is regarded as the truth of the beginning" (W, 126–27). The realized future is now read back into the past.

Sartre's reference to the "mirage" caused by the future's shadow over the present condenses several different ideas which must be distinguished. The "future" of a child before his life has unfolded is different from the "future" of a child viewed from the perspective of his completed adult life. In the first case the future cannot genuinely illuminate the meaning of the present. But this is not the case with the future in the latter sense, where it can be used to illuminate the past events in the life of the child, since this is a future that had already transpired. In this case, the "future" creates a "mirage" only if one's goal is to reproduce the experience of each past moment as it was originally lived. Yet Sartre's own analyses repeatedly show that the full meaning of the events in life goes beyond that immediate experience.

In retrospective analysis, a person's life remains "half-way between . . . the raw fact and the reconstruction. His history becomes a kind of circular essence which is epitomized in each of his moments" (W, 125). A person whose life is complete can be analyzed from the beginning or the middle and extending in any direction. "Chronological order has exploded. . . . His existence has the appearance of an unfolding, but as soon as we try to restore a bit of life to it, it relapses into simultaneity"

(W, 125). When a person's whole life is known, each moment reveals the fundamental meaning or project of his life in its own way, just as each sentence implicitly refers to the rest of the book in which it occurs. As we will see in his analysis of Flaubert, Sartre's methodology requires precisely the retrospective mode of interpretation he seems to criticize in *The Words* as distorting. For example, his progressive-regressive approach makes a point of transversing chronology in all directions. In addition, he analyzes specific moments as symbolic embodiments of the essential structure of a life as a whole.

Sartre is certainly right to criticize his early tendency to judge himself in relation to later anticipated greatness. Indeed, this involves a *false* retrospection since it implies that the future destiny is fixed and merely waiting for present events to bring it into being. Genuine retrospection, however, is the key to all biographical endeavor. It is not illusion, in this case, that the meaning of past events depends upon present ones. Genuine retrospection produces the sense of meaning and necessity in a person's past. Of course, retrospective interpretation necessarily proceeds with a kind of dramatic irony. One views events in light of later events that have already occurred. In this way a contingent set of facts receives a dramatic destiny, but it is a destiny that one creates for oneself. One's life acquires an artistic unity within the context of a specific mythic structure.[58]

In *The Words*, Sartre has reconstructed events of his childhood from the point of view of his later attitudes. The childhood he presents is a kind of confession of heresy, yet heresy only arises from the perspective of the experience of conversion; hence the meaning of his childhood requires the perspective of his "future" life to be fully understood.

SARTRE AS RELIGIOUS BIOGRAPHER

In this chapter, I have focused on certain normative and mythic elements in Sartre's analysis of his own childhood. Sartre's tendency to see a paradigmatic quality in his own life cannot simply be attributed to personal narcissism, however, since his other existential psychoanalyses contain similar elements. All Sartre's studies of lives reveal features characteristic of traditional religious narratives.

In each of his analyses, Sartre focuses on a paradigmatic crisis in the childhood or youth of his subject and the subject's specific response to that conflict. He suggests, moreover, that every life contains a critical event as well as a "fundamental" or "original choice" in response to it. The latter is the key to understanding the development of a person's life. Sartre's critics have sometimes questioned whether he offers adequate evidence for his conjectures about these nodal events. In addition, they often doubt whether the "original choice" is really an actual decision, freely undertaken by a child, which determines the rest of his life. Indeed, if taken literally, Sartre's reconstructions of childhood events and decisions often rest on shaky historical and psychological foundations. Sartre himself admits that they are his own imaginative hypotheses.

The function of such events and choices within Sartre's narratives, however, lies in another direction, overlooked by critics. Students of sacred biography and religious narrative have long realized that events of the past—either in the lives of religious founders (e.g., Moses, Jesus, Buddha) or nations (e.g., Israel)—are often more archetypal than historical. In such cases, the past becomes an exemplary model for the present. In the retrospective analysis of human lives, historical facts are factors within psychic evolution, but they also may become *symbols* of that evolution. The critical events and "original choices" in existential psychoanalysis are condensations of a person's dominant mode of existence. Like most religious biographers, Sartre focuses on critical events more for their thematic and mythic usefulness than their historicity.

Earlier, I noted that Erikson's life histories have a distinct religious quality unrelated to the fact that his main subjects are religious leaders. This is due, in part, to the way his life-cycle theory operates analogously to a traditional theological model for both describing and prescribing the proper course of life. In Sartre's case, the subjects of analysis are anything but traditional religious figures. Nevertheless, as Thomas King points out, Sartre's work has "an overwhelming theological character that often seems to be unaffected by the atheism that he professes."[59] His analysis of the development of identity from childhood through adolescence to adulthood is couched in explicitly theological, and at times even hagiographical, terms.

What, then, are the central categories in Sartre's description of the development of human identity from childhood on, which emerge from his existential psychoanalyses? *Paradise, fall from grace, exile, conversion, death and resurrection, quest for salvation, incarnation in the word, ritual reenactment in sacred time*, and so on. The presence of such traditional theological categories in the work of a confirmed atheist requires explanation. One might be tempted to think that Sartre is merely using such theological language ironically to mock a system of beliefs he has rejected. However, the mythic and theological elements of Sartre's discourse are too central to the force and structure of his narratives for the matter to be so simple.

The explanation, perhaps, lies in a different direction. Unlike Erikson, who uses *psychological* categories as a tacit theology, Sartre uses *theological* categories, purged of their supernatural reference, to explore the dynamics of human consciousness and self-identity. The collapse of the supernatural or transcendent dimension of reality, a characteristic of modern society, encourages protean thinking and elevates psychological introspection to new heights. For Sartre it leads inevitably to the *theologizing of the self*. He desacralizes the Christian model of salvation in order to resacralize the existential task of self-discovery/creation.

Historians of religions such as Mircea Eliade have discussed the homology that archaic thinking perceives between the transcendent cosmos and human life. The archaic person envisions every human life as a microcosm of the universe. Human life reflects the cosmic processes of creation, death, and rebirth. Eliade describes the fundamental religious concern of archaic people as the preservation of cosmic order against the constant threat of chaos. This is often accomplished by means of establishing a sacred center and by continually reenacting creation.

For Sartre, however, the life of the self is the real arena for the theological drama of cosmogony, death, and rebirth. When the traditional theological model is internalized, the "fundamental project" of every person becomes that of self-creation and protection of the ever-changing boundaries of the self where chaos and order meet. Of course, this ideal self represents a permanently elusive goal for human life, since the unstable nature of consciousness prohibits the establishment of any fixed "center" of reference. Neither the center nor the boundaries of the self remain fixed. The goal is to become God, divinely self-sufficient and unchanging. But the goal is impossible to reach. In concluding *Being and Nothingness*, Sartre says "the passion of man is the reverse of that of Christ, for man loses himself as man in order that God may be born. But the idea of God is contradictory and we lose ourselves in vain. Man is a useless passion" (*BN*, 615). More simply, the obsessive concern with the issue of personal identity in the modern world reflects a demythologizing of religious cosmogony in tandem with a remythologizing of the life of the self. The historical drama of Christianity has been translated into a model for the journey of personal consciousness.

Sartre's existential psychoanalysis is not a therapeutic tool or diagnostic technique in any ordinary sense. Like a religious biographer, Sartre uses paradigmatic individuals as a means of presenting the central existential dilemmas and avenues of response for the people of his age. For Sartre, the struggle to achieve an authentic sense of identity is perhaps the only remaining religious drama worth reenacting. To analyze, a person's fundamental project is to uncover a cosmogonic myth and to witness creation of a "world" and a "self" within it.

[7] "WHAT CAN WE KNOW ABOUT A MAN?"

"FOR EXAMPLE, GUSTAVE FLAUBERT"

Sartre's existential psychoanalysis of Gustave Flaubert comprises three large volumes and approximately three thousand pages. It represents a project on which Sartre worked for at least two decades. Like most of Sartre's work, it has provoked strong response from its readers. Some have accused Sartre of having a personal score to settle with Flaubert as well as using the study to come to terms with his own work. One critic has called *The Family Idiot* a "symbolic autobiography in progress."[1] To be sure, Sartre has a deep personal investment in this study which serves in part to resolve his own attitude toward Flaubert and the type of commitment Flaubert represents. After reading *The Words*, moreover, certain parallels between the childhoods of Jean-Paul and Gustave are clear: their refuge in the realm of the imaginary because of the frustrations of the real world, their identification with the salvific role of the writer.[2] One can reasonably argue that the study of Flaubert enables Sartre to understand his role as a bourgeois writer, just as it has been suggested that many of Freud's concerns represented his efforts to confront the meaning of both his Jewishness and his own relation to his father.[3] Similarly, one could doubtless find personal reasons for Erikson's choice of Luther or Gandhi as subjects of psychohistorical inquiry.

Surely, Sartre cannot be taken seriously when he suggests that Flaubert is merely an arbitrary example taken as a concrete case to illustrate the methodological approach of *Search for a Method* (*IF*, 1:7). His casual introduction of the subject of this methodological exercise is perhaps disingenuous. "What can we know about a man, today? It seemed to me that one could only respond to this question by the study of a concrete case: what do we know—for example—about Gustave Flaubert?" (*IF*, 1:7). It would be foolish to think Flaubert was simply the first person who happened to pop into Sartre's mind.

Whatever the personal motivation of Sartre, for the present purposes we may provisionally accept Sartre's claim to be fundamentally concerned with illustrating a sustained (some would say sustained far too long) analysis of a single individual in an effort to elucidate the intricate interconnections of childhood, family, and society in the development of that person's fundamental project. What is most significant about *The Family Idiot* in this context is not its accuracy in specific points of analysis of Flaubert, although for the most part it is argued logically and convincingly. Rather, this study represents the most valuable source of Sartre's mature vision of the nature of human development and the means to understand it.

Sartre contends that a concrete case can provide evidence for the idea that a person is a totalization in which each aspect of his life contributes to a growing, developing truth. He admits the possibility that there might be no singular truth or meaning expressed by a person's life. In juxta-posing social, cultural, family, and individual factors one could end up with "layers of heterogeneous irreducible meanings" (*IF*, 1:7). The purpose of *The Family Idiot* will be to prove that beneath the appearance of irreducibility, every fact is part of a developing whole and is fundamentally related to all the others. This understanding of each fact in a life as an expression of a global frame of reference has been called by one critic the "existential synecdoche."[4] Sartre insists that psychoanalytic, Marxist, and existential methods make it possible today to accomplish such a totalization and thus to understand fully another person.[5]

Bracketing his personal and ideological purposes for the moment, Sartre's choice of Flaubert as a subject is motivated by a methodological consideration. Flaubert has left behind a wealth of material through which his life can be interpreted. Not only has Flaubert objectified himself in his literary works—which can be treated as dreamlike projections of his personality—but he has also left behind thirteen volumes of correspondence and writings of his youth, which offer us "the equivalent of a 'psychoanalytic discourse' " (*LS*, 123).[6] Flaubert reveals himself to us "as though he were lying on the psychoanalyst's couch" (*LS*, 125; *IF*, 1:8). Flaubert seems to have been obsessed with preserving documents about himself. He preserved every word he wrote, including a detailed record of daily events as well as spiritual and psychological conflicts and anxieties.[7] Sartre claims that in one sense Flaubert is an easy subject since he openly reveals his inner problems without knowing it. He believes the data Flaubert has left us is adequate to enable us to understand the quality of his life.

Readers have reacted differently to the specific psychoanalytic content of *The Family Idiot*. Some see this work as showing "greater openness . . . to the language of psychoanalysis, especially that of Dr. Jacques Lacan," and the latter's views of the self as an imaginary creation.[8] Marthe Robert, a prominent commentator on psychoanalysis, admits that Sartre's concern with the hidden traumas of Flaubert's childhood makes this existential psychoanalysis seem like traditional psychoanalysis. However, she concludes that Freudian psychoanalysis is superfluous to *The Family Idiot*; she calls it "une affaire sans ténèbres"[9] because it allegedly ignores unconscious defense mechanisms. It explains Flaubert, she says, completely in terms of his known conscious feelings, and it makes deductions about his family relations based on incomplete and spurious information. Moreover, she insists that the subjective life of a person's childhood cannot be understood simply by means of a historical reconstruction of his parents' character, his childhood care, and so forth, since childhood amnesia and repression make the psychological depths of childhood unknowable, "a rigorously sealed book."[10] Claude Burgelin goes so far as to call *The Family Idiot* "antipsychoanalytic" and a "barrage against Freud," since he believes it fails to explore the Oedipal complex and the child's symbolization of his family relations. He further questions its claims to produce a totalization of knowledge about Flaubert since there are necessary gaps in any knowledge about a person.[11]

It is unfortunate that the massiveness of *The Family Idiot* does not encourage close readings by those intrepid enough to venture within its intricate dialectic. The result is inaccurate appraisals like those of Robert and Burgelin. Robert seems to have completely missed the nuances of Sartre's notion of *le vécu*, which emphasizes precisely those obscure aspects of the psyche she finds lacking in *The Family Idiot*. The facts of childhood amnesia and repression, moreover, surely do not mean that reconstruction is impossible, as a brief glimpse at Freud's case histories will immediately show. Burgelin's objections are likewise misguided. The Oedipal complex is not identified as such in Sartre's work, but the focus on the family triangle and its symbolization reverberates throughout his analysis. Nor is it true that Sartre neglects or denies necessary gaps in our knowledge of Flaubert. Indeed, he is candid about the uncertainties on which parts of his reconstruction rest. His desire for a totalization of knowledge about Flaubert is no different from Freud's desire to conclude an analysis with "an intelligible, consistent, and unbroken case history."[12]

Sartre is also especially concerned with the relation between a person's life and his work. A writer's literary style in particular offers a way to see the conflicts, contradictions, assumptions, and style of his fundamental project exhibited in condensed form. For the writer, it is not simply the decision to write that comprises his fundamental project, but rather "the decision to write in a certain manner in order to manifest himself in the world in a particular way" (*SM*, 147). A literary work is an expression, externalization, and objectification of its author's lived experience. Sartre explains: "The author's style is directly bound up with a conception of the world; the sentence and paragraph structure, the use and position of the substantive, the verb, etc., the arrangement of the paragraphs, and the qualities of the narrative . . . all express hidden presuppositions" (*SM*, 141).[13] An author's style immediately gives us the taste and flavor of his life (*IF*, 1:658). Thus, the frequent use of passive verbs in *Madame Bovary* raises the issue of passivity in Flaubert's personality, just as a psychoanalyst's attention would be aroused by persistent passive constructions in a patient's analytic discourse. Sartre contends that the literary work does not directly reveal secrets about a person's life; rather, "the work poses questions to the life" (*SM*, 142). It gives rise to hypotheses, which can then be used to clarify and illuminate the individual's life, especially his family context and childhood experience. These hypotheses about the author's fundamental project can then be confirmed by comparing them with the personality development that can be detected from biographical information. Under what conditions could this view of the world be possible? What kind of person would objectify himself in his work in this style? What path must Flaubert have followed to reach this destination?

Sartre regards the writing of *Madame Bovary* as a symbolic, dialectical event through which Flaubert can envelop and integrate his childhood traumas. Sartre is less concerned with using Flaubert's life as a guide to understand *Madame Bovary* than with using that work to learn about Flaubert's life. Sartre approaches Flaubert's literary creations as a disguised expression of fundamental values that Flaubert refuses to express in his personal writings or correspondence. Describing *Madame Bovary*, Flaubert said, "I have invented some things, I remembered others, and I put them all together."[14] Flaubert at some level recognized that his own life was the primary source of his most important novel. "Although he admitted it perhaps only three or four times in his life, he always knew that Emma Bovary was himself."[15] By analyzing Flaubert's work, Sartre discovers a style of life that includes narcissism, onanism, idealism, solitude, dependence, femininity, and passivity (SM, 143). These qualities serve as "a schema or conducting thread" (SM, 143) with which he can then investigate the social structures and childhood experiences that influenced Flaubert. That is to say, they comprise Flaubert's "mythology."

Sartre's analysis, however, does not begin with *Madame Bovary*. Nor, for that matter, does Sartre take a strictly chronological approach. Rather he begins by seeking the solution to a puzzle. In a letter Flaubert wrote in his late thirties he describes his work as a response to "a deep and always hidden wound" (IF, 1:9). Sartre begins by looking for the origin of this wound in Flaubert's protohistory. "Protohistory" is a new word in Sartre's vocabulary. He uses it to refer to that early period of life before a person is a genuine historical agent. Protohistory is the real origin of the fundamental project, for at this time social and family situations establish rudimentary structures or styles of acting that form the nucleus for subsequent dialectical development.

It is worth pointing out here that among the major elements of classical psychoanalysis which Sartre appropriates in *The Family Idiot* are Freud's early theories of trauma and hysterical conversion.[16] Sartre clearly gave this material close attention, since his screenplay on Freud for John Huston focuses on Freud's work with Breuer and the early cases described in *Studies on Hysteria*. Accordingly, Sartre's analysis of Flaubert isolates certain childhood traumas that influence Flaubert's perception of the world.

Sartre has described a neurosis as "a specific wound, a defective structure which is a certain way of living a childhood. But this is only the initial wound: it is then patched up and bandaged by a system which covers and soothes the wound" (BEM, 42). This defective structure of childhood is a *psychic* wound, that is, a "trauma" in the psychoanalytic sense; while the system of patches or bandages is equivalent to defense mechanisms in Freud's thought. Sartre's interpretation shows how Flaubert's later experiences exacerbate this wound, ultimately leading to the outbreak of hysterical symptoms whose meaning is crystallized in his nervous collapse one dark night at Pont l'Evêque.

Sartre divides his analysis of Flaubert's development into three major parts. First, he describes the "constitution" of Flaubert; that is, how certain personality structures in Flaubert are constituted by his childhood situation. Next, Sartre presents Flaubert's "personalization" of his constitution in late childhood and adolescence. This involves Flaubert's internalization of the structures imposed by the past and his situation. Finally, the third part presents Flaubert's hysterical crisis at Pont l'Evêque and its consequences. This is what Sartre calls the "last spiral" of Flaubert's development.

In short, while Sartre gives much attention to the impact of Flaubert's childhood on his personality, he always insists that this childhood is merely part of the larger dialectical process which produces a person. There is no determining situation that is not surpassed by one's manner of living it, but, at the same time, there are no actions, however complex or elaborate, that are not rooted in the internalization of family structures (*IF*, 1:653). Consequently, the fundamental project must be seen "reflected from the future in our childhood memories and from our childhood in our rational choices as mature men" (*SM*, 108). In other words, viewing a life as a whole, the picture of childhood is colored by what later happens, while those later actions preserve childhood as their core.

As we have already seen in *The Words*, Sartre proceeds with the appearance of chronological order, though the dialectical links he establishes manipulate chronology at will. The order of analysis need not be either straightforward or linear. Sartre says his method "may be chronological, but it is always prepared to illuminate the chronology by referring to the future" (*LS*, 122). It is often necessary to juxtapose Flaubert's family relationships in childhood with relations from the end of his life so that each will clarify the other. This is not a case of merging "postdestination" and "predestination,"[17] but simply recognizing the multidirectionality of interpretation. The past illuminates the future only to the extent that the future illuminates the past. Sartre says, "The past leads to the present which, at the same time it is formed according to protohistorical schemas, remodels, transforms, and confirms the past" (*IF*, 1:196).

In addition, Sartre's analysis (like many of Freud's analyses) often follows reverse chronology, beginning an inquiry "at the final level of the experience studied, that is to say when it presents itself to the subject himself in the fullness of its development" (*IF*, 1:181). A regressive analysis from this point will discover "prophetic" or "anticipatory" elements in earlier experiences. Early intuitions can be understood as foreshadowings of future developments when they are grasped from the point of view of the "future" (which is already known by the interpreter, of course) and will manifest information and meaning that would otherwise be too obscure, confused, or condensed to understand. In analyzing Flaubert, Sartre finds in the symbols and themes of one particular moment both an outline of deeper and richer experiences that will occur subsequently, and also obscure reminders of the past. For example, Flaubert's first written works in adolescence simultaneously "announce the future ills and are announced by the earliest suffering" (*IF*, 1:182).

It is important at this point to distinguish the two senses of the "retro-spective illusion" which I discussed in relation to *The Words*. Sartre's failure to make this distinction in *The Family Idiot* leads him to make certain dubious statements. When one is dealing with a complete life, it is legitimate to explore all the meanings that early events have acquired in the subsequent course of life. The process of "totalizing" a person's life in interpretation means showing the inevitable course that led from the beginning to the end. False retrospection is what Sartre actually faults himself for when he was a child. This occurs when one interprets the meaning of one's present *while one is living it, as if* one had the perspective of looking back from the end, posthumously. It is fallacious to attempt any complete interpretation of the meaning of experiences before the rest of that life has been played out. Only when one has a complete life to examine, can one use the different parts to clarify each other and discover the appearance of dramatic destiny in the past. But to think such interpretation could have been possible at the time events occurred would require a totally unacceptable concept of fate. Dialec-tical developments cannot be predicted in advance.

The error Sartre occasionally makes is to attribute to Flaubert himself some obscure prophetic understanding of his future. The result is certain awkward passages where the child Gustave is called "the future author," who at the age of fifteen somehow anticipates the specific crisis he will face eight years later and who realizes he will become "the greatest French novelist of the second half of the nineteenth century."[18] It is perhaps best to ignore these lapses as rhetorical excesses.

THE "MYTH" OF FLAUBERT'S CHILDHOOD

Sartre endeavors to reconstruct Flaubert's childhood in order to locate the defective structure or wound within it. He begins by considering Flaubert's difficulty in learning to read and his initially poor relation to language. According to Sartre, Flaubert's adolescent fictions all express the earlier problems of his childhood, particularly his trouble with the alphabet. This failure in his childhood remains "an intolerable memory" (*IF*, 1:31) for the adolescent Flaubert. It is "the Fall," a humiliation for which he will perpetually compensate with "incommunicable ecstacies" (*IF*, 1:40). As a child, Flaubert has great difficulty expressing his feelings in conventional language. This difficulty in the linguistic universe repre-sents the fundamental event of Flaubert's "protohistory." Sartre also finds roots for Flaubert's passive style of life in his relations to his family when he is between the ages of five and nine, the earliest period for which Sartre can decipher any information. This is as far as "regressive anal-ysis" can go.

Sartre is not content to stop here. He insists that without restoring the archaic foundations of Flaubert's mode of existing, the interpretation of his life "remains up in the air, abstract and relatively indeterminate" (*IF*, 1:54). Without the first few years of infancy, the biographer, says Sartre, "only builds on sand: he builds on a haze with a mist" ("sur la brume avec du brouillard") (*IF*, 1:55). Early childhood contains the "dark, hard kernel" of the meaning of subsequent projects (*IF*, 1:54). This "prehistoric past" of the individual, what Freud referred to as the period of infantile amnesia, establishes a kind of destiny for the child. Sartre calls it "the source of permanent impossibilities that later determinations would be incapable of explaining. . . . Either we find the kernel of pitch around which meaning is constituted in its singularity or the profound origins of Gustave Flaubert and, consequently, the course of his idiosyncrasy will forever escape us" (*IF*, 1:55). If one begins a dialectical understanding of a person starting only from the earliest known acts and not from its true point of departure in the obscurity of infancy, any interpretation, however ingenious, will rest on a foundation that has not been fully comprehended, thus undercutting the entire procedure.

While there may be people whose "history" figures more importantly than their "prehistory," in Flaubert's case the influence of early childhood is always keenly felt. In sharp distinction to Sartre's early position, which acknowledged the importance of childhood only in a perfunctory manner and ignored infancy completely, the entire dialectical development of the fundamental project is now seen to receive its initial impetus in infancy. Factors of infancy will not *determine* the later development of the individual, but they form the central axis around which subsequent dialectical spirals revolve. For those accustomed to Sartre's early rhetoric of existential self-creation, this new analysis of the original rudiments of a project is startling.

At this point, Sartre's description of Flaubert's early childhood becomes purely a construction of his imagination. Sartre wishes to retrace the genesis of Flaubert's style of life from its "zero degree" in infancy up to his sixth year. In order to learn of new details that have been neglected, Sartre says that he will "attempt a progressive synthesis, make conjectures on these six years which we lack, forge a comprehensive hypothesis which ties together the new facts to the troubles of the sixth year by a continuous movement. The truth of this restoration cannot be proved; its accuracy is not measurable" (*IF*, 1:56). Sartre asks rhetorically if a hypothesis so punctured by uncertainty and so lacking in definite probability is worth the bother. Not surprisingly, he insists we must go ahead without hesitation.[19]

*A life is a childhood put to every kind of work [mise à toutes les sauces].
Thus, our conjectural understanding will be required by all of Flaubert's subsequent behavior: we will have to introduce the hypothetical*

restoration of infancy in all the manifestations of his idiosyncracy, and
to fill the gaps we have noted with these years which have disappeared
and been reinvented in order to restore to [Flaubert's] sensibility the
dark kernel where the lived body and meaning merge, this nondiffer-
entiation felt as the carnal *texture of passions. In short, our conjecture*
will be required not once, but on every page: the comprehensive synthe-
sis stops only at death (IF, 1:56).

While his reconstruction is to a great extent a product of the imagination, Sartre does not believe that it is arbitrary. If the reconstruction were
not rigorous and did not contain a portion of the truth it would crumble
under the weight of the analysis of the rest of Flaubert's life.

   . . . *trying to illuminate his experience through the black light of*
   infancy, we will see if the slow experience of the adolescent, the young
   man, and the adult is allergic to our hypothesis, tolerates it, or assim-
   ilates it and is changed by it in itself. Thus the adventure of Flaubert,
   to the degree that it approaches its end, will test this rediscovered
   childhood and retrospectively decide its accuracy (IF, 1:57).

In an earlier, more general discussion of method Sartre says:

   The problem is to invent a movement, to recreate it, but the hypothesis
   is immediately verifiable; the only valid one is that which will realize
   within a creative movement, the transverse unity of all the heteroge-
   neous structures (SM, 147–48).

Sartre's desire to locate the origin of the fundamental project at the
origin of life itself should be carefully noted. The "adventure" of a life,
its dialectical unfolding, emerges out of a primitive stage of life where
bodily instincts and consciousness have not yet been differentiated. Of
course, this period of the individual's "constitution" will be radically
transformed when the emergence of self-consciousness begins the process
of "personalization," which Sartre describes as the dialectical surpassing
of one's constituted being. Nevertheless, the organic nucleus of infancy
is preserved within all later stages of development.
   The confidence Sartre expresses in the literal accuracy of his reconstruction is another matter, however. What Sartre is really concerned
about is a narrative account of Flaubert's life that starts at its absolute
beginning. That infancy establishes patterns for the rest of life is Sartre's
presupposition. The accuracy of any specific picture of neonatal experience appears of lesser importance to him than the indication it gives
us of processes involved in a child's relation to his parents.

A child's "first project" starts from the moment his mother begins to nurse him. The beginning of human life is not a sudden upsurge of freedom but the chance meeting of a certain kind of mother and a certain organic disposition in the child. Their intersection begins the process of totalization through which a fundamental project will unfold. The child discovers himself through the kind of nursing and care he receives, the degree of love his mother expresses when her flesh touches his (*IF*, 1:57–59). Through this original primitive relation with his mother, the child establishes the structure of his future actions. Depending on the mother's behavior the child becomes more or less passive. The relationship with the mother in the first two years of life is thus responsible for a general attitude toward the world in later life. It models the "style and shape" of the person's life (*IF*, 2:1515).

To understand the roots of Flaubert's adult personality, Sartre thinks we must first analyze Flaubert's mother and her relations with her husband and her other children. Sartre's analysis returns to the childhood of Flaubert's mother. Sartre describes her childhood as sad: her mother died in childbirth and her father ten years later. Sartre insists that like all orphans she must have felt abandoned and condemned, since her parents had "preferred" to die rather than care for her. Or perhaps her father held her responsible for "killing" his wife, without whom he became so inconsolable that he decided to die. When this child grows up she marries a doctor (like her father was) who serves as both husband and father to her. Her first child is a son, Achille, who is welcomed as the heir to the Flaubert name. Thereafter, Sartre conjectures, Madame Flaubert deeply desires a daughter through whom she can relive her childhood and make up for its frustration and unhappiness. She wants a daughter whom she can love as her mother should have loved her. The factual basis for this elaborate personality profile which Sartre constructs seems to be little more than the fact that Madame Flaubert has no more children after she finally does have a daughter (Gustave's younger sister), and that she gives her daughter her own name—Caroline.

Sartre reconstructs an internal monologue of Madame Flaubert's thought, a technique he employs in many of his analyses. When Madame Flaubert finally does give birth to a daughter, her reaction, as Sartre reconstructs it, is to think: "She's me, me repairing my own childhood, provided with a mother who lives to love me" (*IF*, 1:90–91). This, at least, is what Sartre *imagines* she thought. With this initial premise concerning her fundamental desire it is understandable that after she had provided her husband with a son, Madame Flaubert regarded each subsequent newborn boy as a disappointment. After Achille, the first-born, there were two sons who died in infancy. Not only were these little boys disappointments, but their early deaths in their mother's arms represented her personal failures. Sartre says that there are "heavy odds" that she experienced the death of her two sons as a rebeginning of her original fault ("murdering" her mother) and as a curse on her womb from her mother. ("You killed me; I curse you; the fruits of your womb will rot because your entrails are rotten") (*IF*, 1:132).

While it is not completely clear, Sartre does not seem to regard his reconstruction as an account of what Madame Flaubert *consciously* thought. Instead, it is more likely that she *lived* her situation *as though* she had these thoughts. In this sense Sartre's reconstructions are analogous to the unconscious primal phantasies that Freud reconstructs for his clients. These phantasies are seldom actually remembered. Their function is to assist the process of interpretation in producing a consistent and coherent narrative that links the other known facts of an individual life.

When Dr. Flaubert moves to a new hospital with new responsibilities, his wife, Sartre imagines, "rediscovers without knowing it" (*IF*, 1:132) the unhappiness of her solitary childhood and is disappointed by a "father" for a second time. Her desire for compensation by means of a little girl is especially strong now, and when she soon finds herself pregnant again she eagerly awaits a daughter. Consequently, the birth of Gustave was a tremendous disappointment, which returned her to despair. Sartre says, "If my hypothesis is correct, the young mother saw in him a strange beast: she had hoped too much to reproduce herself—literally— to not feel that a usurper had been incarnated without permission in the flesh of her flesh" (*IF*, 1:133). Only a little over two years later will Madame Flaubert become pregnant with Caroline, the daughter to whom she will show the tenderness she had not received; Caroline is her own rebeginning. During this time Sartre believes Gustave came to know himself as a "poorly-loved-boy-in-front-to-be-followed-by-a-daughter-whose-place-he-usurped" (*IF*, 1:722). Sartre suggests, moreover, that Flaubert's later feminine identification and passive sexuality conceals a fundamental desire to be a daughter loved by a mother (*IF*, 1:723).

These attitudes in Madame Flaubert have devastating consequences for the development of Gustave's personality. Since Gustave is a disappointing "fille manquée" (*IF*, 1:722), his mother treats him with cool solicitude. She does what is necessary to care for him and nurse him, but she does this out of duty rather than tenderness or love. Although no reciprocal tenderness develops between Madame Flaubert and Gustave, she overprotects him and takes every precaution so as not to lose another child. He is changed, fed, washed exactly on time so that he never needs to cry. Yet never does his mother take time to smile or babble with him.

This relationship between Gustave and his mother, as Sartre imagines it to be (*IF*, 1:136–37), is responsible for Gustave's passivity and his later difficulty with language. Since all his needs are anticipated and satisfied, he never develops "aggressiveness" or the capacity to act. Gustave becomes passive. When a well-loved child expresses desires to his mother, this constitutes "a rudimentary form of the project and, consequently, of action" (*IF*, 1:137). A well-loved child knows the primordial basis of all communication: the reciprocity of tenderness and love (*IF*, 1:668). Gustave, however, is prevented by his mother's "cold overprotection" from expressing his demands or hunger. He never has the occasion or the means to break out of the "magical circle of passivity" (*IF*, 1:138). Arrested at the passive stage of development, Gustave will always feel like a receptacle of efforts from outside and not an independent force that actively transcends himself in projects.

Flaubert's passivity, of course, does not continue throughout his life simply because of his infancy. Initially, his apathy and passivity are a way of living his family situation at the most elemental psychosomatic level—in his breathing, sucking, digestion, elimination. Later, however, Flaubert develops a more evolved form of conduct and his passivity serves as a tactic of defense (*IF*, 1:54). His passivity develops within a process of dialectical totalization. Flaubert chooses passivity as his "style of life" (*IF*, 2:1231). He does not fight the passive tendencies established by his early experience, but embraces them willingly. Sartre calls this Flaubert's "active passivity," something analogous to a passive-aggressive personality.

The inadequate love Flaubert experiences as an infant prevents him from developing a sense of self-worth. Sartre attributes the sense of being an effective agent in the world to the presence of maternal affection. From the first day of his life, a child discovers himself in the passive experience of being cared for with love. Whereas in *Being and Nothingness* Sartre argued that shame was the main product of the look of the other and that love was doomed to failure, in this recent work he sees that the loving attention a mother pays to a child's physical needs produces in the child the sense of being an object of value. This "valorization of the infant" (*IF*, 1:136) increases to the degree that the mother expresses her tenderness in words and smiles. Once the child experiences the security of being (at least for several months) "an absolute monarch, always an end, never a means" (*IF*, 1:136), he will never forget it throughout his life. He will retain it even in bad times as "a kind of religious optimism which is founded on the abstract and calm certainty of his value" (*IF*, 1:137). Just as Erikson sees the basic trust established in infancy as the foundation of a person's subsequent attitudes toward the world, Sartre affirms that "in order to love life, at each minute to await the following minute in confidence and with hope, it is necessary to have been able to interiorize the love of the other as a fundamental affirmation of oneself" (*IF*, 1:405).

Flaubert's lack of parental love makes it impossible for him to love himself, or to have a taste for living ("goût de vivre") (*IF*, 2:1509). The treatment Gustave receives as an infant "contains in an implicit state a lack of appetite which will soon make itself explicit as a disgust with living, boredom, 'belief in nothing' " (*IF*, 2:1508–9). Thus the pessimism he develops in college is not a creation of college life, but a reinforcement or totalization of his protohistory. What is important is not a "conscious experience" in college, but "the whole process which precedes the experience and conditions it" (*IF*, 2:1509).

Sartre's account of Flaubert's infancy is punctuated with a number of phrases like "I imagine," "the odds are, . . ." "My hypothesis is, . . ." and the like. So as not to leave any doubt, Sartre admits his account is a heuristic tool:

> *I confess: it's a fable. Nothing proves that it happened this way. And, worse yet, the absence of these proofs—which would necessarily be singular facts—sends us back, when we are telling a fable, to a schematism and to generality: my narrative is suitable to infants, not to Gustave in particular. No matter; I wished to follow it to the end for a single reason: the real explanation, I can imagine, without the least resentment, could be exactly the opposite of that which I invent; in any case, it will have to follow the same paths that I have indicated and it will have to refute my explanation on the ground I have defined: the body, love. I have spoken of maternal love: it's that which fixes for the newborn the objective category of otherness. . . . It is maternal conduct which fixes the limit and intensity of filial love—the oral phase of sexuality—and determines its internal structure. Gustave is immediately conditioned by the indifference of his mother* (IF, 1:139–40).

This confession is problematic, however, in light of Sartre's earlier remarks about the rigor of his reconstruction. Some critics have viewed this confession as an act of epistemological suicide that permanently destroys the possibility of discriminating valid from invalid interpretations. Surely if Flaubert's early childhood were substantially different from what Sartre says, the rest of his analysis would appear to be built on the very misty and hazy foundation he wished to avoid by presenting his reconstruction. Presumably, if Sartre's version were inaccurate, the subsequent course of Flaubert's life would cause it to crumble. It would be unable to illuminate and bear the weight of the known facts of Flaubert's youth and adulthood. As a result, if his reconstruction is completely wrong, Sartre's entire synthesis of Flaubert's life would seem to be in danger. If Sartre really believes that the whole explanatory framework might be totally other than the one he invented, he has seriously undermined the validity of his entire venture. This awkward situation has evoked criticism about *The Family Idiot*, like the following: "A handful of facts induces hypothesis upon hypothesis as the 'true novel' metamorphoses into the pretext for a speculative mania whose relation to anything named 'reality' is purely coincidental."[20]

However, there is another way of reading this confession, which circumvents some of the epistemological problems to which Sartre seems to open himself and explains the kind of "reality" with which Sartre is concerned. On one level Sartre's confession is a disguised challenge to alternate explanations. Sartre knows he has no proof for his interpretation, though he clearly believes it is the most adequate one available. Moreover, since the comprehensive synthesis initiated by his reconstruction implicates the entire course of Flaubert's life and work, any alternate interpretation will have to produce an equivalent synthesis of the same life and work, dealing with or refuting the same issues, the "same paths" that Sartre has explored.

On another level, it is important to consider exactly what aspect of his reconstruction Sartre is describing as a "fable." It is clear that Sartre has little doubt about the validity of his general schema of the crucial developmental factors in early childhood. Although Sartre himself is imprecise, a useful way of regarding his confession is in relation to the distinction Freud came to make between historical and psychic reality. The epistemological uncertainty that Sartre acknowledges can therefore be understood in relation to specific historical facts. Whether Flaubert's mother actually nursed him as Sartre describes, whether someone actually told Flaubert "You are the family idiot," whether Luther's mother actually sang to him as a child as Erikson thinks, and whether Freud's patients actually were seduced by their fathers are all observable historical events that could have been otherwise, as Sartre and (eventually) Freud admit. But the real occurrence of these events is not, in the final analysis, crucial to the reconstructions. The central factors of the psychoanalytic constructions of Sartre or Freud are not historically observable events, nor even explicit attitudes that could have been avowed at the time they allegedly existed.

Even if Madame Flaubert were on a psychoanalyst's couch she would be no more able to remember her desire for a daughter as a disguised wish to relive her own childhood; nor would Gustave, if he were on the couch, recall his mother's indifference in nursing him, if in fact she were indifferent. Sartre's reconstructions in *The Family Idiot* as well as *Saint Genet* concern what is more properly seen as retrospective psychic reality. After examining the course of an individual's youth and adulthood, Sartre conjectures that the initial family situation must have been lived *as though* the feelings or events he described were experienced.[21] But Sartre recognizes that the conditions of childhood are lived "without clearly understanding or reflecting on them" (*SM*, 143). The meaning of these factors will sometimes not emerge until much later and may be projected back onto the past as in Freud's idea of *Nachträglichkeit*. For example, by adolescence Flaubert's childhood trauma has already been "enriched and magnified by pride and resentment" (*IF*, 1:40).

To a certain extent, Sartre sometimes recapitulates the error of Freud's original seduction theory by emphasizing the historicity of his construction. Yet his principle of dialectical totalization implies that reconstructed events function mainly as symbolic condensations of accumulated layers of meaning; it is in this context that they must be evaluated. Here the reconstruction tends to become a mythic structure to which subsequent patterns in life are referred. Thus the question of truth finally rests not in the discovery of external facts but in symbolizing the quality of Flaubert's subjectivity. [22]

While Flaubert's relation to his mother when he was an infant establishes certain fundamental structures in his personality, the major mythic "event" in his life occurs when he is about seven and concerns the nature of his relation with his father. Again Sartre's reconstruction is mainly hypothetical and is based on the simple indication that Gustave had trouble with the "linguistic trial, initiation and rite of passage: alphabetizing" (*IF*, 1:13). He was slow learning the letters and how to read.

To understand the symbolic power and importance of this problem, Sartre analyzes the "domestic religion" (*IF*, 1:112) of the bourgeois family. A son's destiny and purpose is to perpetuate his father's name and status. The son completely identifies with his father and eventually reproduces him. This is a "sacred identification" since the father has a "numinous power" for his children (*IF*, 1:112). In the Flaubert family, the eldest son, Achille, is completely involved in this process. He is a distinguished student and becomes a doctor like his father. In Sartre's view, Achille has completely internalized his father's image. What might be called superego formation by Freud is described by Sartre as a religious process. "The child, at the end of an initiative which begins at birth and finishes at maturity will enter in possession of the *mana* of his father" (*IF*, 1:115). Achille never transcends his perfect identification, nor can he ever accomplish the ritual murder of his father which would give him psychological independence. In Gustave's case as well, this overwhelming father was "unconsciously" internalized in childhood.

In this context Sartre offers a striking interpretation of an anecdote concerning the death of Dr. Flaubert, the father. When his father fell ill, Achille was the doctor who examined him and determined that surgery was necessary. Although Achille was young, his father insisted that he perform the operation. Achille operated, but his father died. Sartre interprets this event as a "rite of succession," a transfer of power.

The father is saying in essence: "You save me or you replace me; if you save me you have proved you will succeed me in several years" (*IF*, 1:121). What is most interesting about this situation, moreover, is that by giving himself to Achille's surgical knife, the father, ironically, takes away Achille's chance to free himself by a murder of the father, ritual or otherwise. Achille has been made into a passive instrument in a "sacred suicide" (*IF*, 1:124). His father's death only serves to seal permanently Achille's identification. He takes over his father's office and clients. There is never a question of really replacing the father, only of incarnating him.

In the case of Gustave, Sartre conjectures that the father is initially warm and tender while Gustave is a small child. A happy relation with his father exists for Gustave from about the ages of three to seven (*IF*, 1:338). When he is young, perhaps four or five, he follows his father on rounds. As Gustave encounters trouble reading, it gradually becomes clear that he can never match his brother's achievements or satisfy the ambitious expectations of his father.

Like similar incidents that Sartre describes in his other case studies, the account of the traumatic event that follows has a mythic quality through which the meaning of a specific period of Flaubert's life is condensed into a single moment. Just as Sartre *constructs* a critical moment of condemnation when Genet is caught stealing, he now conjectures that Gustave is condemned for his problems reading. His father will clearly favor Achille, who fulfills his father's bourgeois ambitions, and will reject his incompetent son as a failure. Achille will carry on the family name; Gustave is superfluous and disgraceful.

Gustave's frustration and the actual or imagined condemnation by his father compounds the passive tendencies and nonvalorization of his self that had begun in infancy. He suffers from a lack of identity and an insufficiency of being. Just as Genet chooses to be the thief others have made him, Flaubert affirms his passivity; he chooses as his fundamental project a solitary life and condemns all action.

Flaubert's passive constitution is thus a kind of deep wound he bears throughout his life. The care his mother gave him as an infant and the crisis in the relation to his father were the two factors which "constituted" Flaubert in this way. Sartre's account of Gustave's fall from his father's grace, which gives the book its title, is essentially just a hypothesis. Sartre imagines that someone, especially his father, must have more or less told Gustave, "You are the family idiot." His parents "must have" told him, "Act like your brother, Gustave" (*IF*, 1:373) and compared his feeble performance with the brilliance of Achille when he was Gustave's age. Again we find that what Sartre describes as a single archetypal event is mainly important for describing the way Flaubert experienced his situation internally, whether or not the verbal condemnation was an actual event. Sartre explains, "The ignorance and passive constitution, the devoted coldness of his mother, and the second weaning, the abrupt disaffection of the father—*or what he had felt as such*—then the jealousy and exasperation of a kid caught between the incapacities that were given to him and the family ambition that he had already internalized, this knot of vipers could not be untied: he had to *live* it, that is, to constitute it obscurely as a *subjective* determination" (*IF*, 3:10–11).

Consequently, as a historical event, Sartre's construction is suggestive but speculative. Treated as a symbolic or mythic event, it acquires structural importance in describing the further course of Flaubert's life and work. Indeed, Sartre himself admits that the problem of reading was not a single event. The condemnation of Gustave was the end of a process spread over several years. For the purpose of analysis (and within Flaubert's memory), however, it condenses into a single event. As I noted in the discussion of *The Words*, a period of life becomes important because it represents a specific stage of dialectical development. More important than any external events, it is the particular quality of a person's life, the way he "lives through" a certain period of life. Consequently, those who complain that there is no evidence that Flaubert's father ever actually condemned or scorned him have misplaced their concern. [23] Sartre calls memory "the crossroads of the real and the imaginary" (*IF*, 2:1526), that is, more or less, the intersection of historical and psychic reality. Every act of memory is partly an act of creation. Sartre acknowledges that when he examines Flaubert's adolescent writings he will not find the "objective truth about his protohistory." Rather we discover another kind of "irrefutable truth": This is the inner feeling Flaubert has of the movement of his life (*IF*, 1:181). [24]

In college Flaubert encounters at a higher dialectical spiral the same situation he lived as a child. He feels humiliated because he knows he is inferior to his brother, who had excelled in college and won his father's approval. Throughout his adolescence and college, Flaubert does not react simply to objective situations, but to interpretations of them based on subjective schemas established in his childhood. For example, he experiences every moment of attention his father shows to his brother Achille as a new condemnation, a repetition of the original crisis. Out of resentment for his brother and father, Flaubert "chooses" to be inferior to Achille. He "refuses" to imitate Achille and pursues law rather than medicine in order to be different.

Of course, Sartre sees his choice of inferiority and refusal of imitation as something Flaubert "lives" without recognizing it or formulating it to himself (*SM*, 106). Thus Flaubert's resentment and refusal function in Sartre's analysis as virtually unconscious feelings. This means that

Flaubert's refusal to imitate Achille is not a decision that preexists individual actions like choosing law rather than medicine. Rather, Flaubert's choice of law is his way of "living" that refusal. Refusal to imitate is not something locatable in Flaubert's personality, but a way of construing certain of his actions. The crisis at Pont l'Evêque will prove to be the ultimate affirmation of Flaubert's choice of inferiority and refusal to imitate his older brother.

FLAUBERT'S HYSTERICAL CONVERSION: THE CRISIS AT PONT L'EVEQUE

Following the condemnation that Flaubert experiences at the age of seven, Sartre describes Flaubert's adolescence as a path leading up inextricably to the central event of Flaubert's life: the crisis at Pont l'Evêque. This is the moment of conversion toward which all that precedes it is pointing. The objective event at Pont l'Evêque is simple. Gustave is driving a carriage along with his brother on a very dark night when suddenly at Pont l'Evêque he collapses at his brother's feet and temporarily lies paralyzed. His father later suspects the problem may be epilepsy and discontinues Gustave's study of law. Gustave, however, rejects this diagnosis and simply refers to the attacks he continues to suffer as his "nervous illness."

Sartre offers a complex and dramatic description of "The Event" using the present tense to emphasize its eternal paradigmatic nature. He spends hundreds of pages trying to show how Flaubert's crisis, far from being a purely physiological disturbance, is a classic case of hysterical conversion, and as such represents Flaubert's response to an impossible situation.[25]

In many ways, Flaubert's crisis is equivalent in nature and effect to the major crisis in Erikson's account of Luther's life—the fit in the choir and the experience of the thunderstorm. Erikson's description of Luther's crisis is perfectly suitable for Flaubert as well. He says, "The crisis in such a young man's life may be reached exactly when he half-realizes that he is fatally overcommitted to what he is not."[26] Luther's fit, like Flaubert's, showed his struggle to affirm his identity while not openly rejecting or hating his father. According to Erikson, Luther's anxiety during the thunderstorm was due to his feeling walled in by the need to please his father by finishing law school, marrying, and being an obedient son in general. The thunderstorm experience revealed only one solution to him: "The abandonment of all his previous life and the earthly future it implied for the sake of total dedication to a new life."[27]

This is precisely the situation Flaubert confronts. When his carriage reaches home, he knows he must set off to Paris to continue the study of law, which will please his father. That is a future he cannot bear. Yet at the same time his passive constitution prevents him from openly disobeying his father. Flaubert has reached a dead end. As he guides his carriage toward home, Flaubert comes closer and closer to what Sartre describes as "two rigorous and contradictory impossibilities: and yet there is urgency. There is no side to take and yet he must take a side. It is then that 'something happens' " (*IF*, 2:1766). [28]

Sartre ends the second part of his study in this melodramatic way, reminiscent of the ending of the first part of *The Words*. [29] Ultimately, literature will supply the support to Flaubert that religion supplied to Luther. Unresolved feelings toward his bourgeois father are reflected in Flaubert's hatred of the bourgeoisie, just as Luther's conflict with the pope expresses his relation to his own father.

Flaubert's fit is not simply an isolated moment in time but the culmination or totalization of the conflicts that have been building throughout the twenty-two years of his life. Sartre uses words such as "strategy," "tactic," "option," "response," "solution," and "adaptation" to describe the event. He characterizes the process that produces the fit as "psychosomatic," "autosuggestion," and "self-hypnosis." But his preferred term has a vaguely theological flavor. He calls the fit the "somatization of an idea." An idea has passed into, or been incarnated in, Flaubert's body (*IF*, 2:1806). Once the idea becomes flesh, so to speak, Flaubert can express with his body what he could not say directly. [30] Sartre's interpretation of the "idea" expressed by the fall at Pont l'Evêque unravels an intricate network of multilayered and interpenetrating meanings equivalent to a classic Freudian interpretation of the "overdetermined" elements of a dream or symptom. Every detail of the situation when the fit occurred—the pitch darkness, Flaubert's position at the reins, the presence of Achille, the act of falling—is analyzed for its levels of significance and symbolism.

Sartre believes the objective situation in which Flaubert finds himself when the crisis occurs is not *in itself* enough to produce a nervous attack. However, Flaubert, like any person, has been "singularized" by all his experiences to that point. Consequently, "the situation, in as much as it is lived, is already structured by the totality of his past" (*IF*, 2:1822). [31] Flaubert experiences and internalizes the objective situation precipitating the crisis in terms of the ongoing totalization of his life. That is, he experiences the situation as a symbolic condensation or crystallization of his entire life. The climactic event constitutes an "image" of the conflicts which have been developing in him (*IF*, 2:1799–1800).

Flaubert's desperation about the future leads him to view the situation not as a chance coincidence of circumstances, but, on the contrary, to give it "the rigorous and necessary unity which belongs only to works of art" (*IF*, 2:1832) (or, as Freud has shown, to dreams and symptoms as well). Flaubert's beliefs and feelings structure the "work" (*oeuvre*) of his apperception. As Sartre has always maintained, the world in which any person lives and acts reveals itself according to the projects of that individual. The objective world reflects the form of one's subjectivity. The unity of each person's lived world corresponds to "the particular style of an enterprise of living and reflects to the subject his objectification . . . in the form of destiny. In this sense the practical field is a language: it's the agent who announces himself to himself through exteriority" (*IF*, 2: 1832).

Sartre insists that Flaubert understands the meaning of both his general situation and the crisis by which he responds to it, however obscure that comprehension may be. The episode at Pont l'Evêque is not the result of a physiological mechanism. Rather, the crisis has an intentional structure. It presents a "living unity of contradictory and complementary intentions" (*IF*, 2:1811). For Flaubert the return trip to Rouen indirectly signifies a return to Paris and the law studies he detests. Thus as he gets closer to home, his fear and anxiety grow, since he feels both the necessity and the impossibility of returning. Sartre suggests that as Flaubert begins his return to Rouen, there is no doubt that the trip "will be lived as a calvary" (*IF*, 2:1821). The events of his life are about to converge in a single climactic event that will permanently alter his life. The reins in Flaubert's hands and the horse he is guiding both symbolize his consent to the direction his father has ordained for his life, and literally are bringing him closer to it.

According to Sartre, however, a deeper intention is disguised by Flaubert's holding the reins that guide his horse home. This active consent to his future permits him to suffer the crisis innocently. Absorbed in his active role of consent and obedience to his father, he does not reflect on the other process occurring within him. Flaubert experiences his crisis as something dreadful that *happens to him*. His disavowal and horror is a fundamental part of the crisis. It enables him to retain his innocence and filial love while fulfilling the wish to disobey his father.[32]

The actual fall and the temporary paralysis that follows provide the richest meanings in Sartre's analysis. To Sartre, they represent a symbolic death and resurrection. Sartre describes the crisis as a virtual religious rite of passage. To a great extent, Flaubert himself shares this view when he later reflects on the crisis. He comes to see the crisis as the most meaningful fact of his life and as an authentic conversion that separates two distinct lives. He says, "He who lives now and is I, only contemplates the other, who is dead. I have had two entirely distinct existences. Exterior events were the symbol of the end of the first and the birth of the second. . . . My active life . . . ended when I was twenty-two."[33]

Thus the crisis is a conversion in two senses. It is a *hysterical conver-*

sion of a conflict into a somatic symptom, and a *religious conversion* that transforms the quality of Flaubert's life. Both hysterical conversion and religious conversion function as "an intentional adaptation of the entire person to his whole past, his present, and the visible forms of his future" (*IF*, 1:176). Following the model of William James,[34] Sartre sees both types of conversion as the result of years of slow, quiet work which allows a former system of values to crumble gradually so that one day a new system can arise. One suddenly finds God, for example, "because one has already begun to invent him" (*IF*, 1:177). Similarly, we might say, that one suddenly *finds* a particular meaning in one's past and present, because one has been slowly *inventing* it for some time.

Flaubert's fall reflects what Sartre calls the negative theology of "Loser wins" (*Qui perd, gagne*) (*IF*, 2:1923–2106 passim). Flaubert sacrifices his active life to gain the life of the artist. He sacrifices his real self for an imaginary one ("La Bovary, c'est moi"). He sacrifices history and profane time for the eternal return to an indefinitely fixed event in circular or sacred time (*IF*, 2:1872). Thus the "event" is elevated to mythic proportions.

As a strategy, the fall resolves the impasse Flaubert had reached. He wins over his father without ever having to say anything. His "neurosis" provides an indirect rebellion against his father's authority and plans for him as a lawyer. Moreover, when his father orders him to quit law school for health reasons, Flaubert can simultaneously obey his father and escape his crushing power. In short, Flaubert's crisis is an indirect dialogue with his father. Since Flaubert cannot actively confront his father, he does it indirectly through his body and at the feet of Achille, a representative of the father, though not the father himself. Lying at the feet of Achille, Gustave symbolizes that he will never attain the success of his favored brother. In order for Flaubert to escape being a lawyer, either father or son must die. Flaubert's solution is to undergo a symbolic death that has parricidal elements. At one level, Flaubert's neurosis is a passive wait for the death of his father (*IF*, 2:1914).

The symbolism of falling, according to Sartre's analysis, has a number of dimensions. It is Flaubert's ultimate declaration of his failure in the real world of action. To some extent, it expresses Gustave's death instinct.[35] To fall is to become inert, reunited with the absolute passivity of matter, unlike *standing* in the world of human action. Furthermore, the fall is an act of regression (*IF*, 2:1863, 1865). It represents an attempt to return to childhood and to become once more an object cared for and loved by his father. Indeed, when Gustave returns home he becomes the center of the family's attention and his stern father appears to him like a tender loving mother.[36]

Although the crisis of Pont l'Evêque obviously is an objective historical event, it also symbolically represents the completion of a "conversion in progress" (*IF*, 1:916), which has been building throughout Flaubert's adolescence. The external event at Pont l'Evêque is the image of a much deeper process that has developed within Flaubert (*IF*, 2:1799). It marks the inevitable outcome of the battle of two elements that clash in all people: what people make of you and what you make of what they make of you. Sartre says dramatically, "The battle of Pont l'Evêque *had to take place*; it was regulated to the smallest detail" (*IF*, 1:191). The crisis serves to clarify, structure, and synthesize opposing and interpenetrating ideas that have been developing in Flaubert for a long time. In this sense the crisis begins at least six years before the actual event at Pont l'Evêque.[37]

Sartre refuses to believe that the vaguely defined problems of Flaubert's adolescence are unrelated to each other, and interspersed with "normal" periods. On the contrary, his analysis tries to show "a single inflexible process which ceaselessly organizes, enriches, and deepens itself until it makes inevitable the bursting in January 1844 [Pont l'Evêque]" (*IF*, 2:1467). The crisis in Flaubert's life is not a single moment, but a "temporal organism," a movement oriented by certain fundamental intentions. A neurosis, in other words, is not simply a malaise one suffers, but an option one has chosen in response to a situation, the culmination of a process that has evolved throughout life.

After Pont l'Evêque, the structure of Flaubert's neurosis is complete. The further attacks he has over the next ten years represent no new development, but only weak, stereotyped reproductions of the original archetypal event that structured and established the neurosis. The neurosis has no "history" after Pont l'Evêque; "it is maintained in the circular time of repetition" (*IF*, 2:1785). The later attacks merely commemorate the crisis as a way to confirm Flaubert in his "neurotic option." His neurosis has the structure of an "eternal return" to the original crisis (*IF*, 2:1785). It is as though the dialectical spiral of totalization has degenerated into a cyclical orbit. The sense of practical, historical time has collapsed into the continual return to a fixed event. The repetitious quality of time for Flaubert represents a return to sacred time and to childhood.

The Family Idiot represents the most recent, most complete, and most satisfactory of Sartre's existential psychoanalyses. Moreover, Sartre himself regarded it as the most representative of his final thought. It demonstrates concretely several avenues where Sartre's relation to psychoanalytic interpretation has been widened and affirmed. Here Sartre shows specifically the actual dynamics of his view of human development—the process of personalization and totalization and its links to early childhood. He examines the interconnection between the earliest relations of mother and child and the ideological issues that are refracted within all of a person's experiences, actions, and creative productions. Sartre believes the final results of *The Family Idiot* are generalizable. The process that produces Flaubert operates in every person; every person is created out of the conditioning factors of family and society.

This work also offers the opportunity to consider further the possibilities and limits of retrospective interpretation and reconstruction. Here one finds the indispensable role that imaginative creation plays in Sartre's construction of an explanatory fable or myth. Sartre has not tried to present an ordinary biography of Flaubert that would focus on a chronology of events. He does not even deal with the whole of Flaubert's life. Like Erikson in the study of the young man Luther, Sartre is only interested in young man Gustave, during the period when he struggled to find a way of coping with the conditions of his situation. Sartre wants to recreate as much as possible the "lived experience" of Flaubert, to imagine how he felt about his position in his family. Sartre pursues this imaginative understanding aggressively and insists that we relive sympathetically Gustave's neurosis without judging its "normality," realize its origins, and see how it solves a fundamental problem.

Sartre's goal is not totally unrelated to the extraordinary length of *The Family Idiot*. Douglas Collins says the length shows that the task of fully understanding a person is endlessly evolving, changing, and never achieved once and for all.[38] In contrast, Ronald Aronson complains that it is "a terrible book, the kind of book that makes you want to throw it down and shout: 'Won't he ever shut up?' "[39] He criticizes Sartre for not distinguishing the activity of study from the results, and forcing us to accompany him on his exploration. This is a very apt observation. Once again, I think Sartre's approach resembles what we demand of good *auto*biography. The life represented in autobiography must reveal the struggle to discover, to understand, and to forge meaning in the very act of narrating that life. In autobiography we expect the activity of investigation and the results of analysis to merge in the self-consciousness of the author. Sartre seems to employ the same approach to recreate genuinely the experience of another person.

[8] *IDENTITY, NARRATIVE, AND MYTH*

This analysis of the issue of interpretation in the study of lives has looked to the work of Jean-Paul Sartre as the basis for reflection on the nature of human meaning and the structures in which it is embodied. One of the recurrent themes in this area has been the imaginative or constructive dimension of interpretation that finds in story and myth a natural form for human meaning to assume. Consequently, the disciplines of literary and religious studies may offer more significant models for the interpretation of lives than traditional positivistic approaches that have deeply influenced psychoanalysts, historians, and others.

All the dimensions of personal meaning I have examined—story, image, memory, myth—must be understood not as exact copies or reproductions of experiences preserved in the mind, but as creative products in which the imagination contributes to reshaping the world. Paul Ricoeur suggests that "fiction 'remakes' reality";[1] by looking at the world in new ways, art provides a means simultaneously to discover and invent reality. The story or myth that interprets a person's life is also more than a copy of his or her past. It both enlarges and condenses the sense of reality created by that life. It is a mixture of poetic and historical elements. Some critics have argued that in modern narrative the boundaries between history, biography, and novel have collapsed. Since knowledge and narration are both subject to artistic and cultural conventions or categories, there is a "modern skepticism of knowing anything about human affairs in an entirely objective (non-fictional) way."[2]

A narrative is a kind of temporal portrait of a subject which, like traditional portraits, aims not at exact reproduction, but at expressing the essential truth of the whole. This position is based on the view that history in general is a process in which one selects and abstracts "in the manner of the artist, for the purpose of constructing a synthesis, of creating a unique 'whole,' of producing a work of art."[3] There is not simply one authentic history to retrieve, Ranke's idea of "what really happened." Historical events require a historian to establish logical and coherent connections, to trace a thread through events. "The 'whole' which he sets forth does not inhere in the happenings of time, but takes form in his imagination."[4] The resulting narrative is judged not by correspondence with past events, but the coherence of the interpretation's view of the past.[5] As in literary interpretation, historical truth is based on constructing an account one believes to be a plausible and meaningful context in which to place various data.

Sartre's idea of the "true novel" as the goal of existential psychoanalysis recognizes that one judges biography and autobiography in terms of the poetics of fiction.[6] An autobiographer, for example, must constantly contend with the artistic power of memory. Those autobiographies that are most successful do not simply recount events chronologically but tend to create the central truth of the person one was. Memories are treated with the status of symbols that magnify and dramatize turning points of the past. In autobiography we view our past from a creative distance that "transforms empirical facts into artifacts."[7] In his confessions, Augustine realized that his memory of the past dealt not with events themselves but with the image of his past in the present. Like autobiography, existential psychoanalysis is fundamentally involved in a myth-making activity, shaping events into patterns of meaning. Fragmentary time becomes continuous, spontaneous actions become prophetic, "trivial" details become significant.

If fiction is "reality remade," existential psychoanalysis is "the self remade." The result is an ideal abstraction, not representing the subject who experienced past events but a revision of the past from the point of view of the present. This does not make its account less true than the original experience, but potentially even more true, since now the original experience is seen in a larger context, with knowledge that was not possessed when the original experiences occurred.

One of the main characteristics of a narrative is the fact that it describes events as part of a unified whole, not simply as one thing after another. This sense of the irreversible direction of a narrative may be called *plot*. As Aristotle observed long ago, the essence of plot (*mythos*) in a tragedy is to have a beginning, middle, and ending. Plot requires an end that is the inevitable result of the events leading up to it. In its original sense, "myth" refers to plot. The sense of myth in the study of lives refers to the overall plot of life which is the goal of interpretation, and which integrates the multiple meanings of events. This plot is largely the product of imagination and memory, for it is not apparent in the immediate quality of experience. The aim of a biographer, therefore, is to develop this plot, to "define the myth that orders his subject's experience and offers the key to his nature. He is a collaborator in the creation of meaning in a life."[8] He seeks to express "the inner myth we all create in order to live."[9]

THE FULLNESS OF TIME

Theological language offers a useful way to describe the construction of a plot or myth about an individual's life. Myth essentially represents the transition from *chronos* to *kairos*.[10] Narration alters mere chronicity by creating the meaningful sequences that Sartre called "adventures" in *Nausea*. The quality of time designated by *kairos* is suggested in Sartre's discussion of the "retrospective illusion," that is, the way in which the conclusion of a story gives meaning to its beginning. Ordinary chronological experience is largely undifferentiated, a succession of unrelated moments. It is quantitative, measured clock time. This formless, contingent quality of immediate living has been captured in the experimental nonnarrative fiction of modern authors like Alain Robbe-Grillet, who is unconcerned with traditional stories or with the minimal plot of beginning, middle, and end; and Samuel Beckett, who sees narrative as inadequate to express the plotless chaotic nature of lived experience.[11] Beckett says "No need of a story, a story is not compulsory, just a life, that's the mistake I made, one of the mistakes, to have wanted a story for himself, whereas life alone is enough."[12]

Sartre, too, initially presents a world without plot, beginning or end. He describes the division of past, present, and future as an "invention of man" (N, 178). He cautions against the illusory nature of stories that transform people into novelistic characters, and create the appearance of narrative coherence that links actions inevitably to an end. This fictive sense of destiny is the result of one's own freedom and imagination by which one transforms chaotic experience into narrative order.

Although Sartre originally saw stories as a way of denying existence, he has reclaimed the value of fiction by recognizing that the natural form for describing a fundamental project is the flexible model of the "true novel." A person with a fundamental project does not have a preformed destiny, but neither does he live simply in the immediacy of the present moment. As a dialectic unfolds, time is purged of its chronicity, new beginnings and endings emerge, and moments are linked together in necessary relationships. "Real time," says Sartre, has nothing to do with clocks. Temporality is not to be confused with chronology (*LPE*, 85). The resulting sense of temporal duration is close to what H. Richard Niebuhr calls "internal history."[13] Internal history, unlike quantitative duration, involves time as an organic unity of past, present, and future that is personally meaningful for a living self. It is the imaginative way in which one finds a context for understanding and ordering experience. "We are not in this time, but it is in us,"[14] says Niebuhr.

Kairos refers to a special "sacred" quality of events and time. It represents a revelatory aspect of time wherein one moment offers the opportunity for "fulfilling" all time up to that moment. *Kairos* is a self-transcending moment "pregnant with a new understanding of the meaning of history and life."[15] All time is illumined and linked by this moment. In Christian theology *kairos* represents God's providential "timing." The divine "plot" is a series of kairotic events leading to the ultimate End. That end radiates its meaning through the present moment.

In this context one can see a new meaning in Sartre's claim that underlying every person's fundamental project is the basic desire to be God. Behind every fundamental project is the desire to establish intelligible time within one's life, to give the present a permanent significance by reference to a projected end. Of course, a person can never achieve the fixed view of the end, which could solidify the meaning of the present. Every individual stands poised between the "original choice" lying in the past and the projected goal that disappears into the future; one's life is viewed as simultaneously destined and indeterminate.

COSMOGONY AND THE SELF

In recent years, a number of scholars of religion have emphasized the centrality of stories for human identity and meaning. While the importance of narrative structure in this area has already been discussed, it is necessary to focus on the *mythic* dimension of such stories to distinguish them from other uses of narrative. The stories that arise in interpretation, what Sartre has designated "true novels," have special qualities which can best be understood in relation to the function of traditional religious myths.

My use of the term "myth" derives from the classic work of Mircea Eliade concerning the primordial structures of religion.[16] Eliade has tried to restore the original existential meaning attached to living, intact myths and to overcome the modern bias that has treated myths as child-ish inventions or fictions that must yield to "objective" history. While I am not directly concerned with Eliade's work on myth in primitive cultures, his general approach can be adapted to a new context.

A myth is fundamentally related to the issue of cosmogony. It narrates a sacred history that describes how the world (cosmos) or some aspect of it comes into being. It delineates what are regarded as the fundamental structures of reality. It reflects a unique vision of reality. The sacred events narrated by a myth represent the beginning or foundation of various aspects of this reality. Such sacred events are important, however, not primarily for their *chronological* priority over other events, but their *ontological* priority.

A mythic event epitomizes the essential structure of a phenomenon, rather than the phenomenon's historical origin seen in a narrow objec-tive sense. In addition, a mythic event occurring in what Eliade calls "sacred time" functions as an exemplary model. It is a symbolic expres-sion of a particular mode of being in the world. Myths provide paradigms in terms of which all human behavior can be meaningfully understood. Eliade calls a myth a "true story" because it establishes what is *truly real* and *significant* for those who believe it. It takes immediate experience and creates an orderly structure or unity within it.

Eliade regards the retelling and reenactment of myths within religious cultures as a means of escaping the terror of history, the pain of existing in time. Reenactment of myths gives one mastery over the irreversibility of time. This means that the traditional religious person posits an *essence* in sacred time that precedes his or her historical *existence* and deter-mines it. In this sense, the return to sacred time might seem like an inauthentic refusal of history and its contingencies, a case of Sartrean bad faith. After all, such an escape from history is the goal that Roquen-tin seeks at the conclusion of *Nausea* and that Sartre himself later recog-nizes as his own literary "neurosis." Roquentin wishes to "wash himself of the sin of existing" (N, 237) by escaping to the timeless, eternal realm of art. For a modern person, literature frequently provides a way to escape ordinary profane duration and to enter a new fresh "sacred time," which is endlessly repeatable.[17]

Certainly, Sartre is commonly associated with the existentialist dictum that a person's existence precedes his or her essence, and that human nature is fundamentally historical. Such a perspective would appear to renounce flatly the mythic view of ancient religious societies. Certainly there is an undeniable breach between the archaic person's demand for mythic archetypes and the modern existential person's refusal of them.

Nevertheless, Sartre's final position seems to attempt a mediation between the two. The dialectical perspective of his later thought makes it difficult to assert the priority of either existence or essence. The meaning of a person's life will involve a constant interplay between objective situations and the *cosmogonic* power of consciousness. The image of the *spiral* of totalization links cyclical time and historical time. In certain cases the spiral collapses and hardens into a single revolution and the individual continually repeats a single "liturgical drama." In any event, the past contains the archetypal core of a person's life. Sartre, therefore, homologizes a person's parents to the supernatural beings of traditional myth who establish patterns to be reenacted in later actions. At the same time, dialectical development implies the perpetual transcendence of the "sacred" or protohistorical core of personality. The work of totalization is an initiatory combat with the past leading to the birth of new syntheses. A person's life develops in a widening spiral of deaths and rebirths of meanings attributed to the past.

Eliade has described psychoanalytic therapy as analogous to the reenactment of religious myths in sacred time. For the postreligious person, the return to the sacred, mythical time of origins is pursued in the primordial past of his or her own childhood. Psychoanalysis returns one to the paradisal beginnings of one's personal history and locates the catastrophic trauma which ruptures childhood bliss and is the basis of future orientation. The resulting dreams and imaginative productions from one's unconscious are a kind of "private mythology." In the same way, Sartre's reconstruction of the "protohistory" of Flaubert recreates the sacred time of his origins.

The fundamental project that Sartre emphasizes as the key to understanding a person, is likewise a mythic structure which shapes that individual's attitudes, ideas, values, and actions. To say that every person has a fundamental project means that every individual's sense of reality rests on a particular myth. According to Yeats, "There is some one Myth for every man which, if we but knew it, would make us understand all that he did and thought."[18]

Eliade describes the experience of the sacred in religious societies as the sense of a meaning which is manifest in the world but which transcends the natural world as such. The natural world is never merely natural to these people, but needs to be "deciphered." This "sacred" quality in experience reflects precisely the way in which Sartre has characterized the manifestation of a fundamental project. The fundamental project is an overall structure of meaning beyond rational explanation. It is revealed in one's experience of the world, in actions, and in attitudes. It is symbolized, moreover, by a primordial event that Sartre calls the "original choice." The "original choice" is a mythic event that manifests the essential characteristics of subsequent situations and activities, as Sartre's various studies reveal. The fundamental project expresses and organizes fundamental beliefs about the world. It thereby retrospectively creates a consistent past, continuous with present situations.

One of the insights to be derived from religious studies is that the understanding of sacred stories involves a mythic form of truth that cannot be judged by comparison with some fixed preexisting events. The stories of the Bible, for example, are significant not as a record of a fixed past, but as an ongoing expression of certain transcendent meanings associated with past events. The effort beginning in the nineteenth century to locate the historical events at the core of these accounts stems from the same misguided approach that led Freud to insist on the historicity of childhood seductions. The recovery of the real significance of religious myth may be compared with the constant revisions that occur in the way a person construes the meaning of his life. Thus Carl Jung notes that what is important in his autobiography is not the truth of the stories he tells about his life in some objective sense. "The only question is whether what I tell is my fable, *my* truth."[19]

When theologians describe the centrality of stories in human life, it is primarily this mythic dimension to which they are referring. The stories that are religiously and psychologically significant are those that are constitutive of personal identity. Steven Crites says, "A man's sense of his own identity seems largely determined by the kind of story which he understands himself to have been enacting through the events of his career, the story of his life."[20] Crites suggests that the mundane stories in an individual's life, those which describe the daily or routine projects of his life, occur within a "sacred story." The sacred story is not an object of consciousness, but rather is what forms or molds consciousness itself, and delineates the horizons of one's world. One interprets everything else in terms of this story.

This inutterable sacred story within ordinary experience constitutes the narrative core of experience. Crites says, "The formal quality of experience through time is inherently narrative."[21] Because experience is immediately temporal, it is immediately narrative, that is, coherent through time. Although Sartre has rightly questioned the narrative quality of reality itself, he does not deny that narrativity is a fundamental structure of reflective consciousness. Indeed, the inutterable sacred story that marks the temporal emergence of the self (in Crites' view) is the same narrative core of identity that can be located in Sartre's idea of the fundamental project. The fundamental project, like Crites' "sacred story," cannot be identified with any specific empirical project, but rather is the transcendent structure of meaning manifested in every one of our activities, simultaneously constituting these activities and being constituted by them. It is a narrative structure that constantly integrates memory and anticipation of the future within a coherent temporal whole. The dialectical notion of totalization implies that as one's fundamental project changes, so too does change occur in the story of one's life, one's consciousness of the world, and one's style of acting. In short, one's personal cosmos is transformed. Insight represents a reconstruction of one's story in terms of new themes and meanings.

Narrative is thus the vehicle through which one discovers what is sacred in one's life. Michael Novak, for example, equates religion with "the awareness of the story dimension of life, . . . awe, reverence, wonder at the risk and terror of human freedom, . . . a sense of being responsible for one's own identity and for one's involvement with the identity of others."[22] The fundamental religious question thus becomes one's personal sense of self. Novak considers all people religious in a weak sense insofar as their completed lives tell a story that retrospectively reveals their ultimate convictions about the world and the way they have constructed their situation. The story expresses a symbolic world that has developed gradually into an organic whole. The "religious" task of each individual is to invent or creatively shape his or her life in a way appropriate to the possibilities determined by the facticities of culture, class, age, and so forth. This is what Sartre has called making yourself out of what others have made of you. When I creatively shape my life I become the author of its story and incorporate it into the cultural stories of my historical period.

All self-interpretation has the potential for becoming a fundamentally religious act. Through it, "man redeems himself from the flux of time and lives again in the word made flesh."[23] Alfred Kazin describes auto-biography as both a personal myth and a resurrection of experience; it takes the seeming insignificance of human existence and reforms it by "a leap of the imagination, an act of faith."[24]

Sartre's approach to human meaning attempts to show that discovering the fundamental structures of meaning in one's life occurs only insofar as one simultaneously invents them for oneself. Jonathan Z. Smith describes this same dialectical quality of human existence in an analysis of the influence of symbols on history. Symbol and history represent the two characteristic forms of human creativity or "work." The creation of a symbolic "work" as well as the "work" of historical action are the necessary means by which man expresses his humanity. Through them he "establishes and discovers his existence, invents and participates in human culture."[25] Human growth and development implies "the discovery or creation of new modes of significance and order."[26] We can work in a world only after we have symbolically transformed it into a meaningful work.

Throughout this investigation into the mythic dimension of meaning, the dual relation between discovery and creation has been stressed. An individual's sense of personal meaning derives from discovering a place in a world whose meaning he or she has created. The fundamental project includes a whole system of symbolic relations based on the initial sense of place. Only after one has symbolically created a space for oneself can meaningful historical action "take place." Like the need to structure the temporal experience of past, present, and future, the need to structure space is one of the fundamental tasks of religion. Moreover, part of every person's project is the need to take a place in the world one has received. Early on, Sartre explains: "Human-reality is that by which something we call place comes to things. Without human-reality *there would have been* neither space nor place, and yet this human reality by which placing comes to things comes to receive its place among things without any say in the matter. In truth there is no mystery here, but the description must proceed from the antinomy; for it is this which will give to us the exact relation between freedom and facticity" (*BN*, 490–91). The place one receives becomes meaningful space only in relation to the goals and values one freely imposes on it. The earliest religious myths of humanity were concerned with the need to introduce orientation or a center of reference into time and space. As modern people search for meaning in their lives, they confront the same mythic task.

NOTES

INTRODUCTION

1. These two aspects of Freud's thought have been frequently noted and documented. Cf. William Barrett and Daniel Yankelovich, *Ego and Instinct*; Paul Ricoeur, *Freud and Philosophy*; Herbert Fingarette, *The Self in Transformation*.

2. Mircea Eliade, *The Sacred and the Profane*, p. 202.

3. Ibid., p. 203.

4. Philippe Lejeune, *L'autobiographie en France*, p. 105.

CHAPTER 1

1. Cf. "His work of construction, or, if it is preferred, of reconstruction, resembles to a great extent an archeologist's excavation of some dwelling-place that has been destroyed and buried or some ancient edifice. The two processes are in fact identical, except that the analyst works under better conditions and has more material at his command to assist him, since what he is dealing with is not something destroyed but something that is still alive." Sigmund Freud, "Constructions in Analysis," p. 275.

2. Freud, "Constructions in Analysis," p. 276.

3. Psychologists such as William James in *The Principles of Psychology*, chap. 10 passim, and Gordon W. Allport in *Personality*, p. 160, have likewise pointed out that conscious experience does not always involve an ego or self. Allport notes that experiences occur which are not tied to personal interests or memories. The sense of a consistent and permanent personality at the root of the flow of experience requires a shift in attitude and a development of consciousness. For the child, consciousness of self is "a gradual and difficult achievement." The infant's consciousness lacks self-reference and a sense of the boundary between what is his and what is not. Allport cites the development of memory and language as essential for adequately conceptualizing experience. The self, far from being present from the start, only develops as experience and memories are accrued and reflectively conceptualized.

4. Sartre, "Intentionality," p. 4.

5. Sartre considers the psychoanalytic notion of thoughts arising from an impersonal unconscious to be a "coarse and materialistic interpretation of a correct intuition" (*TE*, 100), since at least it recognizes that conscious does not come from the "I."

6. Sartre, "Consciousness of Self and Knowledge of Self," p. 135. Cf. Paul Ricoeur, *Freud and Philosophy*, pp. 44–47.

7. This view resembles certain Buddhist ideas of the self.

8. Gabriel Marcel, *The Mystery of Being*, 1:190.

9. Ibid., 1:192.

10. Quoted in Stephen A. Shapiro, "The Dark Continent of Literature: Autobiography," p. 438.

11. Sartre uses the French term *sens*, which might better be translated "opposite direction" in this passage, since he suggests that a story implicitly works backward from the end to the beginning.

12. Sartre, *Situations, II*, p. 253.

13. Louis Mink, "History and Fiction as Modes of Comprehension," p. 557.

14. Sigmund Freud, "The Psychogenesis of a Case of Homosexuality in a Woman," pp. 154–55.

15. Simone de Beauvoir, *La Force de l'Age*, Paris: Gallimard, 1960, p. 377.

16. "New novels" like those of Robbe-Grillet have tried to avoid reflectively ordering experience by eliminating first-person pronouns and offering the direct images of experience. Yet this type of fiction is not likely to be very popular. People need the sense of endings provided by fiction precisely to help them cope with the unending nature of history.

17. Cf., A. N. Whitehead: "The most obvious aspect of this field of actual experience is its disorderly character. . . . This fact is concealed by the influence of language, molded by science, which foists on us exact concepts as though they represented the immediate deliverances of experience. The result is, that we imagine that we have immediate experience of a world of perfectly defined objects implicated in perfectly defined events. . . . My contention is, that this world is a world of ideas, and that its internal relations are relations between abstract concepts." "The Organization of Thought," in *The Limits of Language*, ed. Walker Gibson, New York: Hill & Wang, 1962, p. 12.

18. Sigmund Freud, "The Unconscious," p. 147.

19. Ibid., p. 148.

20. Ibid., p. 116.

21. Serge Viderman, "Interpretation in the Analytical Space," p. 474.

22. Sigmund Freud, *New Introductory Lectures on Psychoanalysis*, p. 95.

23. Viderman, "Interpretation," p. 473.

24. Ibid.; Roy Schafer, *A New Language for Psychoanalysis*, p. 5.

25. Philip Rieff, *Freud*, p. 131.

26. Errol Bedford, "Emotions."

27. Charles Taylor, "Interpretation and the Sciences of Man," p. 15.

28. Sigmund Freud, "From the History of an Infantile Neurosis," p. 189.

29. Ibid., p. 298.

30. Viderman, "Interpretation," p. 474.

31. Ibid.

32. Serge Viderman, *La construction de l'espace analytique*, p. 59.

33. The imagination was the subject of Sartre's thesis for his diploma in advanced studies. In the late 1930s Sartre interrupted his work on the first drafts of *Nausea* to expand his thesis into a longer work on the image. This work was ultimately published as two separate books: *Imagination*, and *The Psychology of Imagination*.

35. On this point, see Mary Warnock's *Imagination*, pp. 176–79.

CHAPTER 2

1. On the idea of a "higher" understanding of Freud, see Peter Homans' *Theology After Freud*, pp. x–xvii.

2. Joseph Fell notes that "the popular antithesis between Sartre as 'radical libertarian' and Freud as 'hard determinist' is misleading." Fell, "Sartre's Theory of Motivation," p. 31. Sartre believes, says Fell, that people do not always know what they are doing, since their actions express specific interpretations of the world which are seldom explicitly known or recognized as interpretations.

3. William Barrett, *Irrational Man*, p. 260.

4. Strictly speaking, Sartre does not equate consciousness with psychic reality. The major part of a person's psychic reality that is not part of consciousness is that person's being-for-others. There are psychological facts about oneself that one learns from other people but that are never part of one's own consciousness. Nevertheless, Sartre does seem to include everything that Freud calls part of the psyche in the realm of consciousness. See "An Interview with Jean-Paul Sartre," [Schilpp], pp. 33, 47.

5. Sartre, "Consciousness of Self and Knowledge of Self," p. 139. Sartre's dialectical approach to consciousness is more explicitly developed in his later thought which will be discussed in chapter 3.

6. Maurice Merleau-Ponty similarly observes that such psychoanalytic "mechanisms" as repression, regression, resistance, and sublimation, do not require Freud's causal notions, and can be explained in terms of systems or structures of consciousness. A complex is not a buried thing producing effects on the surface from time to time, but a structure of meaning or "separated dialectic" in consciousness that has not been integrated into the set of ideas constituting the self. *The Structure of Behavior*, pp. 176–84.

7. Sartre, *Situations*, I, p. 188.

8. Sartre's objection is fairly common, even among psychoanalysts. Cf. "It is hard to avoid the conclusion that Freud's theory of bound and mobile energy has little to do with the concept of energy as used by the 'other natural

sciences,' but that it is really a theory of *meaning* in disguise." Charles Rycroft, *A Critical Dictionary of Psychoanalysis*, p. 43.

9. Sartre, "Freud," unpublished screenplay written for John Huston in 1957–58.

10. Sartre approves of the work of psychoanalyst Wilhelm Stekel, who says the neurotic tends to direct his attention in the "wrong" direction to avoid confronting what he does not wish to accept. The neurotic is like a man who does not wish to accept his wife's infidelity; he represses all thought that would suggest her unfaithfulness. "He is eventually able to convince himself that he believes her to be faithful." Stekel, *Conditions of Nervous Anxiety and Their Treatment*, p. 7. Stekel regards psychoanalysis as a form of retrospective education dealing not with a spontaneous memory of specific traumatic events, but with demonstrating unrecognized patterns in behavior.

11. "Precisely because [consciousness] lives the new aspect of the world by believing in it, it is caught in its own belief, exactly as in dreaming and in hysteria" (*E*, 78; cf. *E*, 80).

12. For example, a person becomes hysterical to avoid a difficult situation.

13. The English translation of *motif* as "cause" rather than "reason" or "grounds" is unfortunate, for then it cannot be distinguished from the French *cause*, which Sartre uses to describe genuinely deterministic relations. Thus the English translation is ambiguous when Sartre says "if there is no act without a cause [French = *motif*], this is not in the sense that we can say that there is no phenomenon without a cause [French = *cause*]. To be a cause [French = *motif*], the cause [French = *motif*] must be experienced as such" (*BN*, 437). Deterministic causes do not need to be experienced as causes to exist but motives or psychological "causes" must be experienced because they have no independent existence outside consciousness. The motivating characteristics of a situation only appear when they are constituted as such by a person who has been motivated.

14. Stuart Hampshire makes much the same point as Sartre in *Thought and Action* when he says that freedom represents the ability to detach oneself from habits and conventions of thought and to redescribe a situation and one's response to us in new terms from a new point of view (p. 213). Like Sartre, Hampshire claims "the situation that confronts a man at any particular time is susceptible to an indefinite set of alternate descriptions. The situation as the agent identifies and describes it is the situation he confronts. He may misdescribe and misconceive the situation and perceive features that are imaginary and not present" (p. 192). Inaction is due not to weakness of will, but to a narrow way of discriminating one's situation. One cannot think of changing habitual action until one thinks of the situation differently (p. 209).

15. Thus when a patient discusses "forgotten" matters, he usually adds, "In a way I have always known that, only I never thought of it." Freud, "Recollection, Repetition, and Working Through," p. 158.

16. Sigmund Freud, "Notes upon a Case of Obsessional Neurosis," p. 59.

17. Ibid., p. 54n.

18. Freud, "Constructions in Analysis," p. 276.

19. Sigmund Freud, *Psychopathology of Everyday Life*, p. 156n.

20. Jacques Lacan has emphasized this phenomenon in the idea of *après-coup*.

21. Sigmund Freud, *The Origins of Psychoanalysis*, p. 170.

22. Erik Erikson, *Young Man Luther,* p. 217.

23. Erik Erikson, *Insight and Responsibility,* p. 68.

24. F. C. Bartlett's classic work *Remembering* shows that memories cannot be treated as simple traces stored in the mind, which preserve a copy of the past, available for a kind of psychic "perception." Rather, Bartlett found memory of the past to involve an "imaginative reconstruction" based on cognitive schema that vary and develop over time. Such schema are used to actively organize past experience into meaningful sequences consistent with a current frame of reference. Bartlett's experiments consisted of telling people a story and asking them to retell it at a later date. Subsequent retellings of the story varied not simply because of decay or distortion of memory, but also because of a shifting interpretative context. This cumulative, ongoing organization operating in long-term memory makes it virtually impossible to distinguish features of an event as it is originally experienced from later versions of it that are remembered. When one recalls a story, certain characteristics and details come to mind. Arranging them within a coherent reasonable story may involve providing links for incompatible material, emphasizing some elements, discarding others, rearranging.

25. Cf. "Toricelli *invented* the weight of air—I say he invented it rather than discovered it because when an object is concealed from all eyes, one must invent it out of whole cloth in order to be able to discover it" (*LE,* 288).

26. Sartre, "Forgers of Myths," p. 37.

27. Here again Sartre uses the French word *sens,* which refers to both the "meaning" and the "direction" of the details in a life.

28. Cf. Hampshire, *Thought and Action,* p. 222: "Every action, even the most inconspicuous voluntary gesture, can be seen as part of a manner of life and of a set of attitudes to experience which can be intentionally changed and controlled when the person acting is made aware of them as finally forming a certain pattern and gradually constituting his character."

29. Joseph Fell, *Emotion in the Thought of Sartre,* p. 154.

30. Ibid., p. 211.

31. Charmé, Critical Review of Morris's *Sartre's Concept of a Person,* pp. 117–19.

32. Barrett, *Irrational Man,* p. 255.

33. Anthony Manser, *Sartre,* p. 122.

34. John F. Mack, "Psychoanalysis and Historical Biography," p. 156.

35. Sigmund Freud, "Screen Memories," pp. 248–49.

36. Sigmund Freud, *Leonardo da Vinci and a Memory of His Childhood,* p. 33; *Psychopathology of Everyday Life,* p. 34; "Notes upon a Case of Obsessional Neurosis," pp. 63–64; "From the History of an Infantile Neurosis," p. 189.

37. Freud, "Screen Memories," p. 249–50.

38. Adler, *The Individual Psychology of Alfred Adler,* p. 287.

39. Sigmund Freud, *An Autobiographical Study,* p. 36.

40. Ernst Kris, "The Personal Myth," pp. 653–81.

41. Freud, *Autobiographical Study,* pp. 63–64.

42. Freud, *The Origins of Psychoanalysis,* p. 216.

43. Viderman, *La Construction de L'Espace Analytique,* pp. 28, 135.

44. Freud, "From the History of an Infantile Neurosis," p. 239.

45. Freud, " 'A Child Is Being Beaten,' " pp. 113–14.

46. Dominick La Capra, *A Preface to Sartre,* p. 173.

47. Roy Pascal, *Design and Truth in Autobiography*, p. 185.

48. The dialectical concept of "totalization" in Sartre's later thought implies a constant retotalizing of one's life as the key to the fundamental project.

49. This error is made by Barrett and Yankelovich in *Ego and Instinct*, p. 428.

50. Cf. "The course of life is, in a way, comparable to a work of art which one creates, shapes and perfects by living it, and if one is fortunate enough, one may even put the finishing touches to it. The person may be only vaguely conscious of this, but it will seem that the life history, the work which he creates by living it, is his greatest concern." Andros Angyal, *Foundation for a Science of Personality*, p. 354. "It is as if a man were regarding his own life and character as a work of art, and asking how it should best be completed." R. M. Hare, *Freedom and Reason*, p. 150.

51. Stanley Hauerwas, "Story and Theology," p. 346.

52. "Of giving the lie," in *The Complete Essays of Montaigne*, p. 504.

53. Sartre, "Entretien: J. P. Sartre et M. Sicard," p. 26.

54. Philosopher Paul Ricoeur has repeatedly discussed the hermeneutical dimension of the human sciences; i.e., the object of study in these disciplines has features in common with a written text and consequently requires a method of interpretation that shares certain characteristics with textual interpretation. See Paul Ricoeur, "The Model of the Text: Meaningful Action Considered as a Text," "The Question of Proof in Freud's Psychoanalytic Writings," and *Freud and Philosophy*.

55. E. D. Hirsch, Jr., *Validity in Interpretation*.

56. Roy Schafer, *Language and Insight*, p. 66. Cf. "Psychoanalysis does not discover truth understood as a correspondence between acts of the past and propositions in the form of interpretations concerning the past. Rather it *constructs truth* in the service of self-coherence for the present and for the future." Wolfgang Loch, "Some Comments on the Subject of Psychoanalysis and Truth," p. 238.

57. Viderman, *La construction de l'espace analytique*, p. 113.

58. Bakan, *Sigmund Freud and Jewish Mystical Tradition*.

59. Bakan's claim that Freud gave the name Dora to one of his patients when writing her case history as a disguised expression of this belief (i.e., Dora = Torah) is highly speculative and not central to the value of the textual analogy.

60. Ibid., pp. 246f.

CHAPTER 3

1. Regarding the French resistance to Freud, see H. Stuart Hughes' *The Obstructed Path: French Social Thought in the Years of Desperation, 1930–1960*, pp. 9–11.

2. Simone de Beauvoir, *The Prime of Life*, p. 22.

3. Ibid., p. 23. Sartre says, "I had known about Freud ever since my philosophy class and I read several of his books. I remember having read *The Psychopathology of Everyday Life* in my first year at Ecole Normale and then, finally, *The Interpretation of Dreams* before leaving the Ecole. . . . then during my years of teaching I went deeper into the doctrine of Freud, though always separated from him, by the way, because of his idea of the unconscious." Sartre, "An Interview with Jean-Paul Sartre" [Schilpp], p. 12.

4. Ibid., p. 106.

5. Christina Howells, "Sartre and Freud," p. 161.

6. Beauvoir, *Prime of Life*, p. 106.

7. Many others among Sartre's contemporaries were initially put off by the mechanistic elements of psychoanalysis, only to return to it later with a more sympathetic interpretation. For example, Merleau-Ponty eventually changed his attitude toward psychoanalysis but noted, "The psychoanalysis we accept and appreciate is not the same which we denied." Preface to A. Hesnard, *L'oeuvre de Freud et son importance pour le monde moderne*, p. 31.

8. Huston reports in his autobiography (*An Open Book*, p. 294): "Sartre was a Communist and an anti-Freudian. Nevertheless, I considered him the ideal man to write the *Freud* screenplay. He had read psychology deeply, knew Freud's work intimately and would have an objective and logical approach."

9. Sartre, "Sartre et Huston," p. 57. Sartre completed an initial draft in December, 1958. He spent some time in Ireland the following September working on the project with Huston.

10. Sartre, "An interview with Jean-Paul Sartre [Schilpp], p. 12.

11. Beauvoir, *Prime of Life*, p. 107.

12. In his defense, Huston takes credit for the main idea of the film and credits Sartre with the idea of making Anna O. a composite of Freud's patients. He says Sartre admired Freud but diminished him a bit. "Interview with John Huston," *Positif* 70 (June 1965): 18.

13. Sartre, "An Interview with Jean-Paul Sartre" [Schilpp], pp. 22–3.

14. Sartre's concept comprehension or understanding is influenced by that of Karl Jaspers (and thus indirectly by Dilthey), whose *General Psychopathology* Sartre helped to prepare for publication in French in 1928. See Michel Contat and Michel Rybalka, *The Writings of Jean-Paul Sartre*, vol. 1: *A Bibliographical Life*, p. 40. Sartre's idea of *le vécu* may have been influenced by the work of French psychoanalyst Angelo Hesnard, who replaced the language of "conscious" and "unconscious" with the terms *vécu actuel* ("the lived that is present") and *vécu inactual* ("the lived that is not present") in order to distinguish experience which can be conceptualized and verbalized vs. experience which is latent and unformulated. Collins, *Sartre as Biographer*, p. 15.

15. Sartre, "Replies to Structuralism: An Interview with Jean-Paul Sartre," p. 113.

16. Sartre's complaint is not entirely fair, since Freud did acknowledge the lack of necessity or inevitability in any particular resolution of childhood conflicts. Leonardo da Vinci's sublimation of his sexuality into "the urge to know," for example, "need not necessarily have taken place; in someone else it might perhaps not have taken place or might have assumed much less extensive proportions. We must recognize here a degree of freedom which cannot be resolved any further by psycho-analytic means." Freud, *Leonardo da Vinci and a Memory of His Childhood*, p. 85.

17. Sartre, *Sartre by Himself*, p. 58.

18. Ibid., p. 59.

19. An empirical study of various "life themes" played out over various individual's lifetimes tends to support Sartre's position and demonstrates how a "life theme" or project serves as an "affective and cognitive representation of a problem or set of problems which constituted the fundamental source of psychic stress for a person in childhood, which triggered adaptive efforts, which identify problems and form the basis for a fundamental interpretation of reality and ways

of dealing with it." Mihaly Csikszentmihalyi and Olga V. Beattie, "Life Themes: A Theoretical and Empirical Exploration of Their Origins and Effects," p. 48.

20. Sometimes, Sartre notes, a totalizing reaction may try to preserve an existing unification by excluding a disturbing element and not linking it to the rest of experience. It is often easier to deny or "forget" a disturbing fact when to assimilate it would require a major change in the totalization in progress. A person may imagine that the rejected element has been forgotten or project it on the external world. Eventually, such a forgotten element may become an "autonomous system" which structures part of experience in its own way, and provokes problems that are unperceived or which are falsely attributed to other factors. The unassimilated element not only detotalizes but becomes active as a "negative totalization" (*IF*, 1:655). Obviously, Sartre is here describing within his own conceptual framework such psychoanalytic phenomena as repression and the return of the repressed. He has never questioned the existence of such phenomena, only their mechanistic explanation in Freudian theory.

21. This is another example of the importance of the "hermeneutical circle" to Sartre's position. Cf. "an individual concept derives its meaning from a context or horizon within which it stands; yet the horizon is made up of the very elements to which it gives meaning. By dialectical interaction between the whole and the part, each gives the other meaning; understanding is circular then. Because within this 'circle' meaning comes to stand, we call this the hermeneutical circle." Richard Palmer, *Hermeneutics*, p. 87.

22. In a similar way, Freud noted that the complete analysis of a particular symptom implicates the whole case history. Therefore, a valid interpretation of a dream or symptom taken in isolation is not possible.

23. Sartre's notion of a dialectical spiral suggests that each new revolution appropriates an old self and inherits its fruits. Fingarette's use of the ideas of karma and reincarnation as metaphors for the process of self-development is very similar in this regard. See Fingarette, *Self in Transformation*, pp. 177–243.

24. Vladimir Nabokov, *Speak, Memory*, p. 275.

25. Eliade, *Cosmos and History*.

26. Sartre contends that Flaubert's "style of life" has been "infinitely condensed" into the style of *Madame Bovary*, so that without knowing Flaubert, the reader already has a "taste" of him. "The flavor which is given immediately [in the book] is what must be restored by the end of a biographical study" (*IF*, 1:658).

27. Barrett and Yankelovich, *Ego and Instinct*, pp. 314–17.

28. Benjamin Nelson, "Sartre, Genet, Freud," p. 162.

29. Barrett and Yankelovich, *Ego and Instinct*, p. 333.

30. Ibid., p. 130.

31. Don S. Browning, *Generative Man*, p. 185.

32. Ibid., p. 180.

33. It is ironic that Sartre is the only major thinker discussed in *Ego and Instinct* whose works do not appear in their bibliography.

34. Browning, *Generative Man*, p. 161.

35. Ibid., pp. 156–57.

36. Erikson, *Identity and the Life Cycle*, p. 116.

37. Ibid., p. 149.

38. Barrett and Yankelovich, *Ego and Instinct*, pp. 311–13.

39. Ibid., p. 436.

40. Erikson, *Gandhi's Truth*, p. 38.

41. Browning, *Generative Man*, p. 157.
42. Erikson, *Young Man Luther*, p. 112.
43. Erikson, *Identity and the Life Cycle*, p. 93.
44. Ibid.
45. Erikson, *Young Man Luther*, p. 261.
46. Sartre, "Replies to Structuralism," p. 112.
47. Sartre, "An Interview with Jean-Paul Sartre," in *Tynan Right and Left*, p. 309.
48. Ibid.
49. Ibid., pp. 309–10.
50. Marjorie Grene, *Sartre*, p. 236.
51. Sartre's change of attitude toward the power of literature to provide salvation is the central theme of his autobiography, *The Words*.
52. Cf. "people—(people everywhere)—wish their own life, with all its dark places that they sense, to be an experience not only lived, but *presented"* (*BEM*, 30).
53. Sartre, "Jean-Paul Sartre on His Autobiography," p. 915.

CHAPTER 4

1. Freud, *An Autobiographical Study*, p. 90.
2. B. A. Farrell, "The Validity of Psychotherapy"; Ernest Glover, "The Therapeutic Effect of Inexact Interpretations: A Contribution to the Theory of Suggestion."
3. Freud, "Recollection, Repetition, and Working Through," pp. 161–62.
4. Schafer, "The Interpretation of Transference and the Conditions for Loving," p. 358.
5. Freud, "Recollection, Repetition, and Working Through," p. 161.
6. Sigmund Freud, *Dora*, p. 96.
7. It is interesting to note that when they were young men, Raymond Aron used to enjoy critically analyzing and cutting up Sartre's various syntheses. Simone de Beauvoir says of Sartre, "There was more imagination than logic in his mental processes." Beauvoir, *Prime of Life*, p. 30.
8. The dialectical relation between literary and historical imagination has begun to receive close attention. See, for example, Barbara Foley, "Fact, Fiction, and 'Reality,' " *Contemporary Literature* 20 (Summer 1979): 389–99.
9. Halpern, *Critical Fictions*, p. 17.
10. Jonas Barish, "The Veritable Genet," p. 279.
11. In a similar way, one might argue that Freud's *Interpretation of Dreams* and *Moses and Monotheism* reveal more truth about his mode of being than his official autobiography. Indeed, Marthe Robert describes these two works as Freud's "family novels" embodying his "personal myth." *From Oedipus to Moses*, p. 165.
12. Maurice Merleau-Ponty notes in *Signs* (p. 57) that art which aims at truth cannot be a mere frozen copy of existence. The exact recording of a conversation which had seemed brilliant later gives the impression of indigence. Both Sartre and Merleau-Ponty agree with Jean Cocteau's famous saying that it is often necessary to lie in order to tell the truth. To a certain extent, one may also look to Sartre's childhood for some roots of this attitude. He says that as a

child he had been told so often about the truth of works of fiction that he saw stories as a way to tell the truth. "I witnessed, helplessly, the telescoping of fiction and reality" (W, 134).

13. Simone de Beauvoir understands this novelistic structure of *The Family Idiot* when she describes it as "a suspense-story, a detective's investigation that ends in the solution of the enigma of the question 'How did Flaubert make himself?' " Beauvoir, *All Said and Done*, p. 53.

14. Gusdorf, "Conditions and Limits of Autobiography," in James Olney, ed., *Autobiography*, p. 48.

15. Ibid., p. 43.

16. Ibid., pp. 37–38.

17. Freud, *Dora*, p. 30.

18. On the notion of following a story, see Gallie, *Philosophy and the Historical Understanding*, pp. 22–50. In one case Freud immediately suspected physiological problems rather than psychological ones when "the story came out perfectly clearly and connectedly in spite of the remarkable events it dealt with" (*Dora*, p. 31n).

19. Freud, *Dora*, p. 30.

20. Sigmund Freud and Joseph Breuer, *Studies on Hysteria*, p. 40.

21. Freud, *Dora*, p. 31.

22. Ibid., p. 143.

23. Ibid., p. 32.

24. Freud, "Constructions in Analysis," p. 274.

25. Michael T. McGuire, *Reconstructions in Psychoanalysis*, p. 90.

26. Freud, *Dora*, p. 24.

27. Freud, "From the History of an Infantile Neurosis," p. 195. Cf. "Consecutive presentation is not a very adequate means of describing complicated mental processes going on in different layers of the mind." Freud, "The Psychogenesis of a Case of Homosexuality in a Woman," p. 147.

28. Rieff, Introduction to *Dora*, p. 9.

29. Ibid., p. 8. The linear, chronological narrative that Freud offers in his official autobiography really tells less about him than the more complex and labryinthine *Interpretation of Dreams*.

30. Steven Marcus, "Freud and Dora: Story, History, Case History," pp. 402–3.

31. Freud and Breuer, *Studies on Hysteria*, p. 201.

32. Marcus, "Freud and Dora," p. 402.

33. James Hillman, "The Fiction of Case History: A Round," pp. 123–73.

34. Ibid., p. 137.

35. Marcus, "Freud and Dora," p. 425.

36. Robert J. Lifton, "On Psychohistory," p. 361.

37. Mircea Eliade, *Myth and Reality*, pp. 5–14.

38. Bernard D. Fine, Edward D. Joseph, Herbert F. Waldhorn, eds., *Recollection and Reconstruction*, p. 76.

39. Freud, "Notes upon a Case of Obsessional Neurosis," p. 40. Emphasis added.

40. See above.

41. Freud, "Notes upon a Case of Obsessional Neurosis, p. 40n.

42. "Constructions in Analysis," p. 282. Similarly, through the interpretation of dreams one acquires "a profound conviction of the reality of these

primal scenes, a conviction which is in no respect inferior to one based on recollection." ("From the History of an Infantile Neurosis," p. 239.)

43. Joseph Margolis, "The Myths of Psychoanalysis," p. 374.

44. Eliade, *Sacred and Profane*, pp. 20–65.

45. Nicholas Hobbs, "Sources of Gain in Psychotherapy," in *Use of Interpretation in Treatment*, ed. Emmanuel F. Hammer, p. 20. Cf. Hans W. Loewald: "In a sense, every patient, and each of us, creates a personal myth about our life and past, a myth which sustains us and may destroy us. The myth may change and in analysis, where it becomes conscious, it often does change. The created life history is neither an illusion nor an invention, but gives form and meaning to our lives, and has to do with the identity Erikson speaks of." Quoted by Schafer in *A New Language of Psychoanalysis*, p. 50.

46. Cf. C. Backès, "Continuité mythique et construction historique."

47. Nicos Nicolaidis, "La réalité du 'mythe' dans la cure psychoanalytique," p. 1011.

CHAPTER 5

1. E.g., Halpern, *Critical Fictions*, pp. 55–56.

2. Ibid., p. 56.

3. Gerald N. Izenberg, *The Existential Critique of Freud*, p. 243.

4. Cf., Roquentin: "I wanted the moments of my life to follow and order themselves like those of a life remembered" (N, 58).

5. Philip Thody, *Jean Genet*, chap. 1.

6. Genet, *The Thief's Journal*, p. 13.

7. Ibid., p. 183.

8. Ibid., p. 89.

9. Ibid., pp. 7–8.

10. I use the term "psychical reality" in the Freudian sense that childhood traumas need not have historical reality to function within personality. See J. Laplanche and J.-B. Pontalis, *The Language of Psychoanalysis*, p. 363.

11. Eliade, *Cosmos and History*.

12. Sartre, "Playboy Interview: Jean-Paul Sartre," p. 70.

13. Erikson offers a very similar description of Martin Luther's transformation of his childhood situation. He traces the dialectical process of "how Martin, at the end of a somber and harsh childhood, was precipitated into a severe identity crisis for which he sought delay and cure in the silence of the monastery; how being silent, he became 'possessed,' how being possessed, he gradually learned to speak a new language, his language; how being able to speak, he not only talked himself out of the monastery, . . . but also formulated for himself and for all of mankind a new kind of ethical and psychological awareness" (*Young Man Luther*, pp. 47–48).

CHAPTER 6

1. Philippe Lejeune, "L'ordre du récit dans *Les mots* de Sartre."

2. Ibid., p. 20.

3. Ibid., p. 23. Lejeune provides a detailed analysis of five stages that can be isolated in this dialectic.

4. Ibid., p. 25.

5. Andre Gide comments that in autobiographical writing "What hampers me most is having to represent stages that are really one confused blend of simultaneous happenings as though they were successive, . . . everything in me is conflicting and contradictory. Memoirs are never more than half sincere, however great the desire for truth; everything is always more complicated than one makes out." Quoted in Shapiro, "Autobiography," p. 438.

6. "I experienced inspiration between the ages of seven and eight" (W, 88).

7. Sartre, "Sartre on His Autobiography," p. 916.

8. Ibid.

9. Sartre, "Jean-Paul Sartre Speaks," p. 95.

10. Similarly, Simone de Beauvoir says in her autobiography: "My life is by no means over yet, but by now it has developed a pattern which the future seems unlikely to modify very much" (*Prime of Life*, p. 10). Writing about old age, she says, "Things change and we with them, but without losing our identity. Our past, our roots in the world remain unalterable. . . . We cannot arbitrarily invent projects for ourselves: they have to be written in our past as requirements" (*Coming of Age*, p. 598).

11. Sartre, "Playboy Interview: Sartre," p. 76.

12. Sartre, *Sartre by Himself*, p. 57.

13. Sartre, "Entretien," p. 21.

14. Ibid., p. 29. Cf. "I think that my taste for coffee and my sexuality are in my books. They have only to be rediscovered and it is up to the critics to find them. In other words, the critics should, on the basis of the books and nothing but the books, together with the correspondence, establish what was the person who wrote these books, reestablish the trends, see the doctrines to which the author subscribed . . . [that is,] a kind of biography that can be done only with documents." "An interview with Jean-Paul Sartre" [Schilpp], p. 50.

15. Sartre, "Sartre on his Autobiography," p. 915.

16. Cf. Barrett and Yankelovich, *Ego and Instinct*, p. 150: "Whether a great man merely expresses his time or creates it is an unreal question. The more decisively he shapes his time, the more deeply he borrows from it, bringing to a head thoughts and insights that were already in the air but halting and half-formed. A great man is, in this respect, only a reminder of how deeply embedded in history man's being is, and this would seem to be a fact which psychoanalysis must also take into account in the case of more ordinary people."

17. Eliade, *Myths, Dreams, and Mysteries*, p. 32.

18. Sartre, "Forgers of Myths," p. 40.

19. Donald Capps, "Theme and Event: *Gandhi's Truth* as Religious Biography," in Capps, ed., *Encounter with Erikson*, p. 168.

20. Erikson, *Life History and the Historical Moment*, p. 20.

21. Erikson, *Young Man Luther*, p. 67.

22. Robert, *From Oedipus to Moses*, p. 7.

23. For a classic sampling of the issues involved in psychobiographical studies, see Roger A. Johnson, ed., *Psychohistory and Religion*, esp. articles by Bainton, Johnson, and Spitz.

24. See, e.g., Erikson, "The Nature of Clinical Evidence," in *Insight and Responsibility*, p. 53.

25. Johnson, "Psychohistory as Religious Narrative: The Demonic Role of Hans Luther in Erikson's Saga of Human Evolution," in *Psychohistory and Religion*, pp. 127–62.

26. Ibid., p. 40.

27. Ibid., p. 129.

28. Erikson, *Young Man Luther*, p. 37.

29. Ibid., p. 83.

30. Ibid., p. 65.

31. Erikson, *Gandhi's Truth*, p. 128.

32. Ibid., p. 133.

33. Erikson, *Young Man Luther*, p. 38.

34. Ibid., p. 123.

35. Capps, "Theme and Event."

36. Donald Capps, "Psychohistory and Historical Genres," in Peter Homans, ed., *Childhood and Selfhood*, p. 213.

37. Don S. Browning, "Erikson and the Search for a Normative Image of Man," in ibid., pp. 264–92.

38. Erikson, *Young Man Luther*, p. 22.

39. Jean Daniel, "We Already Miss his Vigilence . . . ," *Telos* 44 (Summer 1980):.185.

40. Lionel Abel, "The Retroactive 'I'," p. 257.

41. De Man, "Sartre's Confessions," p. 12.

42. Germaine Brée, *Camus and Sartre*, p. 56.

43. Reynolds and Capps, eds., *The Biographical Process*, pp. 1–33.

44. Ernst Kris, "The Image of the Artist," in *Psychoanalytic Explorations in Art*, pp. 64–84.

45. Freud notes that "every child at play behaves like an imaginative writer in that he creates a world of his own or, more truly, he rearranges the things of this world and orders it in a new way that pleases him better." "The Relation of the Poet to Day-Dreaming," p. 35.

46. Sartre, *Sartre by Himself*, p. 88.

47. Jacques Lecarme, "*Les mots* de Sartre: Un cas limite de l'autobiographie?"

48. Robert Jay Lifton, *Boundaries*.

49. Alexander Mitscherlich, *Society without the Father*, p. 268.

50. Browning, "Erikson and the Search for a Normative Image of Man," in Homans, ed., *Childhood and Selfhood*.

51. The absence of a father in childhood is also the major theme in Freud's study of Leonardo da Vinci. One is immediately struck by the number of personality similarities between Leonardo and Sartre that are attributed to their fatherless childhoods. Freud asserts that Leonardo's bold and independent scientific research and his freedom from the support of authority and dogmatic religion were only possible because Leonardo had learned early on to do without his father. Freud, *Leonardo*, pp. 72–73.

52. A useful analysis of Sartre's struggle to establish a sense of self, from a loosely psychoanalytic point of view, can be found in A. J. Arnold and J. P. Piriou, *Genèse et critique d'une autobiographie*, pp. 28–51.

53. Sartre, *L'Existentialisme est un humanisme*, p. 92.

54. Izenberg, *The Existentialist Critique of Freud*, p. 325.

55. Erikson describes how Gandhi adapted his early memories to the moral needs of his later life (*Gandhi's Truth*, p. 97). It is interesting to note that Gandhi entitled his autobiography *The Story of My Experiments with Truth*. Sartre's *Words* is obviously his own experiment with the truth of his life.

56. Beauvoir, *All Said and Done*, p. 101.

57. According to Erikson's analysis, Martin Luther likewise viewed his life

in anticipation of his prospective great deeds. He had a "premature sense of judgment which wishes to receive and render a total accounting of life before it is lived" (*Young Man Luther*, p. 83).

58. Cf. Erikson's description of retrospection: "To the ego the past is not an inexorable process, experienced only as preparation for an impending doom; rather the past is part of a present mastery which employs a convenient mixture of forgetting, falsifying and idealizing to fit the past to the present, but usually to an extent which is neither knowingly delusional nor knowingly dishonest" (*Young Man Luther*, p. 217).

59. Thomas M. King, *Sartre and the Sacred*, p. xi.

CHAPTER 7

1. "Flaubert, c'est moi," *TLS*, 29 September 1972, p. 1157.

2. On the other hand, Sartre claims that the implicit foil to the unloved, insecure Gustave is himself, the well-loved and secure Jean-Paul (*LS*, 114–15).

3. An interesting approach to this issue is presented by John Murray Cuddihy in *The Ordeal of Civility*.

4. Robert Champigny, "Trying to Understand *L'Idiot*," p. 3.

5. Sartre says he welcomes a similar analysis of himself as he has provided of Flaubert. He claims he has left letters and documents of his personal life so that he will be as transparent to posterity as Flaubert was to him (*LS*, 122–23). However, in a later interview Sartre modifies his position in saying, "I can talk about *my* lived experience, but only at risk can I reconstitute yours." "An Interview with Jean-Paul Sartre" [Schilpp], p. 22.

6. In a letter to Fliess, Freud says "the mechanism of creative writing is the same as that of hysterical phantasies" (*The Origins of Psychoanalysis*, p. 208).

7. Benjamin F. Bart, *Flaubert*, p. vi.

8. T. H. Adamowski, "The Condemned of Rouen: Sartre's Flaubert," p. 80. Sartre admits that some of his ideas about Flaubert's constitution are similar to Lacan's, although he was not specifically thinking of Lacan when he wrote *The Family Idiot*, nor has he studied Lacan very much. Sartre seems to agree with elements of Lacan's famous "mirror stage" (*stade du miroir*) whereby a child identifies with the self constituted by social and family designations. At the same time, Sartre maintains that his view of the self as an object of reflection has not changed (*LS*, 117).

9. Marthe Robert, "Le tribunal ou l'analyse," p. 17.

10. Ibid.

11. Claude Burgelin, "Lire *L'Idiot de la Famille*?" pp. 114–15.

12. Freud, *Dora*, p. 32.

13. In some ways Sartre's method resembles the "psychocriticism" of Charles Mauron, which looks for an author's "obsessive metaphors" and organizes them into his "personal myth." However, as Serge Doubrovsky indicates, Mauron presents these themes as fixed and lacks a sense of their dialectical development in time. Serge Doubrovsky, *The New Criticism in France*, pp. 161–67.

14. Letter to Louise Colet, 15 August 1846, quoted in Bart, *Flaubert*, p. 271.

15. Bart, *Flaubert*, p. 271.

16. Cf. *IF*, 1:176, 1040; 3:27.

17. Champigny, "Trying to Understand *L'Idiot*," p. 4.

18. Champigny wryly compares the last statement to a knight announcing his intention to enter the Hundred Years War. Ibid., p. 6.

19. When Erikson confronts the paucity of information about Martin Luther's mother, he shows no hesitation in filling in her portrait. He admits, "A big gap exists here, which only conjecture could fill." Erikson feels compelled to speculate on the kind of mother who could have given rise to a person like Luther: "Instead of conjecturing half-heartedly, I will state, as a clinician's judgment, that nobody would speak and sing as Luther later did if his mother's voice had not sung to him of some heaven; that nobody could be as torn between his masculine and feminine sides, we have such a range of both, who did not at one time feel that he was like his mother; but also that nobody would discuss women and marriage in the way he often did who had not been deeply disappointed by his mother—and had become loath to succumb the way she did to the father, to fate" (*Young Man Luther*, pp. 72–73). There is clearly no genuine historical evidence for this conjecture, nor does Erikson's analysis depend on its accuracy. Like Sartre, Erikson simply has presented his subject as he imagines him. And in reconstructing Luther's childhood, Erikson explains: "A clinician's training permits, and in fact forces, him to recognize major trends even when the facts are not all available. . . . He can and must be able to make meaningful predictions as to what will prove to have happened. . . . In biography, the validity of any relevant theme can only be in its crucial recurrence in a man's development" (*Young Man Luther* p. 50).

20. La Capra, *A Preface to Sartre*, p. 196.

21. Champigny is justified in his criticism that Sartre's narrative is misleading when reconstructed mental "events" are given the appearance of historical facts. See "Trying to understand *L'Idiot*," p. 6.

22. For this reason Marcel Eck complains that *The Family Idiot* is perfectly "logical" but lacks any genuine "historical" basis. Eck is bothered by the absence of hard evidence for Sartre's portrait of the scornful, tyrannical father and the cool, indifferent mother. See "La psychanalyse de Flaubert selon Sartre."

23. E.g., ibid., p. 686.

24. Flaubert himself says, "My life is not facts; my life, it's a thought . . . Oh! Such a long thought" (cited in *IF*, 2:1510).

25. In his study of Dostoevsky, Freud likewise shows that what is taken for "epilepsy" may be assumed to be a neurotic symptom when one considers the relation of the first seizure to the thread of mental life. Sartre follows Freud in seeing parricidal wishes in this kind of seizure. See Sigmund Freud, "Dostoevsky and Parricide," pp. 277–81.

26. Erikson, *Young Man Luther*, p. 43.

27. Ibid., pp. 39–40.

28. In Freud's case of the "Rat-Man," a similar phenomenon occurs. Freud observes: "he resolved this conflict, which was in fact one between his love and the persisting influence of his father's wishes, by falling ill; or, to put it more correctly, by falling ill he avoided the task of resolving it in real life. . . . The results of such an illness are never unintentional; what appears to be the consequence of the illness is in reality the cause or motive of falling ill." Freud, "Notes upon a Case of Obsessional Neurosis," pp. 56–57.

29. Sartre describes this dramatic moment in his life: "I was saved by my grandfather. He drove me, without meaning to, into a new imposture that changed my life" (*W*, 85). This concludes the first half of *The Words*.

30. In Freud's experience, one of the central features of conversion hysteria was the bodily symbolization of an idea. For example, an insult ("slap in the face") may become a facial neuralgia or a sensation in the throat ("I have to swallow this"). Freud and Breuer, *Studies on Hysteria*, pp. 220–22).

31. Freud shows that the symptoms produced by traumas come into existence only with the cooperation of earlier provoking causes. There is a "summation of traumas." Freud and Breuer, *Studies on Hysteria*, p. 215.

32. Sartre compares this phenomenon to the compromise of conflicting intentions which occurs in nightmares. A dream in which a son watches in horror (after futilely trying to stop it) while a soldier shoots his father, unites the desire for the father's death with the refusal of that desire. The wish is expressed while the dreamer avoids the guilt of parricide. This is not an unusual psychoanalytic phenomenon, but it is interesting that Sartre uses it to explain Flaubert's crisis.

33. Quoted in Stratton Buck, *Gustave Flaubert*, p. 48.

34. William James, *The Varieties of Religious Experience.*

35. Sartre admits the death instinct applies to Flaubert, but thinks it was arbitrary of Freud to regard it as universal (*IF*, 2:1745).

36. Sartre's interpretation of the fit as a disguised discourse to Flaubert's father receives some confirmation in the fact that when the father dies two years later, Flaubert experiences it as a deliverance. He has a partial remission of his nervous symptoms, has a strong desire to work again, and has sex for the first time since the attack (Sartre interprets the fall as a symbolic castration) (*IF*, 2:1896). At the same time, however, this remission is accompanied by profound frustration and ambivalence, since Flaubert has never really succeeded in feeling like a genuine object of worth in his father's eyes.

37. In his book on Gandhi, Erikson devotes a large portion of his analysis to reconstructing "the Event," Gandhi's fasting during a local labor dispute in 1918. Retrospectively, the Event appears as the terminus which gives meaning to all that preceded it. Like Sartre's analysis of Flaubert, Erikson returns to Gandhi's beginnings to see "with a mixture of clinical and historical hindsight why what led up to the Event had to happen the way it did" (*Gandhi's Truth*, p. 11).

38. Collins, *Sartre as Biographer*, p. 177.

39. Aronson, "*L'Idiot de la Famille*: The Ultimate Sartre," p. 100.

CHAPTER 8

1. Paul Ricoeur, "That Fiction 'Remakes' Reality."

2. Robert Scholes and Robert Kellogg, *The Nature of Narrative*, p. 151.

3. Frederick J. Teggart, *Theory and Processes of History*, p. 62.

4. Ibid., p. 54.

5. Cf. the construction view of history in Jack W. Meiland, *Scepticism and Historical Knowledge.*

6. See Mandel, "Autobiography—Reflection Trained on Mystery."

7. Louis A. Renza, "The Veto of the Imagination: A Theory of Autobiography," p. 2.

8. Marc Pachter, ed., *Telling Lives*, p. 14.

9. Ibid., p. 30.

10. Frank Kermode, *The Sense of an Ending*, pp. 46–64.

11. See Ted Estess, "The Inerrable Contraption: Reflections on the Metaphor of Story."

12. Samuel Beckett, quoted in ibid., p. 434.

13. H. Richard Niebuhr, *The Meaning of Revelation*, p. 48.

14. Ibid., p. 51.

15. Paul Tillich, *Systematic Theology*, 2:369.

16. Eliade, *Myth and Reality; The Sacred and the Profane*.

17. Eliade, *The Sacred and the Profane*, p. 204.

18. Quoted by Justin Kaplan, "The Naked Self and Other Problems," in *Telling Lives*, ed. Pachter, p. 46.

19. Carl Gustav Jung, *Memories, Dreams, Reflections*, p. 3.

20. Steven Crites, "Myth, Story, History," p. 68.

21. Steven Crites, "The Narrative Quality of Experience," p. 301.

22. Michael Novak, *Ascent of the Mountain, Flight of the Dove*, p. 46.

23. Shapiro, "Autobiography," p. 447.

24. Alfred Kazin, "The Self As History: Reflections on Autobiography," in *Telling Lives*, ed. Pachter, pp. 88–89.

25. Jonathan Z. Smith, "The Influence of Symbols upon Social Change: A Place on Which to Stand," p. 472.

26. Ibid., p. 473.

SELECTED BIBLIOGRAPHY

WORKS BY JEAN-PAUL SARTRE

Baudelaire. Translated by Martin Turnell. New York: New Directions, 1950.

Being and Nothingness: An Essay in Phenomenological Ontology. Translated by Hazel E. Barnes. New York: Philosophical Library, 1956.

Between Existentialism and Marxism. Translated by John Mathews. New York: Random House, Pantheon Books, 1974.

"Consciousness of Self and Knowledge of Self." In *Readings in Existential Phenomenology,* pp. 113–42. Translated by Mary Ellen Lawrence and Nathaniel M. Lawrence. Edited by Nathaniel Lawrence and D. J. O'Connor. Englewood Cliffs, N.J.: Prentice-Hall, 1967.

Critique of Dialectical Reason. Translated by Alan Sheridan-Smith. London: NLB, 1976.

The Emotions: Outline of a Theory. Translated by Bernard Frechtman. New York: Philosophical Library, 1948.

"Entretien: J. P. Sartre et M. Sicard." *Obliques,* nos. 18–19, 1979, pp. 9–29.

L'Existentialisme est un humanisme. Paris: Nagel, 1970.

"Forgers of Myths." In *Sartre on Theatre,* pp. 33–43. Translated by Frank Jellinek. Edited by Michel Contat and Michel Rybalka. New York: Random House, Pantheon Books, 1976.

L'Idiot de la famille. 3 vols. Paris: Gallimard, 1971–73.

Imagination: A Psychological Critique. Translated by Forrest Williams. Ann Arbor, Mich.: University of Michigan Press, 1962; Ann Arbor Paperbacks, 1970.

"Intentionality." *Journal of the British Society for Phenomenology* 1 (May 1970): 4.

"An Interview with Jean-Paul Sartre." In *The Philosophy of Jean-Paul Sartre*. Edited by Paul Arthur Schilpp, pp. 5–51. La Salle, Ill.: Open Court, 1981.

"An Interview with Jean-Paul Sartre." In *Tynan Right and Left: Plays, Films, People, Places and Events*, by Kenneth Tynan, pp. 302–12. New York: Antheneum, 1967.

"Jean-Paul Sartre on His Autobiography." Interviewed by Oliver Todd. *The Listener*, 6 June 1967, pp. 915–16.

"Jean-Paul Sartre Speaks." *Vogue* no. 1, 1 January 1965, pp. 94–95.

Life/Situations: Essays Written and Spoken. New York: Random House, Pantheon Books, 1977.

Literary and Philosophical Essays. Translated by Annette Michelson. New York: Collier Books, 1965.

"Merleau-Ponty." In *Situations*, pp. 156–226. Translated by Benita Eisler, Greenwich, Conn.: Fawcett Publications, 1965.

Nausea. Translated by Lloyd Alexander. Norfolk, Conn.: New Directions, 1964.

"Playboy Interview: Jean-Paul Sartre." *Playboy*, May 1965, pp. 69–76.

The Psychology of Imagination. Translated by Bernard Frechtman. New York: Washington Square Press, 1966.

"Replies to Structuralism: An Interview with Jean-Paul Sartre." *Telos* 9 (Fall 1971): 110–16.

Saint Genet: Actor and Martyr. Translated by Bernard Frechtman. New York: New American Library, 1963.

"Sartre et Huston." *Magazine Littéraire*, nos. 103–4, September 1975, p. 57.

Sartre by Himself. Translated by Richard Seaver. New York: Urizen Books, 1978.

Search for a Method. Translated by Hazel E. Barnes. New York: Alfred A. Knopf & Random House, 1963; Vintage Books, 1968.

Situations, I. Paris: Gallimard, 1947.

Situations, II. Paris: Gallimard, 1948.

Situations, X. Paris: Gallimard, 1976.

The Transcendence of the Ego: An Existentialist Theory of Consciousness. Translated by Forrest Williams and Robert Kirkpatrick. New York: Noonday Press, 1957.

What Is Literature? Translated by Bernard Frechtman. New York: Harper & Row, 1965.

The Words. Translated by Bernard Frechtman. New York: George Braziller, 1964; reprint ed., Greenwich, Conn.: Fawcett Publications, 1969.

OTHER WORKS CONSULTED

Abel, Lionel. "The Retroactive 'I'." *Partisan Review* 32 (1965): 255–61.

Adamowski, T. H. "The Condemned of Rouen: Sartre's Flaubert." *Novel* 6 (Fall 1972): 79–82.

Adler, Alfred. *The Individual Psychology of Alfred Adler: A Systematic Presentation in Selections from His Writings*. Edited by Heinz L. Ansbacher and Rowena R. Ansbacher. New York: Basic Books, 1956.

Allport, Gordon W. *Personality: A Psychological Interpretation.* New York: Holt, 1937.

Angyal, Andros. *Foundation for a Science of Personality.* New York: Viking Press, 1969.

Arnold, A. J., and Piriou, J. P. *Genèse et critique d'une autobiographie: "Les Mots" de Sartre. Archives des Lettres Modernes* no. 144. Paris: Minard, 1973.

Aronson, Ronald. "*L'Idiot de la Famille:* The Ultimate Sartre." *Telos* no. 20 (Summer 1974): 90–107.

Avenberg, R., and Guiter, M. "The Concept of Truth in Psychoanalysis." *International Journal of Psychoanalysis* 57 (1976): 11–18.

Bachelard, Gaston. *The Poetics of Reverie: Childhood, Language, and the Cosmos.* Translated by Daniel Russell. Boston: Beacon Press, 1971.

Backès, C. "Continuité mythique et construction historique." *L'Arc* no. 34.

Bakan, David. *Sigmund Freud and the Jewish Mystical Tradition.* New York: Schocken Books, 1969.

Barish, Jonas. "The Veritable Genet." *Contemporary Literature* 6 (Winter–Spring 1965): 267–85.

Barratt, Barnaby B. "Freud's Psychology as Interpretation." *Psychoanalysis and Contemporary Science* 5 (1976): 443–78.

Barrett, William, and Yankelovich, Daniel. *Ego and Instinct: The Psychoanalytic View of Human Nature—Revised.* New York: Random House, 1970; Vintage Books, 1971.

Barrett, William. *Irrational Man: A Study in Existential Philosophy.* Garden City, N.Y.: Doubleday, Anchor Books, 1962.

Bart, Benjamin F. *Flaubert.* Syracuse: Syracuse University Press, 1967.

Bartlett, F. C. *Remembering.* Cambridge: Cambridge University Press, 1932.

Beauvoir, Simone de. *All Said and Done.* Translated by Patrick O'Brian. New York: Warner Books, 1975.

———. *The Prime of Life.* Translated by Peter Green. New York: Harper & Row, 1976.

Bedford, Errol. "Emotions." *Proceedings of the Aristotelian Society* 62 (1956–57): 281–304.

Bensimon, Marc. "D'un mythe à l'autre: Essai sur les 'Mots' de Jean-Paul Sartre." *Revue des Sciences Humaines* no. 119 (July–September 1965): 415–30.

Brée, Germaine. *Camus and Sartre: Crisis and Commitment.* New York: Delta Books, 1972.

Brombert, Victor. "Sartre et la Biographie Impossible." *Cahiers de l'Association Internationale des Etudes Françaises* no. 19 (March 1967): 155–66.

Browning, Don S. *Generative Man: Psychoanalytic Perspectives.* Philadelphia: Westminster Press, 1973.

Buck, Stratton. *Gustave Flaubert.* New York: Twayne Publishers, 1966.

Burgelin, Claude. "Lire *L'idiot de la famille?*" *Littérature* no. 6 (May 1972): 111–20.

Capps, Donald, ed. *Encounter with Erikson: Historical Interpretation and Religious Biography.* Missoula, Mont.: Scholars Press, 1977.

Champigny, Robert. "Trying to Understand *L'Idiot.*" *Diacritics* 2 (Summer 1972): 2–6.

Charmé, Stuart. Critical Review of Morris's *Sartre's Concept of a Person: An Analytic Approach. NOUS* 14 (1980): 117–19.

Cohen, Gilbert. "De Roquentin à Flaubert." *Revue de Metaphysique et de Morale* 81 (January–March 1976): 112–41.

Collins, Douglas. *Sartre as Biographer*. Cambridge, Mass.: Harvard University Press, 1980.

Contat, Michel, and Rybalka, Michel, comps. *The Writings of Jean-Paul Sartre*. Translated by Richard McCleary. Vol. 1: *A Bibliographical Life*. Evanston, Ill.: Northwestern University Press, 1974.

Crites, Steven. "Myth, Story, History." In *Parable, Myth and Language*. Edited by Tony Stoneburner. Cambridge, Mass.: Church Society for College Work, 1968.

————. "The Narrative Quality of Experience." *Journal of the American Academy of Religion* 39 (September 1971): 291–311.

Csikszentmihalyi, Mihaly and Olga Beattie. "Life Themes: A Theoretical and Empirical Exploration of Their Origins and Effects." *Journal of Humanistic Psychology* 19 (Winter 1979): 45–63.

Cuddihy, John Murray. *The Ordeal of Civility: Freud, Marx, Levi-Strauss and the Jewish Struggle with Modernity*. New York: Basic Books, 1974.

De Man, Paul. "Sartre's Confessions." *The New York Review of Books*, 6 November 1964, pp. 12–13.

Doubrovsky, Serge. *The New Criticism in France*. Translated by Derek Coltman. Introduction by Edward Wasiolek. Chicago: University of Chicago Press, 1973.

Eck, Marcel. "La psychanalyse de Flaubert selon Sartre." *La Nouvelle Presse Medicale* 10 (4 March 1974): 685–88, 825–28.

Eliade, Mircea. *Cosmos and History: The Myth of the Eternal Return*. Translated by Willard R. Trask. New York: Harper & Row, 1959.

————. *Myth and Reality*. Translated by Willard R. Trask. New York: Harper & Row, 1963.

————. *Myths, Dreams, and Mysteries: The Encounter Between Contemporary Faiths and Archaic Realities*. Translated by Philip Mairet. New York: Harper & Row, 1975.

————. *The Sacred and the Profane*. Translated by Willard R. Trask. New York: Harcourt, Brace, & World, 1959.

Erikson, Erik. *Gandhi's Truth*. New York: W. W. Norton & Co., 1969.

————. *Identity and the Life Cycle: Selected Papers*. Psychological Issues Monograph. Vol. 1. New York: International Universities Press, 1959.

————. *Insight and Responsibility*. New York: W. W. Norton & Co., 1964.

————. *Life History and the Historical Moment*. New York: W. W. Norton & Co., 1975.

————. *Young Man Luther: A Study in Psychoanalysis and History*. New York: W. W. Norton & Co., 1962.

Estess, Ted. "The Inerrable Contraption. Reflections on the Metaphor of Story." *Journal of the American Academy of Religion* 42 (September 1974): 415–34.

Farrell, B. A. "The Validity of Psychotherapy." *Inquiry* 15 (Summer 1972): 146–70.

Fell, Joseph P. III. *Emotion in the Thought of Sartre*. New York: Columbia University Press, 1965.

————. "Sartre's Theory of Motivation: Some Clarifications." *Journal of the British Society for Phenomenology* 1 (May 1970): 27–34.

————. "Sartre's *Words*: An Existential Self-Analysis." *Psychoanalytic Review* 55 (Summer 1968): 426–41.

Fine, Bernard D., Joseph, Edward D., and Waldhorn, Herbert F., eds. *Recol-*

lection and Reconstruction—Reconstruction in Psychoanalysis*. Kris Study Group of the New York Psychoanalytic Institute, Monograph no. 4. New York: International Universities Press, 1971.

Fingarette, Herbert. *The Self in Transformation: Psychoanalysis, Philosophy and the Life of the Spirit*. New York: Harper & Row, 1963.

Freud, Anna. "Observations on Child Development." *Psychoanalytic Study of the Child* 6 (1951): 18–30.

Freud, Sigmund. "The Aetiology of Hysteria." In *Early Psychoanalytic Writings*, pp. 175–203. Edited by Philip Rieff. New York: Collier Books, 1969.

————. *An Autobiographical Study*. Translated by James Strachey. New York: W. W. Norton & Co., 1952.

————. " 'A Child Is Being Beaten.' " In *Sexuality and the Psychology of Love*, pp. 107–32. Edited by Philip Rieff. New York: Collier Books, 1963.

————. *Civilization and Its Discontents*. Translated and edited by James Strachey. New York: W. W. Norton & Co., 1965.

————. "Constructions in Analysis." In *Theory and Technique*, pp. 273–86. Edited by Philip Rieff. New York: Collier Books, 1963.

————. *Dora: An Analysis of a Case of Hysteria*. Introduction by Philip Rieff. New York: Collier Books, 1963.

————. "Dostoevsky and Parricide." In *Character and Culture*, pp. 274–93. Edited by Philip Rieff. New York: Collier Books, 1963.

————. "Formulations Regarding the Two Principles in Mental Functioning." In *General Psychological Theory*, pp. 21–28. Edited by Philip Rieff. New York: Collier Books, 1963.

————. "From the History of an Infantile Neurosis." In *Three Case Histories*, pp. 187–316. Edited by Philip Rieff. New York: Collier Books, 1963.

————. *The Interpretation of Dreams*. Translated and edited by James Strachey. New York: Avon Books, 1965; Discus Books, 1967.

————. *Leonardo da Vinci and a Memory of His Childhood*. Translated by Alan Tyson. New York: W. W. Norton & Co., 1964.

————. *New Introductory Lectures on Psychoanalysis*. Translated and edited by James Strachey. New York: W. W. Norton & Co., 1965.

————. "Notes upon a Case of Obsessional Neurosis." In *Three Case Histories*, pp. 15–102. Edited by Philip Rieff. New York: Collier Books, 1963.

————. *The Origins of Psychoanalysis: Letters to Wilhelm Fliess, Drafts and Notes: 1887–1902*. Translated by Eric Mosbacher and James Strachey. Edited by Marie Bonaparte, Anna Freud, and Ernst Kris. New York: Basic Books, 1954.

————. "The Psychogenesis of a Case of Homosexuality in a Woman." In *Sexuality and the Psychology of Love*, pp. 133–59. Edited by Philip Rieff. New York: Collier Books, 1963.

————. *Psychopathology of Everyday Life*. Translated by A. A. Brill. New York: New American Library, Mentor Books, n.d.

————. "Recollection, Repetition, and Working Through." In *Therapy and Technique*, pp. 157–66. Edited by Philip Rieff. New York: Collier Books, 1963.

————. "The Relation of the Poet to Day-Dreaming." In *Character and Culture*, pp. 34–43. Edited by Philip Rieff. New York: Collier Books, 1963.

————. "Screen Memories." In *Early Psychoanalytic Writings*, pp. 229–54. Edited by Philip Rieff. New York: Collier Books, 1963.

————. "The Unconscious." In *General Psychological Theory*, pp. 116–50. Edited by Philip Rieff. New York: Collier Books, 1963.

Freud, Sigmund, and Breuer, Joseph. *Studies on Hysteria*. Translated and edited by James Strachey. New York: Avon Books, Discus Books, 1966.

Gabel, Peter. "Freud's Death Instinct and Sartre's Fundamental Project." *Psychoanalytic Review* 61 (Spring 1974): 221–27.

Gallie, W. B. *Philosophy and the Historical Understanding*. New York: Schocken Books, 1968.

Gedo, John. "The Methodology of Psychoanalytic Biography." *Journal of the American Psychoanalytic Association* 20 (1972): 638–49.

Genet, Jean. *The Thief's Journal*. Translated by Bernard Frechtman. Forward by Jean-Paul Sartre. New York: Grove Press, 1973.

Gibson, Walker. *The Limits of Language*. New York: Hill & Wang, 1962.

Glover, Ernest. "The Therapeutic Effect of Inexact Interpretations: A Contribution to the Theory of Suggestion." *International Journal of Psychoanalysis* 12 (October 1931): 397–411.

Grene, Marjorie. *Sartre*. New York: New Viewpoints, 1973.

Hakim, Elearnor. "Jean-Paul Sartre: The Dialectics of Myth." *Review of Existential Psychology and Psychiatry* 13 (1974): 1–29.

Halpern, Joseph H. *Critical Fictions: The Literary Criticism of Jean-Paul Sartre*. New Haven: Yale University Press, 1976.

Hammer, Emanuel F., ed. *Use of Interpretation in Treatment: Technique and Art*. New York: Grunet & Stratton, 1968.

Hampshire, Stuart. *Thought and Action*. New York: Viking Press, 1959.

Hare, R. M. *Freedom and Reason*. New York: Oxford University Press, 1965.

Hauerwas, Stanley. "Story and Theology." *Religious Life* 45 (Autumn 1976): 339–50.

Hertz, Neil. "Flaubert's Conversion." *Diacritics* 2 (Summer 1972): 7–12.

Hesnard, Angelo. *L'oeuvre de Freud et son importance pour le monde moderne*. Paris: Payot, 1960.

Hillman, James. "The Fiction of Case History: A Round." In *Religion as Story*, pp. 123–73. Edited by James B. Wiggins. New York: Harper & Row, 1975.

Hirsch, E. D., Jr. *Validity in Interpretation*. New Haven and London: Yale University Press, 1967.

Homans, Peter. *Theology after Freud: An Interpretive Inquiry*. New York: Bobbs-Merrill Co., 1970.

―――, ed. *Childhood and Selfhood: Essays on Tradition, Religion, and Modernity in the Psychology of Erik H. Erikson*. Lewisburg, Pa.: Bucknell University Press, 1978.

Hook, Sidney, ed. *Psychoanalysis, Scientific Methods, and Philosophy*. New York: New York University Press, 1964.

Howells, Christina. "Sartre and Freud." *French Studies* 33 (April 1979): 157–76.

Hughes, H. Stuart. *The Obstructed Path: French Social Thought in the Years of Desperation, 1930–1960*. New York: Harper & Row, 1968.

Huston, John. *An Open Book*. New York: Knopf, 1980.

Izenberg, Gerald N. *The Existentialist Critique of Freud: The Crisis of Autonomy*. Princeton, N.J.: Princeton University Press, 1976.

James, William. *The Principles of Psychology*. New York: Dover, 1918.

―――. *The Varieties of Religious Experience*. New York: New American Library, 1958.

Johnson, Roger A., ed. *Psychohistory and Religion: The Case of Young Man Luther*. Philadelphia: Fortress Press, 1977.

Jung, Carl Gustav. *Memories, Dreams, Reflections.* New York: Random House, 1963.

Kazin, Alfred. "Autobiography as Narrative." *Michigan Quarterly Review* 2 (Fall 1964): 210–16.

Keen, Ernest. "A Rapprochement in the Psychologies of Freud and Sartre." *Psychoanalytic Review* 58 (Spring 1971): 182–88.

Kermode, Frank. *The Sense of an Ending.* New York: Oxford University Press, 1967.

King, Thomas M. *Sartre and the Sacred.* Chicago: University of Chicago Press, 1974.

Klauber, John. "On the Dual Use of Historical and Scientific Method in Psychoanalysis." *International Journal of Psychoanalysis* 49 (1968): 80–88.

Kris, Ernst. "The Personal Myth." *Journal of the American Psychoanalytic Association* 4 (1956): 653–81.

———. *Psychoanalytic Explorations in Art.* New York: International Universities Press, 1952.

———. "The Recovery of Childhood Memories in Psychoanalysis." *Psychoanalytic Study of the Child* 11 (1956): 54–88.

Lacan, Jacques. *The Language of the Self: The Function of Language in Psychoanalysis.* Translated by Anthony Wilden. New York: Delta Books, 1968.

La Capra, Dominick. *A Preface to Sartre.* Ithaca, N.Y.: Cornell University Press, 1978.

Laplanche, J., and Pontalis, J.-B. *The Language of Psychoanalysis.* Translated by Donald Nicholson-Smith. New York: W. W. Norton & Co., 1973.

Leavy, Stanley. "Psychoanalytic Interpretation." *Psychoanalytic Study of the Child* 27 (1973): 305–30.

Lecarme, Jacques. *"Les mots* de Sartre: Un cas limite de l'autobiographie?" *Revue d'Histoire Littéraire de la France* 75 (November–December 1975): 1047–67.

Lejeune, Philippe. *L'autobiographie en France.* Paris: A. Colin, 1971.

———. "L'ordre du récit dans *Les mots de Sartre." Scolies* nos. 3–4 (1973–74): 7–54.

Lifton, Robert Jay. *Boundaries: Psychological Man in Revolution.* New York: Simon & Schuster, 1969.

———. "On Psychohistory." In *Psychoanalysis and Contemporary Science: An Annual of Integrative and Interdisciplinary Studies,* vol. I. Edited by R. R. Holt and E. Peterfreund. New York: Macmillan, 1972.

Loch, Wolfgang. "Some Comments on the Subject of Psychoanalysis and Truth." In *Thought, Consciousness, and Reality,* pp. 217–55. Edited by Joseph H. Smith. New Haven and London: Yale University Press, 1977.

Loewenstein, Rudolph M. "Some Thoughts on Interpretation in the Theory and Practice of Psychoanalysis." *Psychoanalytic Study of the Child* 12 (1957): 127–50.

McGuire, Michael T. *Reconstructions in Psychoanalysis.* New York: Appleton-Century Crofts, 1971.

MacIntyre, A. C. *The Unconscious.* Atlantic Highlands, N.J.: Humanities Press, 1958.

Mack, John E. "Psychoanalysis and Historical Biography." *Journal of the American Psychoanalytic Association* 19 (1974): 143–79.

Mandel, Barrett John. "Autobiography—Reflection Trained on Mystery." *Prairie Schooner* 45 (Winter 1972–73): 323–29.

Manser, Anthony. *Sartre: A Philosophic Study.* New York: Oxford University Press, 1966.

Marcel, Gabriel. *The Mystery of Being.* 2 vols. Chicago: Henry Regnery Co., 1960.

Marcus, Steven. "Freud and Dora: Story, History, Case History." *Psychoanalysis and Contemporary Science* 5 (1976): 389–442.

Margolis, Joseph. "The Logic of Interpretation." In *Philosophy Looks at the Arts,* pp. 108–18. Edited by Joseph Margolis. New York: Scribner's, 1962.

––––––. "The Myths of Psychoanalysis." *Monist* 56 (July 1972): 361–75.

Mehlman, Jeffrey. *A Structural Study of Autobiography.* Ithaca, N.Y.: Cornell University Press, 1974.

Meiland, Jack W. *Scepticism and Historical Knowledge.* New York: Random House, 1965.

Merleau-Ponty, Maurice. *Signs.* Evanston, Ill.: Northwestern University Press, 1964.

––––––. *The Structure of Behavior.* Translated by Alden L. Fisher. Boston: Beacon Press, 1963.

Mink, Louis. "History and Fiction as Modes of Comprehension." *New Literary History,* vol. 1 (1969): 541–558.

Mitscherlich, Alexander. *Society without the Father: A Contribution to Social Psychology.* New York: Harcourt, Brace, & World, 1969.

Molnar, Thomas. *Sartre: Ideologue of Our Time.* New York: Funk & Wagnalls, 1968.

The Complete Essays of Montaigne. Translated by Donald M. Frame. Stanford, Calif.: Stanford University Press, 1965.

Morris, Phyllis. *Sartre's Concept of a Person: An Analytic Approach.* Amherst, Mass.: University of Massachusetts Press, 1976.

Mouchard, Claude. "Un roman vrai?" *Critique* 27 (December 1971): 1029–49.

Nabokov, Vladimir. *Speak, Memory.* New York: G. P. Putnam's Sons, 1947.

Nelson, Benjamin. "Sartre, Genet, Freud." *Psychoanalytic Review* 50 (Fall 1963): 155–71.

Nicolaidis, Nicos. "La réalité du 'mythe' dans la cure psychanalytique." *Revue Française de Psychanalyse* 35 (September–December 1971): 1011–13.

Niebuhr, H. Richard. *The Meaning of Revelation.* New York: Macmillan, 1941.

Novak, Michael. *Ascent of the Mountain, Flight of the Dove.* New York: Harper & Row, 1971.

Novey, Samuel. "The Significance of the Actual Historical Event in Psychiatry and Psychoanalysis." *British Medical Journal of Psychology* 37 (1964): 279–90.

Olney, James, ed. *Autobiography: Essays Theoretical and Critical.* Princeton, N.J.: Princeton University Press, 1980.

––––––. *Metaphors of Self.* Princeton, N.J.: Princeton University Press, 1972.

Pachter, Marc, ed. *Telling Lives: The Biographer's Art.* Washington, D.C.: New Republic Books, 1979.

Palmer, Richard. *Hermeneutics.* Evanston, Ill.: Northwestern University Press, 1969.

Pascal, Roy. *Design and Truth in Autobiography.* Cambridge, Mass.: Harvard University Press, 1960.

Peterson, Joel. "Problems in the Sartrean Paradigm of Life as a Project." *Philosophical Forum* 7 (Spring 1976): 188–202.

Pike, Burton. "Time in Autobiography." *Comparative Literature* 28 (Fall 1976): 326–42.

Renza, Louis A. "The Veto of the Imagination: A Theory of Autobiography." *New Literary History* 8 (Autumn 1977): 1–26.

Reynolds, Frank E., and Capps, Donald, eds. *The Biographical Process*. Paris: Mouton, 1976.

Ricoeur, Paul. *The Conflict of Interpretations: Essays in Hermeneutics*. Edited by Don Ihde. Evanston, Ill.: Northwestern University Press, 1974.

———. *Freud and Philosophy: An Essay on Interpretation*. Translated by Denis Savage. New Haven and London: Yale University Press, 1970.

———. "Language and Image in Psychoanalysis." In *Psychoanalysis and Language*, pp. 293–324. Edited by Joseph H. Smith. New Haven and London: Yale University Press, 1978.

———. "The Model of the Text: Meaningful Action Considered as a Text." *Social Research* (Autumn 1971): 529–62.

———. "The Question of Proof in Freud's Psychoanalytic Writings." In *The Philosophy of Paul Ricoeur*, pp. 184–210. Edited by Charles E. Reagan and David Stewart. Boston: Beacon Press, 1978.

———. "That Fiction 'Remakes' Reality." *Journal of the Blaisdell Institute* 12 (Winter 1978): 44–62.

Rieff, Philip. *Freud: The Mind of the Moralist*. Garden City, N.Y.: Doubleday, Anchor Books, 1961.

Robert, Marthe. *From Oedipus to Moses: Freud's Jewish Identity*. Translated by Ralph Manheim. Garden City, N.Y.: Anchor Books, 1976.

———. "Le tribunal ou l'analyse." In *Le Monde*, 2 July 1972, p. 17.

Rycroft, Charles. *A Critical Dictionary of Psychoanalysis*. London: Thomas Nelson & Sons, 1968.

Schafer, Roy. "The Interpretation of Transference and the Conditions for Loving." *Journal of the American Psychoanalytic Association* 25 (1977): 335–62.

———. *Language and Insight: The Sigmund Freud Lectures at University College London*. New Haven and London: Yale University Press, 1978.

———. *A New Language for Psychoanalysis*. New Haven and London: Yale University Press, 1976.

Schimek, J. G. "The Interpretations of the Past: Childhood Trauma, Psychical Reality, and Historical Truth." *Journal of the American Psychoanalytic Association* 23 (1975): 845–62.

Scholes, Robert and Robert Kellogg. *The Nature of Narrative*. New York: Oxford University Press, 1966.

Scriven, Michael. "Sartre on Flaubert: Problems of Biography." *Degré Second* no. 2, 1978.

Shapiro, Stephen A. "The Dark Continent of Literature: Autobiography." *Comparative Literature Studies* 5 (December 1968): 421–54.

Sherwood, Michael. *The Logic of Explanation in Psychoanalysis*. New York: Academic Press, 1969.

Sicard, Michel. *La critique littéraire de Jean-Paul Sartre*. Archives des Lettres Modernes no. 159. Paris: Minard, 1976.

Smith, Jonathan Z. "The Influence of Symbols upon Social Change: A Place on Which to Stand." *Worship* 44 (October 1970): 457–74.

Spence, Donald P. "Clinical Interpretation: Some Comments on the Nature of the Evidence." *Psychoanalysis and Contemporary Science* 5 (1976): 367–88.

Stekel, Wilhelm. *Conditions of Nervous Anxiety and Their Treatment*. New York: Dodd, Mead, & Co., 1923.

Stern, Alfred. "Existential Psychoanalysis and Individual Psychology." *Journal of Individual Psychology* 14 (May 1958): 38–50.

———. *Sartre: His Philosophy and Existential Psychoanalysis.* New York: Delta Books, 1967.

Suhl, Benjamin. *Jean-Paul Sartre: The Philosopher as a Literary Critic.* New York: Columbia University Press, 1970.

Taylor, Charles. "Interpretation and the Sciences of Man." *Review of Metaphysics* 25 (September 1971): 3–51.

Teggart, Frederick J. *Theory and Processes of History.* Berkeley and Los Angeles: University of California Press, 1962.

Thody, Philip. "Existential Psychoanalysis." *Journal of the British Society for Phenomenology* 1 (May 1970): 83–90.

———. *Jean Genet.* London: Hamish Hamilton, 1968.

Tillich, Paul. *Systematic Theology.* 3 vols. Chicago: University of Chicago Press, 1951–63.

Viderman, Serge. "The Analytic Space: Meanings and Problems." *Psychoanalytic Quarterly* 48 (April 1979): 257–91.

———. "La bouteille à la mer." *Revue Française de Psychanalyse* 38 (February–March 1974): 323–84.

———. *La construction de l'espace analytique.* Paris: Editions Denöel, 1970.

———. "Interpretation in the Analytical Space." *International Review of Psychoanalysis* 1 (1974): 467–79.

Warnock, Mary. *Imagination.* Berkeley and Los Angeles: University of California Press, 1976.

Weisman, Avery D. *The Existential Core of Psychoanalysis.* Boston: Little, Brown & Co., 1965.

INDEX

Abel, Lionel, 114
Adler, Alfred, 42
Allport, Gordon W., 160n.3
Aristotle, 151
Aron, Raymond, 167n.7
Aronson, Ronald, 148
Augustine, 150
Autobiography, 4, 21, 34, 44, 81–82, 148, 150, 156; Sartre's, 48, 53, 56, 79, 101–8, 114. See also *Words* (Sartre)

Bach, Johann Sebastian, 121
Bad Faith, 26–29, 57, 106, 153
Bakan, David, 52, 164n.59
Barish, Jonas, 78
Barrett, William, 39, 67–68, 170n.16
Bartlett, F. C., 163n.24
Baudelaire, Charles, 3, 39, 73, 87–92, 94, 101
Baudelaire (Sartre), 56, 87–91

Beauvoir, Simone de, 13, 55–56, 102, 167n.7, 168n.13, 170n.10
Beckett, Samuel, 151
Being and Nothingness (Sartre), 23, 38, 59, 60, 61, 62, 119, 125, 137
Biography, 4, 9, 10. *See also* Narrative; Religious biography
Brée, Germaine, 114
Breuer, Josef, 130
Browning, Don S., 68, 69, 112
Burgelin, Claude, 128

Capps, Donald, 109, 112
Character, 61
Childhood: Allport on, 160n.3; Baudelaire's, 88–91; Flaubert's, 132–43; Genet's, 93–95; and "original choice," 39–42, 101; and psychoanalysis, 17, 75; Sartre on, 62–65, 88; Sartre's, 102–6, 120–23

Collins, Douglas, 148
Conditioning, 61. *See also* Determinism
Consciousness, 2, 19, 20, 22, 24–30, 48, 57, 161n.4
Conversion, hysterical, 130, 145–46; religious, 31, 95–96, 145–46
Crites, Steven, 155
Critique of Dialectical Reason (Sartre), 3, 71
Cuddihy, John Murray, 172n.3

De Man, Paul, 114
Descartes, 18
Determinism, Sartre's response to, 2, 23–25, 27, 29, 33, 35, 87, 162n.13
Dialectic: and the fundamental project, 37–38, 48, 99, 152; in psychological development, 33, 45–46, 60–61, 68, 70, 75, 131, 154; in *The Words*, 102–5
Dos Passos, John, 14
Doubrovsky, Serge, 172n.13

Eck, Marcel, 173n.22
Ego Psychology, and Sartre, 2, 24, 67–70
Eliade, Mircea, 3–4, 86, 95, 108, 113, 125, 153–54
Erikson, Erik H.: ego psychology of, 2, 3, 33–34, 55, 67–70, 137, 171n.58; on Gandhi, 109–11; on Luther, 109–13, 143, 148, 169n.13, 171–72n.57, 173n.19. *See also* Religious biography
Existential Psychoanalysis, 1–4, 25, 34–35, 48, 54, 67, 73–74, 78, 80–81, 84, 91, 107–9, 150

Family Idiot (Sartre), 3, 80, 81, 91, 126–48, 168n.13, 173n.22
Fell, Joseph, 38, 161n.2
Fingarette, Herbert, 166n.23
Flaubert, Gustave, 3, 56, 73, 80, 81, 107–8, 126–48, 174nn.32, 36
Fliess, Wilhelm, 33
Freedom: in Freud's thought, 165n.16; in Sartre's thought, 2, 24, 60–61, 99, 162n.14
Freud, Sigmund, 127, 168n.29, 174nn.30–31; and analysis of Dostoevsky, 173n.25; and analysis of Leonardo da Vinci, 76, 165n.16, 171n.51; and the case of Dora, 82–84, 164n.59, 168n.18; and the case of the "Rat-Man," 32, 85, 173n.28; and

the case of the "Wolf-Man," 83; and Helmholtz school, 27–28; and Jewish mysticism, 52–53; and memory, 41–43; Sartre's attitude toward, 1–2, 24, 128, 130, 164n.3, 165nn. 8, 12, 174n.35; Sartre's screenplay about, 56. *See also* Psychoanalysis
Fundamental project, 2, 152; changes in one's, 44–46; Genet's, 99; literary elements of, 47–52, 59, 66–67; and the "original choice," 39–41, 90, 123, 134, 154–55; as a totality, 34–38, 60, 68, 90

General Psychopathology (Jaspers), 165n.14
Genet, Jean, 3, 73, 76, 78, 92–101, 141
Gide, André, 10, 57, 114, 170n.5
Grene, Marjorie, 71–72
Gusdorf, Georges, 81–82

Halpern, Joseph, 78
Hampshire, Stuart, 162
Hauerwas, Stanley, 46
Hegel, G. W. F., 37, 48, 68
Hermeneutics, 2, 34, 51; and hermeneutical circle, 48, 49, 164n.54, 166n.21
Hesnard, Angelo, 165n.14
Hillman, James, 84
Hobbs, Nicholas, 86
Howells, Christina, 56
Hume, David, 18
Husserl, Edmund, 6, 36
Huston, John: work with Sartre, 56, 57, 130, 165nn. 8, 12

Identity: American, 118; Sartre on, 64, 67–68
Ideology: in Erikson, 110–14; and existential psychoanalysis, 107–8; in *The Words*, 114–116
Image, characteristics of, 18–22
Imagination, 13, 17–22, 44, 81, 149, 161n.33, 167n.8
Instincts, 16, 35, 70–72, 88, 98
Intentionality, 7
Interpretation of Dreams (Freud), 164n.3, 167n.11, 168n.29

James, William, 7, 146, 160n.3
Jaspers, Karl, 165n.14
Johnson, Roger, 110–12
Jung, Carl, 155

Kazin, Alfred, 156
King, Thomas, 124
Kris, Ernst, 43, 115

Lacan, Jacques, 17, 67, 78, 128, 162n.20, 172n.8
LaCapra, Dominick, 44
Language, 15–17, 47, 59, 77
Leibniz, G. W., 18
Lejeune, Philippe, 4, 102
Lifton, Robert, 84, 117
Literature, Sartre's theory of, 3, 14–15, 48–49, 59, 76, 116, 120–21, 129
"Lived experience" *(le vécu)*, 58–60, 165n.14, 172n.5
Loewald, Hans W., 169n.45

McGuire, Michael, 83
Mack, John, 40
Madame Bovary (Flaubert), 129–30, 166n.26
Manser, Anthony, 39
Marcel, Gabriel, 9–10
Marcus, Stephen, 84
Marx, Karl, 54, 71, 87
Mauron, Charles, 172n.13
Meaning: and the fundamental project, 35, 38, 71; in human experience, 1, 2, 25, 44, 67, 69, 72, 74, 85; and language, 15–17, 47–49; and narrative, 9, 12, 47; and the past, 30–32, 41, 44, 172n.58
Memory, 34; of childhood events, 41–43, 120; Freud's view of, 32–33, 41–43; and imagination, 21–22, 163n.24; Sartre's view of, 30–31
Merleau-Ponty, Maurice, 79, 161n.6, 165n.7, 167n.12
Mink, Louis, 12
Mitscherlich, Alexander, 117
Molière, 121
Morris, Phyllis Sutton, 38
Moses and Monotheism (Freud), 84, 167n.11
Myth, 151, 153–55; in Erikson, 111–12; in existential psychoanalysis, 3–4, 34, 40–41, 78, 113–16; and Genet, 92, 94–95; of the hero, 115; in psychoanalysis, 43, 44, 83, 84–86, 169n.45; in religion, 85–86

Nabokov, Vladimir, 65
Nachträglichkeit, 33, 140
Narrative: characteristics of, in novels, 14–15; and the fundamental project, 46–47; and human experience, 9–14, 20, 150–51, 155–56; and psychoanalysis, 82–84
Nausea (Sartre), 9–15, 17–18, 53, 72, 79, 92, 116, 153
Nelson, Benjamin, 67
Niebuhr, H. Richard, 152
Novak, Michael, 156

Oedipal complex: and Baudelaire, 88; and Flaubert, 128; and Freud, 110

Pascal, Roy, 44
Past: Sartre's attitude toward his own, 105–6; and transference, 75. *See also* Meaning
Protean style, and meaning of fatherlessness, 117–19, 171n.51
Proust, Marcel, 50, 81
Psyche. *See* Self
Psychoanalysis: archeological model of the mind in, 5–6, 19, 33, 52; Eliade on, 154; interpretation in, 6, 29, 51–52, 166n.22; mechanistic elements in, 56–57, 161n.6, 165n.7; psychic reality vs. material reality, 43; resistance in, 28; Sartre's attitude toward, 2, 3, 19–20, 23, 26–27, 35, 54–57, 66, 67; therapeutic setting in, 74; transference in, 74–75. *See also* Freud; Unconscious
Psychohistory, 109–10
Psychopathology of Everyday Life (Freud), 164n.3

Reflection, and self-consciousness, 7, 8–10
Religion, 4. *See also* Myth; Sacred
Religious biography: and Erikson, 109–13, 124–25; existential psychoanalysis as, 4, 109, 124–25
Repression, 5, 28, 166n.20
Ricoeur, Paul, 149, 164n.54
Rieff, Philip, 16, 83
Robbe-Grillet, Alain, 151, 160n.16
Robert, Marthe, 110, 128, 167n.11
Rousseau, Jean-Jacques, 121

Sacred: and life of Genet, 93, 97–98; in parent-child relationship, 88; and Sartre's death, 114; traditional religious vs. modern sense of, 3–4, 85–86, 125, 152–56

Saint Genet (Sartre), 56, 92, 139

Schafer, Roy, 51, 75

Schopenhauer, A., 32

Schweitzer, Charles, 116, 120

Search for a Method (Sartre), 61, 90, 127

Self, 2, 46, 160n.3; and religion, 4, 125; Sartre's analysis of, 6–8, 90, 166n.23

Smith, Jonathan Z., 156

Stekel, Wilhelm, 162n.10

Story. *See* Narrative

Studies on Hysteria (Breuer and Freud), 130, 174nn.30–31

Superego, Sartre's equivalents for, 62, 140

Theology, and existential psychoanalysis, 4, 119, 124–25, 152

Thief's Journal (Genet), 92, 93

Time: cyclical vs. historical, 65, 154; *kairos* vs. *chronos*, 151–52; in novels, 14–15; sacred vs. profane, 98, 153–54

Totalization, 45–46, 62–64, 79–80, 90, 127, 164n.48, 166n.20. *See also* Dialectic

Transcendence of the Ego (Sartre), 6–9, 10

Truth: and art, 167–68n.12; and autobiography, 82, 93, 155, 171n.55; in existential psychoanalysis, 3, 78–82, 92, 127, 142; in psychoanalysis, 164n.56

Unconscious: and fundamental project, 39; and language, 15–17; and "lived experience," 58–60; Sartre's attitude toward, 2, 18–20, 24–28, 56–57, 160n.5

Viderman, Serge, 16, 17, 43–44, 52, 86

What is Literature? (Sartre), 48

Whitehead, A. N., 160n.17

Words (Sartre), 3, 53, 79, 92, 101–6, 115–16, 119, 123, 126, 131, 142, 167n.51, 173n.29

Yankelovich, Daniel, 67–68, 170n.16

Yeats, W. B., 154

Young Man Luther (Erikson), 110–11